ARKANSAS TRAVELERS

Arkansas History

JEANNIE WHAYNE, GENERAL EDITOR

ARKANSAS TRAVELERS

Geographies of Exploration and Perception, 1804–1834

ANDREW J. MILSON

THE UNIVERSITY OF ARKANSAS PRESS
FAYETTEVILLE
2019

Manufactured in the United States of America

ISBN: 978-1-68226-096-8 (cloth)
ISBN: 978-1-68226-232-0 (paper)
eISBN: 978-1-61075-665-5

Library of Congress Cataloging-in-Publication Data
Names: Milson, Andrew J., author.
Title: Arkansas travelers : geographies of exploration and perception, 1804-1834 / Andrew J. Milson.
Description: Fayetteville : The University of Arkansas Press, [2019] |
Series: Arkansas history | Includes bibliographical references and index. |
Identifiers: LCCN 2018041475 (print) | LCCN 2018051462 (ebook) | ISBN 9781610756655 (electronic) | ISBN 9781682260968 | ISBN 9781682260968 (cloth : alk. paper)
Subjects: LCSH: Arkansas—Discovery and exploration. | Arkansas—History—19th century. | Dunbar, William, 1749-1810—Travel—Arkansas. | Nuttall, Thomas, 1786-1859—Travel—Arkansas. | Schoolcraft, Henry Rowe, 1793-1864—Travel—Arkansas. | Featherstonhaugh, George William, 1780-1866—Travel—Arkansas. | Explorers—Arkansas—Biography.
Classification: LCC F411 (ebook) | LCC F411 .M657 2019 (print) | DDC 976.7/04—dc23
LC record available at https://lccn.loc.gov/2018041475

23 22 21 20 19 5 4 3 2 1

Designer: April Leidig

∞ The paper used in this publication meets the minimum requirements of the American National Standard for Permanence of Paper for Printed Library Materials Z39.48–1984.

The cartography for this book was supported in part by an award from the University of Texas at Arlington College of Liberal Arts Endowment for Faculty Research.

In memory of my dad,

James Lee Milson

(1937–2017)

Contents

Illustrations

Acknowledgments

I AM GRATEFUL FOR my colleagues and the administration at the University of Texas at Arlington (UTA) for their support, both financial and moral, during various phases of this project. My department chair until 2016, Marvin Dulaney, funded visits to Arkansas and to conferences such as the American Historical Association (AHA), International Conference of Historical Geographers (ICHG), and the American Association of Geographers (AAG). In the fall of 2015, the UTA Division of Faculty Affairs, under the leadership of Maria Martinez-Cosio, organized a faculty book-writing group that was immensely useful to me. John Garrigus, my history department colleague, was an outstanding leader for the group, and my conversations with him and other colleagues helped me to complete a book proposal to the University of Arkansas Press. In the spring of 2016, I received a Digital Humanities research award from the College of Liberal Arts at UTA. This award assisted me as I sorted through various approaches to mapping travelers' perceptions. My conversations with my history department colleagues and coinvestigators John Garrigus, Katy Beebe, Patryk Babiracki, and Imre Demhardt about digital humanities and mapping were invigorating. My fellow geographer at UTA, Charlie Travis, has been very helpful with suggestions and ideas for tapping into the scholarship of digital humanities and Historical Geographic Information Systems (HGIS). William Hansard served as my student assistant in the early phases of this project and provided excellent assistance with the data management needed for mapping the routes of the travelers in this book. Since the fall of 2016, my new department chair, Scott Palmer, and Dean Elisabeth Cawthon have been very supportive of my scholarly goals and activities. I am also grateful for the funding I received from the UTA College of Liberal Arts Endowment for Faculty Research and the University of Arkansas Press that allowed me to hire a professional cartographer, Erin Greb, to produce the maps that you will find in this book.

As I sought to focus my ideas while writing chapters for the book, I delivered presentations at conferences and symposia such as the International Conference of Historical Geographers (ICHG) in London in July 2015, the

American Association of Geographers (AAG) in San Francisco in April 2016, the Social Science History Association (SSHA) in Chicago in November 2016, the UTA Libraries Digital Scholarship Series in March 2017, the Texas Map Society in Washington-on-the-Brazos, Texas, in April 2017, the Arkansas Historical Association in Fort Smith in April 2018, the Butler Center Symposium on Mapping Arkansas Territory in Little Rock in June 2018, and the Red River Heritage Symposium in Historic Washington, Arkansas, in July 2018. I benefited tremendously from conversations at these conferences with Dick Nostrand, Innes Keighren, Charlie Withers, John Bauer, Larry Dilsaver, Terry Young, Bob Schwartz, Jeannie Whayne, Brooks Blevins, Blake Perkins, Billy Higgins, George West, Conevery Valenčius, Peggy Lloyd, Keenan Williams, Josh Williams, and many others. I am particularly indebted to and appreciative of Dick Nostrand and Jeannie Whayne for their advice and tremendously helpful review of the entire book manuscript, and to David Scott Cunningham, Mike Bieker, and the staff of the University of Arkansas Press for their encouragement and support through all phases of this project.

My family has been a vital source of inspiration and strength in ways that I cannot effectively express in words. For my mom, Judy; my sister, Amy; my uncle, Tom; my mother-in-law, Carol; my son, Colin; and my wife, Lori—love you!

ARKANSAS TRAVELERS

Introduction

A WEARY TRAVELER on horseback arrives at a ragged cabin in the backwoods of Arkansas just as the sun is setting. He approaches a scruffy man playing a fiddle near the doorway of the hovel and asks for lodging for the night. The Arkansawyer continues to fiddle. A disheveled woman eyes the traveler from the threshold as children play recklessly in the background and a dog barks nervously. A dialogue begins.

Traveler: Hello, stranger.

Arkansawyer: Hello yourself.

Traveler: Can you give me a night's lodging?

Arkansawyer: No room, stranger.

Traveler: Can't you make room?

Arkansawyer: No, sir. It might rain.

Traveler: What if it does rain?

Arkansawyer: There's only one dry spot in this house and me and Sal sleeps on that.

The Arkansawyer continues to play a tune on the fiddle.

Traveler: Why don't you put a roof on the house?

Arkansawyer: When it's dry I don't want a roof; when it's wet I can't.

The fiddling continues.

Traveler: Which is the way to the Red River Crossing?

Arkansawyer: I've lived hyar twenty years and never knowed it to have a crossin'.

Once again, the Arkansawyer scratches out the same tune on his fiddle.

Traveler: What are you playing that tune over so often for?

Arkansawyer: Only heard it yesterday. 'Fraid I'll forget it.

Traveler: Why don't you play the second part of it?

Arkansawyer: I've knowed that tune ten years, and it ain't got no second part.

Traveler: Pass it here!

The Arkansawyer hands the fiddle to the traveler who tunes it and then skillfully launches into a new part of the tune. The Arkansawyer leaps off his whiskey barrel and begins to dance, the unkempt woman smiles, and the dog wags his tail. As the traveler finishes the tune, the Arkansawyer exclaims, "Walk in stranger! Tie up your horse 'side of ol' Ball. Give him ten ears of corn. Pull out the demi-john and drink it all. Stay as long as you please. If it rains, sleep on the dry spot."[1]

There are multiple versions of the dialogue for the Arkansas traveler story, but its essence is the repartee between the annoyed traveler and the churlish, fiddle-playing Arkansawyer. The story has comedic value on multiple levels. Foremost, it plays on stereotypes of the coarseness of backcountry settlers and their suspicions toward outsiders. The frontiersman is poor, dirty, obtuse, and uncouth. The traveler is educated, experienced, and refined. The contrast proves humorous to those who would laugh with contempt at the foolishness and filth of the backcountry squatter. On another level though, there is humor in a poor man rebelling against the expectations and sense of superiority of the out-of-his-element traveler. The cunning and carefree independence of the squatter is a source of pride to rural residents who have suffered the sneers and snobbery of their urban counterparts. Another level of amusement arises as their differences are transcended by the "turn-of-the-tune." The social divides between rural and urban, rich and poor, are not so great among Americans when they are imbibing the frontier spirit through dance and song. The multiple layers of the Arkansas traveler legend help to explain its endurance in folklore, art, theater, music, and comedy, and the Arkansas Traveler moniker has also been adopted and co-opted by Arkansans in a variety of forms from newspapers to baseball teams. Yet, some Arkansans have voiced displeasure with the resilience of the tale and label in its many manifestations. Indeed, toward the end of the nineteenth century, William Foote Pope, an Arkansan who had lived through the early period of Arkansas statehood, grumbled about the damage the silly tale had done to the reputation of the state.

> So much has already been written and sung anent the "Arkansas Traveler" that I would fain pass the subject by with the silence it deserves were it not for the fact that many intelligent people believe to this day that the humorous caricature represents a leading type of Arkansas character . . . The [legend] has had a widespread circulation, [and] has done untold injury to the good name of the State and her people.[2]

Historian Brooks Blevins has skillfully examined the dual Arkansas/Arkansaw image and explained that the negative attributes often associated with the image—"violence, ignorance, shiftlessness, laziness . . . racism, moonshining, clannishness, inbreeding, barefootedness, floppyhattedness, and general cussedness"—simultaneously conjure positive representations of the Arkansawyer as "independent, resourceful, nonconformist, close to nature, unpretentious, generous, and nonmaterialistic."[3] This multifaceted image is captured in the Arkansas Traveler legend.

Geography of Travel: Exploration and Perception of Place and Landscape

My purpose in this book is neither to reexamine the origins of the Arkansas Traveler legend nor to explain why the moniker has proven so resilient. These topics have been explored expertly by others.[4] Instead, I aim to explore the stories of actual Arkansas travelers from the early nineteenth century through the lens of geography. When examined through a geographical lens, another facet of the multi-faceted Arkansas Traveler mystique is revealed. Geography is particularly relevant to a study of the original Arkansas travelers because travel is at its core a geographical act. Traveling engages the traveler in a geographical movement through spaces, places, and landscapes. A traveler traverses geographical space by physically moving from one location to the next. The geography of travel at its most basic level can be represented as a line on a map showing which spaces a traveler traversed. Yet, travelers do more than move through space. Travelers interact with the peoples and the natural environments they encounter. These interactions with fellow humans and with nature are fodder for travel narratives. Travelers have written, publishers have sold, and readers have consumed travel narratives in a variety of forms for centuries.[5] Travel narratives are enjoyable to read because the genre is characterized by dramatic imagery, provocative epithets, and anecdotes filled with danger, conflict, and an occasional pinch of hyperbole.[6] While these literary devices make for entertaining reading, they can result in a distorted geographical understanding of a place. Exotic peoples, titillating insults, and spectacular scenery are privileged in the geographical memory of the reader, even when most of the narrative is more mundane. The mental map of the reader can be distorted easily by the sensational language travelers use to describe the peoples and environments they encountered. The Arkansas travel narratives described in this book are excellent examples of this phenomenon. When first reading the journals of early nineteenth-century travelers, one might be tempted to focus on the travelers' abusive critiques of Arkansas society. Indeed, some of the travelers' most provocative passages are those most frequently quoted as evidence of the state of early Arkansas societies and the bad reputation that followed.[7] The language of these Arkansas travelers also provides a window into the ethnic, class, and political biases common among early nineteenth-century men of privileged social stations. But, like the Arkansas Traveler tale itself, it is necessary to scratch beneath the superficial and the sensational to understand how these Arkansas travelers mapped the geography of the Arkansas past.

As I tell the stories of the travels of William Dunbar, Henry Rowe Schoolcraft, Thomas Nuttall, and George William Featherstonhaugh in the chapters ahead, I hope to illustrate how geographical ideas can serve as a useful interpretive lens. Specifically, I will focus attention on two themes—place and landscape—that are important to historical geographers like myself. From the perspective of historical geography, travel literature can be understood as a traveler's exploration and perception of places and landscapes. Place is often used in everyday conversation as a synonym for location. For geographers, place is more than location. Place as a geographical concept involves both objective and subjective characteristics that bring human meaning to a physical space. The difference between location and place can be understood as the difference between the question *where is it?*—a locational query—and the question *what is it like there?*—a query that conjures the human emotions and subjectivities associated with the concept of place. The meanings that are associated with a place are created by both insiders and outsiders. Insiders—those who live in a place—construct ideas about what they like about the place, what they dislike about the place, what the place represents, who and what belongs in the place, what is to be valued in that place, how the place makes them feel, how they think others view their place, and so on. These ideas are necessarily contested by those with and without power, as well as by those in and outside of the mainstream culture. Outsiders also construct ideas about places. Some outsiders physically visit a place, but many simply imagine it. Whether visited or imagined, an outsider's sense of a place is colored by the positive and negative prejudices that they reference as they react to different cultures and environments. The multiple meanings that are attached to a place are thus a combination of the ideas of those who live in a place, those who have visited a place, and those who imagine the place at a distance. While the concept of place is useful for geographers seeking to explain the meanings that people ascribe to spaces, the idea of landscape is used to understand the human imprint on the world, as well as how people *see* the world and how people *inhabit* the world. Landscape is more than scenery. People view, interpret, and shape their landscapes daily. As people interact with and interpret landscapes, they develop perceptions about their world and make decisions about how to act in the world. Power is an important factor in how landscapes are perceived, who controls landscapes, who benefits from landscapes and the ways in which they are perceived, who may act to shape landscapes over time, and how landscapes reinforce existing social relationships.[8]

Witnesses to the Transformation of Arkansas Landscapes

Arkansas in the early nineteenth century is a particularly relevant setting for an exploration of the ways in which travelers constructed place and landscape. The territory that is now the state of Arkansas experienced a significant transformation during this period. Prior to the American acquisition of the territory in 1803, eighteenth-century Arkansas was populated by a small French-Indian society. Although the 1541 Spanish expedition of Hernando de Soto was the first European contact with the native peoples of Arkansas—an encounter that resulted in drastic population reduction due to the introduction of European disease—it was the French in the 1680s, led by explorers René-Robert Cavelier, Sieur de La Salle and Henri de Tonti, who established relationships with the Quapaws near the confluence of the Arkansas and Mississippi Rivers. The territory was officially claimed by Spain in 1769 in the aftermath of the Seven Years' War, but a culturally accommodative French-Indian society persisted. In 1800, Napoleon Bonaparte reacquired Louisiana territory from Spain, but he quickly sold the French claim to the United States in 1803 in the famous Louisiana Purchase.

In the first few decades following the American purchase, a significant transformation occurred in the human geography of Arkansas. The cultural accommodation and relatively peaceful coexistence that had been practiced by the French settlers and the Quapaws of the Arkansas River valley yielded to a new American agricultural society that was less tolerant of native neighbors. Between 1810 and 1820, the non-native population of Arkansas increased from about one thousand to more than fourteen thousand. Much of this population growth is attributed to the migration of Anglo-American settlers during the second half of the decade following the War of 1812. Many of these new settlers aimed to extend the social, economic, and political structures of the American South to Arkansas, while others aimed to flee organized society for the perceived independence of the backcountry.

Furthermore, the Indian removal schemes of the U.S. government forced the relocation of numerous southeastern groups, such as the Cherokees and Choctaws, to Arkansas. While the Quapaws of southeastern Arkansas generally sought peaceful accommodation with new arrivals, both native and white, the Osages in the region of northwestern Arkansas violently resisted the encroachment of Cherokees and Americans. In addition to the cultural upheaval posed by migration and population growth, the statehood petition of neighboring Missouri in 1819 brought the controversy over the extension of slavery to the fore. In the aftermath of the Missouri Compromise of 1820, Arkansas was established as a slave territory and the political and economic influence of southern plantation owners further transformed the region. When Arkansas became a full-fledged state of the United States in 1836, it was a vastly different place and landscape than it had been thirty-three years earlier when it was purchased by President Thomas Jefferson.[9]

The four travelers presented in this book were eyewitnesses to critical moments in the transformation of Arkansas places and landscapes during the first decades of the nineteenth century. William Dunbar explored south-central Arkansas along the Ouachita River to Hot Springs in 1804 shortly after the area was acquired by the United States in the Louisiana Purchase. Henry Rowe Schoolcraft and Thomas Nuttall toured the Ozarks and the Arkansas River valley, respectively, in 1819 when Arkansas had just become an official territory of the United States. The final traveler, George William Featherstonhaugh, traversed Arkansas in 1834, just two years before it was granted statehood by the United States. The geographies of the Arkansas past that emerge from the writings of these travelers are multifaceted—just like the Arkansas Traveler legend itself. Dunbar, Schoolcraft, Nuttall, and Featherstonhaugh each explored and perceived Arkansas landscapes and places that brought both the cultural and the environmental attributes of Arkansas to the fore. The cultural landscapes and places that surface in their writings reveal that Arkansas has always been multicultural. One set of cultural landscapes and places that all four travelers explored and perceived is the native landscapes and places of the Quapaws, Cherokees, Osages, and the hybrid French-Indian society. Another layer of landscapes and places concentrates attention on the white settlers and their African-American slaves that transformed the cultural map of Arkansas during this period. Finally, each traveler explored and perceived commercial landscapes and places and assessed the current state of commerce, the industry of the settlers, and the future commercial potential of the place. The environmental landscapes and

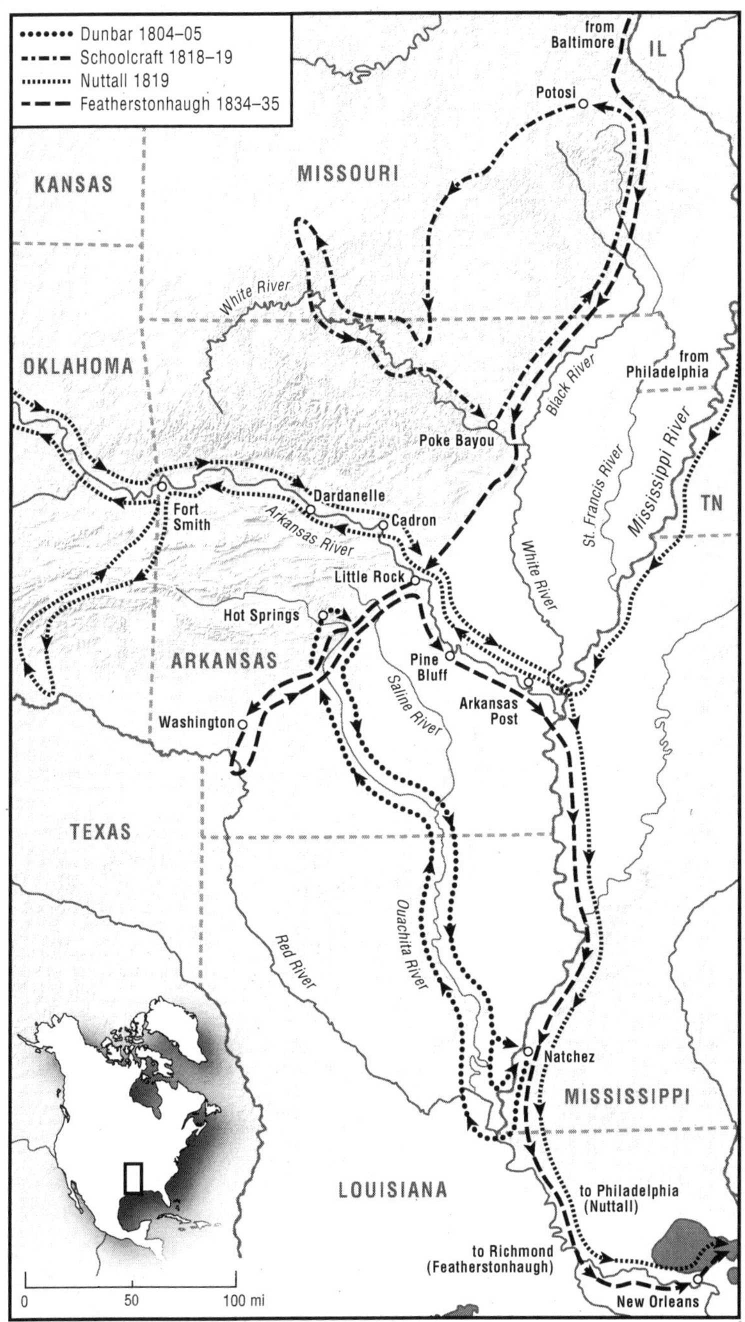

FIG. 0.1. Routes of Four Arkansas Travelers. Cartography by Erin Greb.

places that are explored and perceived by the travelers include a range of perceptions from the sublime to the mundane. The sublime conjures the idea of a physical space that is both beautiful and frightening, while the mundane suggests a space that is unremarkable and possibly unworthy of further attention. Below, I discuss each of these layers of landscape and place in turn.

The transformation of native landscapes and places in Arkansas between 1804 and 1834 is remarkable. In 1804, William Dunbar had very little direct interaction with any of the tribes of Arkansas. The native landscapes and places that he perceived are those of distant and dangerous Osages in conflict with Cherokees and others. His few interactions with natives were in the form of serendipitous encounters with hunting parties of white men and their native partners. These limited interactions form only faint tracings of the landscapes of the hybrid French-Indian society of the period. Had Dunbar chosen the Arkansas River over the Ouachita River, he could have provided a view of the Quapaw-French landscapes and places near Arkansas Post. But Dunbar intentionally chose a path that traversed sparsely inhabited lands and, as a result, the native landscapes and places that he mapped are imagined at a distance rather than experienced firsthand. Henry Schoolcraft also described distant and dangerous Osage landscapes and places. The tales his informants told of the treacherous Osages were not unlike those that Dunbar heard fifteen years earlier. Unlike Dunbar, though, Schoolcraft traveled into Osage territory and observed some of the Osages' abandoned camps. Though he did not interact with the Osages directly, he described Osage landscapes and places with respect and empathy. He speculated about the causes of conflict between Osages, Cherokees, and whites in a way that deepens and humanizes the map of these landscapes and places. Thomas Nuttall was the only traveler of the four discussed in this book who had direct contact with the Osages. Nuttall's life-threatening episode in present-day Oklahoma provides some confirmation of the dangers posed to white trespassers. But Nuttall's account provides much more depth and diversity to native landscapes and places than is evident in either Dunbar's or Schoolcraft's writings. Nuttall had more extended contact with the Quapaws and the Cherokees along the Arkansas River than any of the other four travelers discussed in this book. Thus, Nuttall's explorations and perceptions of native landscapes and places are more complex. He did not rely on informants to map these landscapes and places, but instead interviewed and spent time with the peoples he encountered. His geography of native landscapes and places then, though filtered through his own cultural lenses, is deeper than any other account discussed in this book. In stark contrast to Nuttall, native landscapes and places are nearly absent from George Featherstonhaugh's narrative. The native landscapes and places of Featherstonhaugh's Arkansas are only apparent in traces—an ancient Caddo mound and the "Quapaw blood" that he detected in the wife of a settler. It is telling that, despite the continuous presence of Cherokees, Quapaws, Choctaws, and other groups in Arkansas in 1834, Featherstonhaugh has so little to say about them and that he had no encounters with them that he recorded. Thus, a transforming set of native landscapes and places is apparent across the four narratives. Dunbar's native landscapes and places are simplistic reports of dangerous Indians-in-the-Distance and useful Indians-as-Partners. Fifteen years later, Nuttall and Schoolcraft explored and perceived native landscapes and places that were much more diverse and nuanced. Nuttall's writing, in particular, reveals Osages, Cherokees, and Quapaws as individuals with a full range of attributes. Rather than Indians-as-Objects who are either dangerous or useful to whites, Nuttall perceived landscapes and places that portray Indians-as-Humans. Yet, only fifteen years after Nuttall's and Schoolcraft's tours, Featherstonhaugh perceived native landscapes and places that suggest Indians-as-Remnants. The cycle of distance-presence-neglect of native landscapes and places in Arkansas is one layer of the Arkansas travelers' stories of which one should be aware.

A second layer of landscapes and places that are revealed in these four travelers' writings are the cultural landscapes and places of non-native hunters and settlers. The regional differences across Arkansas are illuminated by the different groups with whom each traveler interacted. Dunbar encountered almost no one along the Ouachita River in the south-central portion of Arkansas. The lack of settlement suggested an empty cultural landscape, devoid of place, with a transitory population of white hunters. By contrast, the other three travelers all encountered numerous non-native settlers and hunters. The landscapes and places explored and perceived by the travelers though are a function of the region through which they traversed. Henry Schoolcraft's non-native landscapes and places are those of Ozark seclusion teetering on the edge of civilization. He maps a geography of landscapes and places on a spectrum of civilization to savagery. The two extremes—and all shades in between—co-existed across Schoolcraft's Arkansas landscapes and places. Thomas Nuttall also explored non-native cultural landscapes and places along the Arkansas River that suggest his perception of degrees of civilization and savagery in Arkansas society in 1819. But the societies with whom Nuttall interacted constituted a much broader social range than those that Schoolcraft encountered in the Ozarks the same year. From the French-Quapaw communities near Arkansas Post, to the "vortex of swindling and idleness" at the Cadron Settlement, to the American military at Fort Smith, Nuttall encountered a wide assortment of cultural landscapes and places that exemplify the transformation of the heart of Arkansas during this pivotal period. Finally, George Featherstonhaugh also evaluated the non-native people he encountered in Arkansas in 1834, but the geography of landscapes and places are perceived by Featherstonhaugh less as a spectrum of savagery to civilization than as one of poverty to prosperity. Featherstonhaugh is also the first to describe the presence of slaves in Arkansas, and thus to explore and perceive Arkansas landscapes and places that included African Americans.

Commercial landscapes and places are another layer of the geographies of the Arkansas past that are mapped in the stories of these travelers. Each man imagined a future in which American commerce would extend into the territory and made predictions about which places and landscapes were ripe for commercial harvest. On one level, commercial reconnaissance for these travelers involved assessing the value of Arkansas soils, minerals, metals, coal, wildlife, plants, and other natural endowments. All four men kept their eyes wide open for any trace of commercially viable nature. This level of reconnaissance is prominent in William Dunbar's narrative. In addition to exploring the "great natural curiosity" of the hot springs, an important mission for Dunbar was to report to President Jefferson on the potential for American commercial development in this newly acquired and mostly unknown land. Dunbar was also an entrepreneur who understood how personally lucrative it could be for him to expand his operations into Arkansas. Similarly, Henry Schoolcraft was engaged in a reconnaissance of the lead deposits of the Ozarks with a view toward entering the mining business. Thomas Nuttall was perhaps the least commercially motivated of the four travelers discussed in this book, but his inspection and sampling of the botanical landscapes of Arkansas was not without a view toward selling plants and making note of flora that could be harvested and processed for commercial use. By the time of Featherstonhaugh's tour in 1834, an American commercial presence had become evident in much of Arkansas. Nevertheless, Featherstonhaugh persuaded his allies in the United States government that a geological survey of the mineral resources of Arkansas and the other western territories could improve mining operations and bring about more efficient and profitable industrial production for the country. His commercial reconnaissance was less about imagining an Arkansas commercial geography than about expanding and improving it. Featherstonhaugh's purpose hints at another level of commercial reconnaissance that is apparent in the other three travel narratives. In addition to resource extraction, commerce depends on labor, modes of transportation, and infrastructure for processing raw materials. Thus, each traveler recorded his perceptions of the navigability of rivers, the quality of roads, and the places that could develop industrial processing facilities or serve as an entrepôt for trade. Furthermore, the travelers evaluated what they saw to be the current level of industry and know-how among the peoples they observed and with whom they interacted. Importantly, much of the negative commentary about the cultural characteristics of Arkansas residents can be understood as a judgment by the travelers that the people were not taking proper commercial advantage of the natural bounties of Arkansas. Where people were praised by the travelers, it is often in situations in which the traveler perceived that the people were diligent, resilient, and otherwise in harmony with their vision of American commercial progress. This set of moral judgments about the industriousness of Arkansas settlers is a significant layer in the geography of the Arkansas past that is evident in the narratives of these travelers.

A fourth layer in the geography of the Arkansas past is the natural environment. The narratives of each traveler are replete with commentary and reflections upon natural places and landscapes. As with the cultural and commercial judgments made by each of these travelers, the environmental features of Arkansas are both admired and maligned. On one level, the natural features to be admired were those that provided commercial potential or opportunities for scientific examination. Conversely, landscapes and places were maligned when they seemed devoid of either commodities or curiosities. On a deeper level though, each man responded to natural features along a perceptual range from the sublime to the mundane. Sublime features provoke a response in the observer that mixes a sense of wonder with a sense of dread. Each of the travelers was astonished by both the aesthetic beauty of Arkansas and the perils of its wilderness. In contrast with the poetic passages that each traveler penned in his attempt to capture the natural splendor of Arkansas, some places and landscapes were perceived by the men as mundane. Occasionally, these ordinary places and landscapes were a refreshing break from the hardships of travel. While the sublime will make a traveler's heart beat faster, the mundane provides a necessary emotional respite. Yet mundane places and landscapes were also maligned by the travelers. While the natural environment of Arkansas treated the travelers to moments of splendor, it also disappointed them when it appeared too familiar.

Organization of the Book

In the first chapter, I introduce each of the four travelers to situate their tours of Arkansas within the broader context of their lives, interests, and goals. In chapters two through five, I describe each of their tours respectively, with attention to the ways in which their descriptions of Arkansas environments and peoples reveal their perceptions of places and landscapes. What emerges from the discussion of the places and landscapes explored and perceived by these four Arkansas travelers is a geography of the Arkansas past. This geography of the Arkansas past encompasses many layers and is thus deeper than the shallow mapping of invectives and accolades pervasive in travel writing. By attending to the many layers of cultural and environmental landscapes explored by these travelers, my goal is to build an understanding of the geographies of exploration and perception in this transformative period in Arkansas history through the writings of these four eyewitnesses. In the final chapter, I present a new approach to mapping the perceptions of travelers. The goal of this cartographic experiment is to reveal and interpret the spatial patterns of these travelers' cultural and environmental landscape perceptions.[10]

Chapter One

Eyewitnesses to Geographical Transformation

THE FOUR TRAVELERS featured in this book had much in common. All four were literate white men. All but the American Henry Schoolcraft were immigrants to the United States from Great Britain. George Featherstonhaugh, Thomas Nuttall, and Henry Schoolcraft were all of the same generation—born within thirteen years of each other in the 1780s and 1790s as the United States was securing independence from Britain and establishing a fledgling republic. At the times of their travels through Arkansas, all but Henry Schoolcraft were well connected with the influential networks of political and scholarly elites on the American East Coast. As such, all but Schoolcraft were funded by either the U.S. government or the American Philosophical Society. Schoolcraft would gain admission to these circles shortly after his Ozark excursion. William Dunbar and George Featherstonhaugh both traveled in Arkansas while in their mid-fifties. For Dunbar, this was near the end of his life. Both Nuttall, at thirty-three, and Schoolcraft, at twenty-five, were relatively young at the time of their Arkansas excursions. Beyond their commonalities in gender, age, social standing, and nationalities, the characteristic that unites all four of these men was their love of science. All four were autodidacts to some degree. Though they received the primary education and tutoring that was common for eighteenth-century boys of their social standing, none of them received formal training at the post-secondary level. All four of them were fascinated by scientific discovery and sought out opportunities to learn. As their biographies reveal, each man had a different path to Arkansas, but each path was paved with an interest in science and the possible discoveries to be made on the Arkansas frontier.

William Dunbar, 1750–1810

The first Arkansas traveler discussed in this book, William Dunbar, was born in approximately 1750 to a privileged family in northeastern Scotland. William's father, Sir Archibald Dunbar, engaged in the sporting pursuits of the Scottish landed gentry, such as hawking, fishing, and dog breeding; he also managed the affairs of the three estates that he owned. His primary country estate, the three-storied Duffus House overlooking a large garden and an orchard, was the birthplace of William. Archibald's first wife, Helen, died in 1748 after giving birth to a daughter and three sons. William was the first child of Anne Bayne Dunbar, Archibald's second wife, whom he had hired to tutor his sons. Dunbar's biographer, Arthur H. DeRosier Jr., explained the importance of William's mother, Anne, in her son's intellectual development.

> Her emphasis on and respect for learning were more important than Dunbar titles, holdings, and money. He inherited from his mother an insatiable curiosity, a love for learning, and a desire to make a difference. What he got from his Dunbar ancestors was the economic and social security to make that difference.[1]

Young William was apparently disinterested in the blood sports of the Scottish gentry. Instead of conquering nature, William preferred to study it by collecting and examining rocks, plants, and insects. Anne encouraged her son's interest in science, and Archibald hired tutors for all his sons during their grammar school years. One of these tutors, John Brulet, taught William to speak fluent French and engaged his interest in science with long talks and explorations of the countryside. In 1763, William entered King's College in Aberdeen, where he studied a classical curriculum of history, philosophy, science, mathematics, geography, economics, religion, English, Latin, and Hebrew. His mathematics professor Alexander Rait was particularly influential in cultivating William's belief in mathematics as vital to the progress of civilization. Following his graduation from King's College in 1769, William continued to study natural science, collect specimens, and work with the Museum of Natural History in Aberdeen. It was most likely the indignities of primogeniture in Scotland and a desire to seek economic and social opportunities in America that led William at the age of twenty-one to sail for Philadelphia in 1771. William's elder half-brother Alexander inherited the family estate and titles upon Archibald's death in 1769. With a small

FIG. 1.1 William Dunbar, 1750–1810.
Courtesy of the Library of Congress.

inheritance and encouragement from his mother and sisters, William had the means and motivation to seek a new life across the Atlantic.[2]

John Ross, a Dunbar family acquaintance and successful Scottish merchant in Philadelphia, was the magnet that drew William Dunbar to Philadelphia in favor of other American ports. Dunbar sought to become involved in the Indian trade, so Ross suggested that William move to Pittsburgh and partner with his son, Alexander Ross. For the next two years, Dunbar developed a strong and lasting partnership with the Rosses. By 1773, Dunbar had learned of liberal land policies in British West Florida and, with a loan from the Rosses, descended the Ohio and Mississippi Rivers with visions of building a plantation. Dunbar selected land east of Baton Rouge, sailed to Jamaica to purchase slaves, proceeded to Pensacola to secure a land grant from the governor, and returned to his new property to direct his slaves in the construction of buildings, roads, and fences. The twenty-three-year-old planted indigo, rice, corn, and other crops common for export and personal use, but he decided early to focus his plantation efforts on manufacturing barrel staves for export to the Caribbean. Dunbar's journal entry in late May of 1776 noted the activities of his plantation three years after his arrival.

> The Plantation Negroes are in Number 14 of whom 7 Men & 4 Women work in the field & 3 Women are at present in the House—There are also 23 New Negroes for sale who are employed about the business of the Plantation as occasion requires. The Dry lands Cleared have been planted with Corn Rice & a little Indigo, together with peas &c. We have also begun the making of Staves, of which there are already made 13 hundred of white oak Puncheon Staves—A Hired Man is employed in building Negro houses.[3]

Over the next year, Dunbar recorded in his journal the daily activities on his plantation. The people he enslaved—Barra, Castor, Cato, Jamie, Timbo, Primus, Abraham, Isaac, Adam, Paul, Solomon, Pollux, Bessy, Ketty, Tango, Polly, Silvia, Juliet, and Mamma—were worked year-round felling timber, rolling logs, splitting wood, sawing, dressing boards, weeding, planting, hoeing, harvesting, burning, carting, washing, digging canals, cutting cane, beating indigo, thrashing rice, building fences, clearing a road, raising a smokehouse, daubing the chimney and any other chore necessary to the maintenance and growth of plantation operations. The most prevalent daily activity for those enslaved by Dunbar, though, was the making of staves. From eight to seventeen slaves on any given day were dedicated to manufacturing the thousands of staves per week that became the staple product of the Dunbar plantation. Dunbar and the enslaved people on his plantation were frequently ill with cholera, yellow fever, and other ailments of life in eighteenth-century Louisiana. When Bessy attempted to run away in late July 1776, she was placed in irons for a few days and then received "25 lashes with a Cow Skin as a punishment & Example to the rest."[4] Earlier that month, Dunbar was astonished to learn from his neighbors of a slave conspiracy that involved three of his men. He lamented the perceived betrayal.

> Of what avail is kindness & good usage when rewarded by such ingratitude; 'tis true indeed they were kept under due subordination & obliged to do their duty in respect to plantation work, but two of the three had always behaved so well that they had never once received a stroke of the whip.[5]

When one of the men drowned as he attempted to escape, Dunbar interpreted the tragedy as "sufficient evidence of his guilt." The other two men were hanged.

William Dunbar's plantation was growing prosperous when the war for American independence came to his doorstep. Dunbar detailed in his journal the destruction of his plantation in late February 1778.

> We were alarmed . . . by a report . . . that a party of Americans had arrived . . . I instantly determined to send my negroes for protection to the Spanish side. . . . [I] set out for Point Coupee that I might gain the earliest possible intelligence of the numbers and intent of the Americans, not suspecting that any mischief was intended to the peaceable inhabitants; therefore . . . I took nothing out of my house . . . Mr. Alexander . . . informed me that he had learnt that the intention of the Americans was to rob & plunder every English subject who had property of any value . . . and further I was informed that the party was commanded by James Willing of Philadelphia, a young man who had left this country the year before; perfectly & intimately acquainted with all the gentlemen upon the river at whose houses he had been often entertained in the most hospitable manner & frequently indulged his natural propensity of getting drunk.[6]

Willing's party fired shots, seized slaves, plundered and burned houses, killed hogs and livestock, and set fire to indigo works and staves. When they arrived at Dunbar's plantation, the men took "every thing that cou'd be carried away—all my wearing apparel, bed & table linen . . . blankets, pieces of cloth, sugar, silver ware . . . [and] destroyed a considerable quantity of bottled wine."[7] Dunbar responded to the destruction and uncertainty by obtaining a land grant from the Spanish governor in New Orleans for land on the west side of the Mississippi River where he attempted to rebuild his stave manufacturing operations in Spanish territory. Unfortunately for Dunbar, the Spanish joined France in the fight against the British and on the side of the American colonists in 1779. By 1780, his holdings on the Spanish side of the river had also been pillaged and many of his slaves had run away. Despite these severe setbacks, Dunbar rebuilt his Spanish plantation, purchased new slaves, developed good commercial and political relationships in New Orleans, and diversified his operations by planting rice, corn, pumpkins, and peas. Many of these agricultural endeavors involved experimentation with varieties of seeds and methods. Dunbar studied agronomy and carefully recorded the results of his plantings. In 1784, as his plantation once again began to grow, Dunbar married Diana Clark. William and Diana, often spelled Dinah, would have several children together and remain married until Dunbar's death.[8]

Despite the tumult of the 1780s, Dunbar acquired more than five thousand acres of land in the fertile Natchez district where he established a plantation and built a grand house of his own design. In addition to managing his plantations and traveling between New Orleans, Natchez, and Manchac, Dunbar assembled a significant library, served as an interpreter for Spanish officials, acquired equipment for experimentation, tinkered with methods for determining latitude and longitude in the field, invented five types of plows, and studied horticulture, architecture, botany, zoology, and surveying. In 1789, a survey of the thirty-first parallel was conducted to settle the boundary between Spain and the United States. Andrew Ellicott led the United States commission and Dunbar was selected as the lead Spanish commissioner on the strength of his relationship with Governor Manuel Gayoso de Lemos and his reputation as an honest and dependable broker and skilled surveyor. The chronically ill and perpetually busy Dunbar agreed to serve as Spanish commissioner on the arduous survey in return for additional Spanish grants of land and in hopes of currying favor with the Americans—in whose territory he now resided. Although Dunbar left the survey expedition early due to illness and obligations to his plantation and family, he earned the respect of Andrew Ellicott. On Ellicott's recommendation, Thomas Jefferson sponsored Dunbar for membership in the American Philosophical Society.[9]

Although his budding reputation as a scientist was relevant, it was *where* William Dunbar resided that was perhaps most significant to Jefferson and other Americans on the Atlantic coast. Natchez, situated in southwestern Mississippi on a bluff overlooking the Mississippi River, served as a vital commercial entrepôt for overland transportation to the Tennessee River near present-day Muscle Shoals, Alabama, and the Cumberland River at present-day Nashville, Tennessee. Natchez also served as a significant station on the Mississippi River north of the newly surveyed thirty-first parallel marking the boundary between Spanish Florida and the United States. Furthermore, the Natchez area had been a cultural crossroads for generations of Indian, European, and African peoples. The broad lower Mississippi Valley in which it was situated was a borderland region of shifting imperial claims for several decades before the American purchase in 1803. Thus, Natchez was a significant outpost on the southwestern frontier of the nascent United States and, importantly, William Dunbar had proven himself to be a skillful negotiator of regional politics and a resilient and creative entrepreneur, as well as an intelligent and capable scientist. During the Mississippi territorial governorship of Winthrop Sargent, 1798–1801, Dunbar ascended to a variety of political appointments, including cotton gin inspector, quarter session court judge, conservator of the peace, probate judge, legislator, and trustee of the short-lived Jefferson College. Despite his Federalist political leanings, Dunbar's political influence continued during the Democratic-Republican governorship of William C. C. Claiborne, 1801–5, including service as Speaker of the House of the territorial legislature from which he guided legislation on taxes, vaccinations, dueling, debtors, orphans' courts, education, and the militia. In the summer of 1799, Jefferson commented in his letter to Dunbar that "it is . . . with great pleasure I have learnt that so advanced a post as the Natchez possesses a gentleman so well qualified as yourself to extend enquiries into the regions beyond that."[10] Jefferson saw the value in cultivating a bond with a man of Dunbar's talents and situated in Dunbar's geographical location, and the two men began a regular correspondence. Shortly before his inauguration as the third president, Jefferson wrote to Dunbar in 1801 and remarked that a "philosophical vedette at the distance of one thousand miles, and on the verge of the terra incognita of our continent, is precious to us here."[11]

Even if they are not familiar with all the details, most Americans have heard of the Lewis and Clark Expedition. The stories of the other early attempts to explore the Louisiana Territory have been mostly forgotten, though. Arkansas was included in the purchase and was of significant interest to President Jefferson. As Meriwether Lewis, William Clark, and the Corps of Discovery began their northwestern journey along the Missouri and Columbia Rivers in 1804, Jefferson was planning an equally ambitious expedition to explore the Red and Arkansas Rivers. Much of the land recently acquired by the United States from France was a terra incognita to the American president. Largely unknown were the sources, courses, and navigability of the major rivers of this territory, along with the flora, fauna, minerals, and soils to be found. Of political concern was the disposition of the peoples in the region toward the Americans, as well as the Spanish claims to the unknown boundaries of the purchase territory. South of the confluence of the Missouri River with the Mississippi River at St. Louis, there were known to be two major western rivers that flowed into the Mississippi—the Red River and the Arkansas River. Jefferson considered it possible that the Red River might rival the Missouri as a passageway to the West. Therefore, Jefferson proposed to the United States Congress an expedition to ascend the Red River to its source, to explore the highland territory of the West, and to return via the Arkansas River to the Mississippi. The expedition would be a southwestern counterpart to the northwestern expedition of Lewis and Clark. If both expeditions succeeded, the Americans would have a wealth of geographical knowledge to add to their limited understanding of this distant territory they now ostensibly owned.[12]

President Jefferson turned to William Dunbar to inquire about the prospects for this so-called Grand Expedition. There were numerous obstacles to American exploration of this terra incognita and the signs that the Grand Expedition was doomed came quickly. First, the Spanish and American governments had yet to resolve the western boundary of Louisiana that served as the division between American and Spanish claims. Although Dunbar had word from his sources that the Spanish military official Marqués de Casa Calvo might grant permission to the Americans for scientific exploration, Dunbar wondered with pride whether it "might seem as improper condescension to ask the approbation of any man to explore our own rivers." A second group of people unlikely to welcome American explorers were the Osages along the Arkansas River. In the summer of 1804, Jefferson was visited in Washington by the Osage chief Pawhuska, or White Hair, who informed him of a schism in the Osage Nation. The president was told that the splinter group of Osages who inhabited the Arkansas River valley would "undoubtedly oppose [American] passage . . . and perhaps do worse." The third major obstacle is a familiar one to modern Americans: funding. Jefferson asked Congress for $12,000 to fund both the Red-Arkansas expedition and another expedition on the Platte River. Congress granted only $3,000 for both. The president decided to place the Platte River mission on hold and asked Dunbar to lead the Red-Arkansas expedition. Dunbar knew that $3,000 would not be enough money for the ambitious journey. With this "scanty appropriation," he would not be able to acquire appropriate instruments, provisions, the services of another scientist, an officer to command the soldiers, an interpreter and guide for each river, or much else on his list of necessities. The president wrote to Dunbar in July 1804 that he was suspending the Red-Arkansas expedition until the following year when relations with the Spanish and the Osages might be improved and funding from Congress might be more generous. In lieu of the Grand Expedition, Jefferson told Dunbar to use the money and supplies already procured to go forward with a shorter expedition "to what distance and in what direction you please." Dunbar had contemplated exploring the Ouachita River and wrote to Jefferson that this tributary of the Red River "is supposed to offer many Curious objects;" among these was the "boiling spring" that had a reputation for therapeutic effects. He resolved to use the opportunity given him by the president to explore the Ouachita River and the legendary hot springs and assured Jefferson that the expedition "shall collect information sufficient to induce Congress to make liberal provisions for the important Expedition of the ensuing season."[13]

The river voyage from Natchez to the hot springs, primarily on the Ouachita River, from October 1804 to January 1805 is described in chapter two. Upon his return, Dunbar wrote President Jefferson that "the objects which have presented themselves to us are not of very high importance, it must however be acknowledged that the hot springs are indeed a very great natural curiosity."[14] He went on to brief the president about the temperatures of the water, the charting of the rivers, the moss and cabbage he found, and the deposits he observed around the springs. While Dunbar busied himself through the early months of 1805 preparing his journal, specimens, and maps for shipment to the president, he was also called upon to plan another expedition. In March 1805 Jefferson wrote to Dunbar, "It will be necessary for us now to set on foot immediately the Arcansa & Red river expedition, Congress having given an additional appropriation of 5000D for these objects."[15] It appeared that the Grand Expedition would go forward after all. Over the next few months, Dunbar corresponded with Jefferson and his secretary of war Henry Dearborn and convinced them to abandon the plan to explore both rivers in one expedition. Dearborn wrote to Dunbar in May 1805 to let him know, "Your remarks, and further reflection, have induced the President of the United States to confine the object of the proposed exploring expedition to the Red river, and some of its principal branches, together with the country immediately adjacent."[16] Dunbar agreed to oversee the planning of the expedition. He corresponded with John Sibley of Natchitoches, Louisiana, about the Red River and coordinated with officials in New Orleans to secure supplies, soldiers, and Spanish passports for the expedition leaders. He also offered his opinions about the various men who were considered by Jefferson and Dearborn to lead the expedition. More than one year after President Jefferson had written that the expedition should "set on foot immediately," Thomas Freeman, Peter Custis, Richard Sparks, and their crew departed Fort Adams, Mississippi, in April 1806 to begin their ascent of the Red River. Three months later, the expedition came to an end along the current border between Arkansas and Texas. Thomas Freeman explained the dramatic confrontation with the Spanish:

> The Spanish commanding officer stated that his orders were not to suffer any body of armed troops to march through the territory of the Spanish government; to stop the exploring party by force, and to fire on them if they persisted in ascending the river before the limits of the territory were

> defined. I stated that the object of my expedition was to explore the river to its source under the instructions of the President of the U.S. and I requested the Spanish commander to state in writing his objections to the progress of the party, and the authority upon which it was made. This was refused by the Spaniard, but he pledged his honor for the truth of his assertion, that he was acting under the orders of the government, who would be answerable for his conduct in the affair. He then asked if the American party would return, and when. The great superiority of the Spanish force, and the difficulty the party had already experienced in ascending the river . . . rendering a further progress impracticable, I replied that I should remain in my present position that day and would return the day following.[17]

Despite the failure of the Freeman-Custis-Sparks expedition on the Red River, Dunbar continued planning for an 1807 expedition on the Arkansas River. Unfortunately for Dunbar and others interested in further exploration of the southern portion of the Louisiana Purchase, Congress would not appropriate funds for additional expeditions and secretary of war Henry Dearborn informed Dunbar that the Arkansas River expedition would not materialize. Ultimately, there would be no southern counterpart to the famous Lewis and Clark expedition—no Grand Expedition. Dunbar published several articles in the *Transactions of the American Philosophical Society*, and his journal was excerpted in a U.S. government publication entitled *Message from the President of the United States, Communicating Discoveries Made in Exploring the Missouri, Red River, and Washita, by Captains Lewis and Clark, Doctor Sibley, and Mr. Dunbar: With a Statistical Account of the Countries Adjacent: February 19, 1806*. Dunbar was frequently ill and feverish throughout his adult life, and though the exact cause of his death is uncertain, his passing in October 1810 at the age of sixty could be attributed to his general poor health. In his biography of Dunbar, Arthur DeRosier Jr. offered that Dunbar died of "inquisitiveness" because he could "never stop studying, pondering, inventing, inquiring, and learning."[18]

Henry Rowe Schoolcraft, 1793–1864

The second traveler featured in this book, Henry Rowe Schoolcraft, differed from William Dunbar in many ways. Unlike the seasoned, politically connected, and federally funded Dunbar, Schoolcraft was young, inexperienced, and seeking opportunity without notice or support from the federal government. Schoolcraft's travels occurred fourteen years after the Dunbar and Hunter expedition and introduced readers to an altogether different region of Arkansas. Also, unlike the other travelers featured in this book, Schoolcraft was born in the United States and held deep family roots in New York. Henry's great-grandfather, James Schoolcraft, came to America around 1727 as a member of the British army and settled near Albany, New York. One of James' sons, John, also served in the military and settled along the Normans Kill, a tributary to the Hudson River near Albany. Henry was born in 1793 to John's son, Lawrence Schoolcraft, and Margaret Anne Barbara Rowe. Lawrence served in the New York militia and subsequently the Continental Army. Henry Schoolcraft recorded with pride that his father was "present, in 1776, when the Declaration of Independence was read to the troops drawn up in hollow square at Ticonderoga" and that he "continued to be an indomitable actor in various positions, civil and military, in the great drama of the Revolution during its entire continuance."[19] Following his Revolutionary War service, Lawrence returned to farming along Normans Kill, remained a member of the militia, and was active in the Reformed Protestant Dutch Church of Helderberg. Shortly after Henry's birth, Lawrence became superintendent at the local glass factory, and in 1808 organized a new glass factory near Utica, New York. Henry learned the glass business from his father, and at the age of twenty he became superintendent of a new factory on Lake Dunmore in Vermont. While directing the factory in Vermont, Henry was tutored in mineralogy and chemistry by Frederick Hall, Professor of Natural Philosophy at Middlebury College. As Schoolcraft's biographer explained, "Hall deeply influenced Schoolcraft's intellectual development as his was the first trained academic mind to which the latter had been exposed."[20]

Within two years, the Vermont Glass Factory under Henry's leadership had proven to be unprofitable. As the Vermont venture began to fail, Lawrence organized a New Hampshire Glass Factory in Keene and invited Henry to become superintendent. By 1817, the factory at Keene was also uncompetitive and Henry Schoolcraft was deeply in debt. Whether the collapse of the two factories directed by Henry was due to the failure of the young man to lead a business, the broader economic instability of the time, bad luck, or some combination of these factors is difficult to discern, but the result was that the twenty-four-year-old Henry Schoolcraft was forced to declare insolvency in 1817. His only remaining assets were his clothes. Thus, in early 1818, Schoolcraft left the humiliation he must have felt at home to seek new opportunities in the American West.[21] Rufus Pettibone, Henry's

FIG. 1.2. Henry Rowe Schoolcraft, 1793–1864.
Courtesy of the Library of Congress.

lawyer during his insolvency hearings, was moving to St. Louis with his brother Levi and others, so Henry joined them with an eye toward investigating prospects in the lead mining district of southeastern Missouri.

Shortly after his arrival in Missouri, Schoolcraft was introduced to another twenty-five-year-old named Stephen F. Austin and his father, Moses Austin, who offered Henry lodging and a place to store his mineral collections.[22] Schoolcraft spent the next few months surveying the mining and smelting operations in the region and collecting mineral specimens. As he toured the Missouri mines and spoke with experienced miners, Henry heard reports of large, unworked lead deposits along the James River in the rugged Ozarks to the southwest and became determined to visit the area. He convinced his fellow migrant Levi Pettibone to join him on the journey but failed to secure a commitment from any of the experienced backwoodsmen in the area.[23] In early November 1818, Schoolcraft and Pettibone set out over the hills surrounding Potosi, Missouri, for a tour of the Ozarks. In chapter three, I explore what I call their greenhorn expedition through the Ozarks from November 1818 to February 1819.

Upon his return from the harrowing journey through southern Missouri and northern Arkansas, Schoolcraft met Major Stephen H. Long, zoologist Thomas Say, and geologist Augustus Jessup, who were about to embark on the U.S. government–sponsored expedition to the Yellowstone River.[24] The meeting was a "lightbulb" moment for young Schoolcraft.

> This expedition was the first evidence to my mind of the United States Government turning attention, in connection with practical objects, to matters of science, and the effort was due I understand, to the enlightened mind of Mr. Calhoun, then Secretary of War. It occurred to me . . . that the subject of the mines which I had been inquiring about, so far as relates to their management as a part of the public domain, was one that belonged properly to the United States Government . . . I determined to visit Washington, and lay the subject before the President.[25]

Schoolcraft quickly set to work on a report on lead mining that was published later that year as "A View of the Lead Mines of Missouri Including Some Observations on the Mineralogy, Geology, Geography, Antiquities, Soil, Climate, Population, and Productions of Missouri and Arkansaw, and Other Sections of the Western Country." In this report, Schoolcraft made recommendations that he hoped to bring to the attention of president James Monroe and secretary of war John C. Calhoun.

> Respecting the present state of the lead mines, it is only necessary here to add, that they are worked in a more improved manner than at any former period; that they are more extensive than when the country came into the hands of the United States, and of course giving employment to a greater number of miners, while every season is adding to the number of mines; and that the ores may be considered of the richest kind. Every day is developing to us the vast resources of this country in minerals, and particularly in lead; and we cannot resist the belief that in riches and extent, the mines of Missouri are paralleled by no other mineral district in the world. In the working of the mines—in raising the ore, and smelting it—and in the establishment of the different manufactures dependent upon it, there is much to be done. Though the processes now pursued are greatly superior

> to those in use under the French and Spanish governments, there is still ample room for improvement. The earth has not yet been penetrated over 80 feet![26]

The primary obstacles to further progress in mining in the region, according to Schoolcraft, were "the want of capitalists in the mine country . . . of scientific knowledge in those by whom mining is conducted, and of practical skill in the boring, blasting, sinking shafts, and galleries, draining and ventilating . . . [and] but one hearth furnace for smelting in the whole district."[27] Schoolcraft proposed that with better infrastructure, management, skill, laws, and a "mineralogical school located in the mine country" the vast mineral wealth of the country could be tapped by the United States.

Schoolcraft returned to New York in 1819 and, after publishing his report of the lead mines, secured a meeting with President Monroe, Secretary Calhoun, and Treasury Secretary William H. Crawford. Calhoun was apparently impressed with Schoolcraft and selected him to serve as the mineralogist for a war department expedition to northern Michigan and the Upper Mississippi River. The Cass Expedition of 1820, led by Lewis Cass, governor of the Michigan territory, was charged with improving relations with the Indians of the region, investigating the mineral resources of the upper Great Lakes, and locating sites for forts along the unstable border with Canada. When the expedition concluded in October 1820, Schoolcraft returned to New York, where he prepared for publication his "Narrative Journal of Travels through the Northwestern Regions of the United States Extending from Detroit through the Great Chain of American Lakes to the Sources of the Mississippi River, Performed as a Member of the Expedition under Governor Cass in the Year 1820." One of the strategic points of interest to the United States was the rapids of the St. Mary River, or the Sault Ste. Marie, that formed a natural barrier to navigation between Lake Huron and Lake Superior. Schoolcraft was impressed with the area on his first visit in the summer of 1820.

> Several wooded islands upon the inclined plane of the falls, by contrasting the deep green foliage of the hemlock, spruce, and pine, with the snowy whiteness of the rapids, produce a contrast which has a pleasing effect; and the shadowy outlines of the distant mountains of Lake Superior, the singular mixture of forest trees upon the shores, and the fishing canoes of the savages, which are constantly seen at the foot of the falls, render it one of the most picturesque views of northern scenery. . . . The village of the Sault de St. Marie, is on the south or American shore, and consists of from

> fifteen to twenty buildings, occupied by five or six French and English families. . . . In the hospitality and politeness, which during our stay at the Sault, we experienced in this family [of John Johnston], we have been made to forget our insulated situation, and to observe how short a participation in the blandishments of refined society, is sufficient to obliterate the effect of the fatigues and privations of travelling.[28]

It is fortunate that Schoolcraft found the Sault to be so pleasant. In 1822 he was appointed by President Monroe to serve as the U.S. Indian Agent at Sault Ste. Marie to oversee a district that included most of upper Michigan, northwest Wisconsin, and northeast Minnesota. He was responsible for maintaining day-to-day relations with the Chippewas in the region and reducing British influence with the tribe. Schoolcraft took his post during the summer of 1822 under the supervision of Governor Cass, but with scant regulations or funding to guide and support him. As Schoolcraft settled into his new office overlooking the St. Mary River, his transition from mineralogist to ethnologist was in motion. Schoolcraft became absorbed in studying the Chippewa language and creating a vocabulary and grammar guide. He was also fascinated by the allegorical tales told by the Chippewas, and saw this as evidence of their high intellect. John Johnston, an Irish immigrant who came to America in the 1790s, settled at the Sault as a fur trader, married a Chippewa woman, and had numerous children, welcomed Schoolcraft into his home. Both Johnston and his wife, Susan, or Oshauguscodaywayqua, helped Schoolcraft with his study of the Chippewa language, customs, and folklore. The relationship with the Johnstons proved to be fruitful to Schoolcraft for more than academic and political reasons. In 1823, Henry married the daughter of John and Susan, Jane Johnston, or Bamewawagezhikaquay, and their first son, William Henry "Willy" Schoolcraft, was born the following summer. Henry and Jane would have two more children over the next five years: Jane Susan Anne "Janee" Schoolcraft in 1827, and John Johnston Schoolcraft in 1829. Willy died suddenly of croup in 1827, before Janee was born. In 1833 the Schoolcraft family left Sault Ste. Marie for Mackinac so that the children could attend a Presbyterian school, and three years later they moved to Detroit where Henry accepted an appointment as Michigan Superintendent of Indian Affairs. The departure from the Sault was difficult for Jane, in part due to her mixed-race identity. As one historian explained,

> the daughters of Indian women and Anglo officials and traders grew up as first ladies of the fur-trade country. Jane had been that in Sault Ste. Marie, where so many visitors at her father's table had admired her grace and

accomplishments. Her marriage to a rising government official might have assured her place in society had she stayed in Sault Ste. Marie. . . . But in the larger settlements, white ladies were beginning to arrive; for them, "half-breeds" were a lesser caste, unfit to be known or visited.[29]

Shortly after the Schoolcrafts' move to Detroit, their family savings were seriously depleted in the economic collapse of 1837 due to Henry's aggressive investments. The election of the Whig candidate William Henry Harrison in the presidential election of 1840 would prove to be another blow to Schoolcraft, who was a staunch supporter of New York Democratic president Martin Van Buren. Schoolcraft was removed from his post by the incoming administration in 1841 after serving as an Indian agent and superintendent in Michigan for nineteen years. In his biography of Schoolcraft, Richard G. Bremer assessed this defining portion of Schoolcraft's career as follows:

> Schoolcraft's basic distaste for the Indians themselves remained subordinated to his belief in the moral obligation of the white man to provide them with a fair compensation for their lands together with the opportunity to embrace civilization and Christianity. Thus, despite the obvious self-interest that lay behind many of his actions, he did what he could, according to his own lights, to protect the red man. If he did not delve into his own pocket to help out his charges in times of extreme need, as certain other agents did, . . . his performance compares favorably with that of the horde of political hacks and corrupt self-seekers who swarmed into office after the early [1840s]. In an essentially untenable situation, he did what he could for a cause doomed by the realities of power and the cultural assumptions of the day.[30]

If the loss of his savings and employment were not tragic enough, his wife Jane died the next year in 1842. Jane and Henry engaged in literary projects together during their nineteen-year marriage, including distribution of a magazine called *Muzzeniegen* that included poetry written by Jane and provided Henry an outlet for his ethnological work, as well as *The Myth of Hiawatha* that served as inspiration for Henry Wadsworth Longfellow's more famous work *The Song of Hiawatha*. Following Jane's death and the loss of his job, Schoolcraft spent much of the 1840s lobbying publishers and politicians to support additional publication projects, such as an encyclopedia on Native Americans. Shortly after he married his second wife, Mary Howard, in 1847, Schoolcraft finally landed a political appointment as the director of a new federal Indian statistics program at the Office of Indian Affairs in Washington, D.C. In his new position, Schoolcraft was focused on conducting a comprehensive census of the Indian population and collecting ethnographic data on the history and present condition of the tribes of North America. The immense complexity of the project, resistance among some tribes to participate in a federal project of this sort, the use of outdated research methods, and Schoolcraft's failing health resulted in a flawed and rambling six-volume assemblage that was published from 1851 to 1857. Henry Schoolcraft's final years were marked by financial insecurity and significant physical deterioration. His publications did not sell well, and his efforts to secure new publication projects proved to be fruitless. Schoolcraft also suffered a series of strokes that left him progressively more paralyzed and bedridden. He passed away in December 1864 at the age of seventy-one.

Thomas Nuttall, 1786–1859

While Henry Rowe Schoolcraft and Levi Pettibone were canoeing down the White River in northern Arkansas in mid-January 1819, Thomas Nuttall, the third traveler presented in this book, arrived at Arkansas Post on the Arkansas River. Unlike William Dunbar and Henry Rowe Schoolcraft, Nuttall was an experienced traveler. Nuttall developed an interest in natural history while traveling as a young man in the Craven district of North Yorkshire in his native England. After immigrating to the United States in 1808 at the age of twenty-two, he met Benjamin Smith Barton, a professor at the University of Pennsylvania and author of the textbook *Elements of Botany*.[31] Barton recognized potential in young Thomas and agreed to tutor him and to allow the use of his library. On Barton's recommendation, Nuttall embarked on an excursion in 1810 tasked with gathering plant specimens along the Missouri River path of the Lewis and Clark expedition. Nuttall traveled through the Great Lakes, descended the Mississippi River to St. Louis, and ascended the Missouri River to Fort Mandan. Following this excursion, Nuttall returned to England in late 1811 where he remained until the War of 1812 was over. In 1815, Nuttall returned to the United States and embarked on a southern expedition during which he explored the Potomac River and the Chesapeake, as well as Georgia and the Carolinas. The following year, Nuttall journeyed down the Ohio River to Cincinnati, overland across Kentucky and Tennessee, east through the Cumberland Gap and across the Carolinas to Charleston. Thus, in less than ten years, Thomas

FIG. 1.3. Thomas Nuttall, 1786–1859.
Courtesy of the Wellcome Collection.

Nuttall had traversed much of the eastern part of the United States and the Old Northwest.

In 1817, at the age of thirty-one, Nuttall had become a rising star among the scientists of the United States and was elected to the American Philosophical Society and the Academy of Natural Sciences of Philadelphia. In 1818 the publication of his first book, *Genera of North American Plants*, bolstered his international reputation as a botanist. But Nuttall was not ready to rest on his laurels. His goal was to travel to the Rocky Mountains in hopes of discovering new plant species. Nuttall probed his numerous connections to make known his desire to serve as a naturalist on a U.S. government–sponsored expedition to the Rockies.[32] Whether it was suspicion about Nuttall's English nationality during a period of Anglophobia in the United States or simply shifting priorities and politics regarding western exploration, Nuttall was unable to secure government backing. Instead, his colleagues at the American Philosophical Society agreed to fund his Rocky Mountains excursion.[33] He departed Philadelphia in October 1818, traveled overland to Pittsburgh, sailed down the Ohio River, and arrived at the confluence of the Mississippi and Ohio Rivers one week before Christmas in 1818. It is at this point that we join Nuttall's journey in chapter four.

Following his Arkansas tour, Nuttall returned to Philadelphia in the late spring of 1820 and would spend the next two years delivering botanical lectures and attending the meetings of the American Philosophical Society and the Academy of Natural Sciences. Perhaps these academic pursuits were the salve needed to soothe the sting of his failure to reach the Rocky Mountains. His colleagues urged a reluctant Nuttall to publish an account of his travels to Arkansas, and in 1821 his narrative appeared as *A Journal of Travels into the Arkansa Territory During the Year 1819, with Occasional Observations on the Manners of the Aborigines.* Nuttall made clear to his readers that he intended this to be a scientific work and not one for the casual reader of traveler tales.

> To those who vaguely peruse the narratives of travellers for pastime or transitory amusement, the present volume is by no means addressed. It is no part of the author's ambition to study the gratification of so fastidious a taste as that, which but too generally governs the readers of the present day; a taste, which has no criterion but passing fashion, which spurns at every thing that possesses not the charm of novelty, and the luxury of embellishment.[34]

In his 1823 review of *A Journal of Travels into the Arkansa Territory*, Harvard professor Jacob Bigelow noted with approval that

> Mr. Nuttall, from an early attachment to natural history, and from the attractions offered by the unexplored wilds of North America, has followed our plants and minerals with indefatigable perseverance, not only to the confines of civilization and cultivation, but into the remote and desert recesses of the continent. We have few individuals, at least men of education, whose survey of our territory has been equally extensive.[35]

In 1823 Nuttall was appointed to the position of Curator of the Botanic Garden at Harvard College in Cambridge, Massachusetts. From 1823 to 1834, Nuttall served as curator, taught botany at Harvard, published papers in scientific journals, and embarked on several field tours through New

England and the American Southeast to study and collect botanical, mineralogical, and ornithological specimens. His ornithological studies led to the publication of his two-volume series entitled *A Manual of the Ornithology of the United States and Canada*. The first volume, published in 1832, focused on *The Land Birds*, while the second volume of 1834 introduced *The Water Birds*.

Nuttall resigned from Harvard in 1834 so he could join an expedition led by Nathaniel Jarvis Wyeth, a Boston entrepreneur, and Milton Sublette of the Rocky Mountain Fur Company on a journey across the Rocky Mountains to the Oregon Country. John Kirk Townsend, a twenty-four-year-old ornithologist, was invited by Nuttall to join the expedition.[36] In his *Narrative of a Journey across the Rocky Mountains to the Columbia River*, Townsend recorded that he and Nuttall arrived in St. Louis on March 24, 1834, and that on April 28, 1834, the large party departed Independence, Missouri. Townsend recounted his excitement about embarking on this stage of the journey with his friend and fellow naturalist Thomas Nuttall.

> On the 28th of April, at 10 o'clock in the morning, our caravan, consisting of seventy men, and two hundred and fifty horses, began its march; Captain Wyeth and Milton Sublette took the lead, Mr. N. and myself rode beside them; then the men in double file, each leading, with a line, two horses heavily laden, and Captain Thing (Captain W.'s assistant) brought up the rear. The band of missionaries, with their horned cattle, rode along the flanks. I frequently sallied out from my station to look at and admire the appearance of the cavalcade, and as we rode out from the encampment, our horses prancing, and neighing, and pawing the ground, it was altogether so exciting that I could scarcely contain myself. Every man in the company seemed to feel a portion of the same kind of enthusiasm; uproarious bursts of merriment, and gay and lively songs, were constantly echoing along the line.[37]

The prospect of reaching and surpassing the Rocky Mountains must have filled Nuttall with scarcely contained excitement as well. Indeed, Nuttall collected a bounty of specimens. Along the North Platte River in western Nebraska, the party traversed rugged bluffs that were carpeted with flowers at their bases. At this moment in the journey, Townsend depicts the devotion of Nuttall to his botanical endeavors.

> It was a most enchanting sight; even the men noticed it, and more than one of our matter-of-fact people exclaimed, *beautiful, beautiful*! Mr. N.

> was here in his glory. He rode on ahead of the company, and cleared the passages with a trembling and eager hand, looking anxiously back at the approaching party, as though he feared it would come 'ere he had finished, and tread his lovely prizes under foot.[38]

Many such moments of eager collecting must have occurred as the party crossed western Nebraska, Wyoming, and southern Idaho. Here Nuttall was crossing territory that had not been seen by a Euro-American botanist. The expedition paused at a point along the Snake River in southeastern Idaho, north of present-day Pocatello, to construct Fort Hall, a fur-trading post that became an important location along the Oregon Trail. Townsend joined a group of men on a buffalo hunt, while Nuttall stayed behind where the men were on a tight food allowance. When he returned to the fort, Townsend noted a change in Nuttall.

> My companion, Mr. N., had become so exceedingly thin that I should scarcely have known him; and upon my expressing surprise at the great change in his appearance, he heaved a sigh of inanity, and remarked that I 'would have been as thin as he if I had lived on old *Ephraim* for two weeks, and short allowance of that.' I found, in truth, that the whole camp had been subsisting, during our absence, on little else than two or three grizzly bears which had been killed in the neighborhood; and with a complacent glance at my own rotund and *cow-fed* person, I wished my *poor* friend better luck in the future.[39]

After a difficult four-week trek from Fort Hall to Fort Walla Walla, the party was relieved to arrive at the Columbia River. But during their journey to Fort Vancouver the river fought back with winds and waves that soaked some of Nuttall's carefully collected specimens. Townsend relates the story of a resolute Nuttall working to rescue his botanical discoveries.

> Mr. N.'s large and beautiful collection of new and rare plants was considerably injured by the wetting it received; he has been constantly engaged since we landed yesterday, in opening and drying them. In this task he exhibits a degree of patience and perseverance which is truly astonishing; sitting on the ground, and steaming over the enormous fire, for hours together, drying the papers, and re-arranging the whole collection, specimen by specimen, while the great drops of perspiration roll unheeded from his brow. Throughout the whole of our long journey, I have had constantly to admire the ardor and perfect indefatigability with which he has devoted

himself to the grand object of his tour. No difficulty, no danger, no fatigue has ever daunted him, and he finds his rich reward in the addition of nearly *a thousand* new species of American plants, which he has been enabled to make to the already teeming flora of our vast continent.[40]

On September 16, 1834, Nuttall and Townsend arrived at Fort Vancouver along the Columbia River north of present-day Portland, Oregon, where they were "greeted and received with a frank and unassuming politeness" by Dr. John McLoughlin of the Hudson's Bay Company.[41] The men remained in the area, where the local Chinooks and Klikatats referred to Nuttall as "Grass Man," until December when they continued on the Columbia River to Astoria and then departed for the Sandwich Islands, present-day Hawaii. Following a three-month tour of the botanical glories of the Islands, Nuttall and Townsend arrived back in Oregon in late April 1835. The following September, Nuttall again departed for Honolulu and spent the winter of 1835 to 1836 in Hawaii. In the spring of 1836, he sailed for California to begin his oceangoing return to Boston. From April to September, Nuttall sailed on trading vessels down the California coast, around Cape Horn, and up the eastern coast of South and North America to Boston.[42]

After a nearly two-year absence, Nuttall resumed his scientific endeavors in Boston and Philadelphia in 1836. He busied himself over the next five years arranging the vast quantity of specimens that were collected on the expedition, attending meetings of the Academy of Natural Sciences and the American Philosophical Society, meeting with other naturalists, such as John James Audubon, who were interested to hear about his travels and discoveries, delivering lectures, publishing papers, and contributing to the multivolume work *Flora of North America* prepared by Asa Gray and John Torrey.

In 1841, Nuttall's mother and his Aunt Frances both passed away in England. Nuttall was to inherit the estate of his late Uncle Jonas, Frances's husband, but with the stipulation that he was not to be away from England for more than three months out of each year. He could have renounced his inheritance had his financial situation been more secure, but the expenses of his travels, his lack of a steady salary after resigning from Harvard, and his inability to sell his collections during a time of national economic distress in the late 1830s left him with little choice. In late December 1841, he reluctantly left the United States and returned to England to live at his uncle's Nutgrove manor in Lancashire. Nuttall would manage to return to the United States only once more in the winter of 1846–47. He would live another eighteen

FIG. 1.4. George William Featherstonhaugh, 1780–1866.
Courtesy of the Library of Congress.

years in England and spend his final years visiting the Craven district of his Yorkshire youth, corresponding with and visiting fellow naturalists in England and cultivating rhododendrons sent to England from India. Thomas Nuttall died in September 1859 at the age of seventy-three.

George William Featherstonhaugh, 1780–1866

George William Featherstonhaugh, or Fenston as his friends called him, was born in London in 1780 to George and Dorothy Simpson Featherstonhaugh.[43] Following the death of George Sr. soon after Fenston was born, Dorothy moved with her two young children to her native Scarborough. Fenston's childhood in the resort town on the North Sea provided him opportunities to interact with visitors and other children from across Great Britain, and he received a boarding school education in history and the classics along with tutoring in Latin and Greek. In his spare time, Fenston cultivated his interest in natural history and mineralogy by collecting fossils and shells on the beach. In his early twenties, Fenston pursued business opportunities with import-export firms that allowed him the chance to travel widely through continental Europe. In 1806, at the age of twenty-six, he sailed for Boston with his one-hundred-pound inheritance from his grandfather and ambitions for arranging commercial work in the United States that would allow him to tour the country, and perhaps to study Native American languages.

Shortly after his arrival in the United States, Fenston moved to New York City, where he became acquainted with the Duane family of Schenectady. He was impressed with Schenectady and the beauty of the Mohawk River valley. He was also impressed by the beauty of one of the Duane daughters. He and Sarah "Sally" Duane were married in late 1808. Sally and Fenston moved to Duanesburg, New York, southwest of Schenectady, where they acquired land, built a house, studied languages together, and started a family. On approximately fifteen hundred acres, Fenston grew a variety of crops and developed a focus on sheep raising. His successful breeding program led to accolades from the agriculturalists in New York, and this encouraged him to venture into breeding cattle and horses. When not absorbed in the details of overseeing his laborers and perfecting his breeding programs, Fenston pursued other interests such as mineralogy, writing, and politics. He developed a friendship with Archibald Bruce, who had founded the *American Mineralogical Journal* and who kept Fenston up-to-date on new developments in the field. He also found time to write poems, essays, and plays, some of which were published in literary journals, and to write a translation of Dante's *Inferno.*

Following his selection in 1820 as an officer of the newly formed New York Board of Agriculture, Fenston became involved in agricultural policy and legislation efforts in New York and beyond. His duties included correspondence with significant American leaders such as James Madison, Henry Clay, Albert Gallatin, and Oliver Wolcott Jr. Another of his duties involved the preparation of annual reports for which he wrote agricultural essays that were widely praised by his peers. In 1823 Fenston traveled to Washington, D.C., to lobby for protective agricultural tariffs and met with president James Monroe, secretary of state John Quincy Adams, speaker of the House of Representatives Henry Clay, congressman Daniel Webster, recent president of the Second Bank of the United States Langdon Cheves, and Louisiana senator and newly appointed minister to France James Brown. His efforts came to fruition when a tariff bill was passed in 1824 under Henry Clay's leadership. Though he could not vote because he lacked U.S. citizenship,

Fenston became a strong supporter of Clay's bid for the presidency in 1824 and corresponded with him regularly.

In 1826 Fenston successfully lobbied for legislation in New York that established the Mohawk and Hudson Rail Road Company, for which Fenston would serve as one of the commissioners. Although the railroad that would eventually become the New York Central began operations in 1831, Fenston had sold his shares during a period of personal and financial distress: two daughters died of scarlet fever in 1825, Sally died in 1828, and his home was destroyed by fire in 1829. Geology and writing became tools for coping with the immense grief that afflicted Fenston in the wake of this series of personal tragedies. Fenston moved to Philadelphia, attended meetings of the American Philosophical Society, was elected a member of the Academy of Natural Sciences of Philadelphia, and immersed himself in the transatlantic theoretical controversies that enraptured geologists at the time. He earned money by writing essays and reviews for scientific publications and by delivering lectures at the Franklin Institute in Philadelphia. He also founded and edited a short-lived scientific journal that counted President Andrew Jackson among its subscribers.

The fifty-one-year-old Fenston married eighteen-year-old Charlotte Carter, of a prominent Virginia family in 1831, and the following year the couple were hosted by former president James Madison at Montpelier during a visit to Virginia. Having earned respect and recognition as a prominent figure in American geology and drawing upon his political connections and prior experience with petitioning powerbrokers in Washington, Fenston promoted the idea of a federally sponsored geological survey of the United States. Chief among his arguments was that a study of the available minerals of the United States would lead to more systematic mining, enhanced industrial production, and greater prosperity. Fenston's lobbying efforts proved successful and in the summer of 1834, he was appointed to the new position of Geologist to the United States. Congress appropriated $5,000 for a geological survey of the lands between the Missouri River and the Red River and would compensate Fenston six dollars per day and twelve cents per mile to carry out the excursion. In July 1834, Fenston was directed to proceed to the Territory of Arkansas to complete the survey and to return to Washington with a report by February 1835.[44] Chapter five presents the portion of Fenston's journey through Missouri and Arkansas in final months of 1834.

Upon arriving at home in late January 1835, Fenston wrote and published his report entitled "Geological Report of an Examination Made in

1834, of the Elevated Country between the Missouri and Red Rivers." Like Schoolcraft before him, Fenston reported significant sources of mineral wealth for the country in the deposits of Missouri and Arkansas.

> I had occasion to observe, in numerous instances, that the mineral indications on the public lands were quite as encouraging as at the established mines; but the mineral of lead, to judge from obvious appearances, exists in such inconceivable profusion in the metalliferous region of the south of Missouri and the north of Arkansas, that . . . it may be relied on for countless ages as a source of national wealth, and an interminable supply of the most useful metals.[45]

Later in the report, he remarked with awe that the iron deposits in the region offered all the resources of Sweden in one locality and declared the White River of Arkansas to be "one of the most important and beautiful rivers in the United States."[46] His report is bursting with positive adjectives about the beauty, scenery, and economic potential of Arkansas, given its bounty of minerals and fertile soils. He concluded that Missouri and Arkansas possessed "an amount of the ores of lead and iron, of an excellent quality, not only more than adequate to any estimate of the domestic consumption of this nation, but such as may justify the expectation that it will form an important element hereafter of commercial exportation from that part of the world."[47] Both Missouri and Arkansas newspapers carried excerpts from the report, and Fenston distributed copies of it to friends in the United States and Europe.

In addition to his official geological report, Fenston wished to publish an account of his travels for a popular audience. A friend of his carried the proposal to John Murray, a London publisher with a growing list of popular travel narratives. Murray was apparently so enthusiastic about the idea that he began advertising the forthcoming book in London periodicals, but, after drafting much of the manuscript, Fenston decided to postpone completing it when a few of his friends convinced him that his sharp critiques might upset many Americans. It was not until 1843, when he was no longer employed by the U.S. government, that Fenston returned to the project. He completed the revisions of his journals in 1844, and the work was published in two volumes by John Murray as *Excursion through the Slave States from Washington on the Potomac to the Frontier of Mexico; with Sketches of Popular Manners and Geological Notices.* A one-volume American edition of the book was published later in 1844 by Harper and Brothers. As expected, the book received very positive reviews outside of the United States, while American periodicals attacked the author as superficial, unqualified, and mean.[48]

Between his return in 1835 to Washington, D.C., following the excursion to Arkansas and the publication of his travel narrative in 1844, Fenston was engaged in nearly constant travel. In July 1835 Fenston was sent in his role as United States Geologist to Wisconsin and Minnesota to complete a survey of the geology of the Wisconsin River, the Upper Mississippi River, and the Coteau des Prairies formation. Fenston stopped in Detroit on his way to Wisconsin and spent a few days with Henry and Jane Schoolcraft from whom he received advice about touring the Upper Mississippi, lessons on Chippewa language and customs, a tour of the town, and assistance with shipping specimens. Following his two-month expedition, Fenston published another geological report in 1836 entitled "Report of a Geological Reconnaissance Made in 1835, from the Seat of Government, by the Way of Green Bay and the Wisconsin Territory, to the Coteau de Prairie, an Elevated Ridge Dividing the Missouri from the St. Peter's River." Fenston's next government mission was to conduct a geological investigation of the Cherokee territory in Georgia. In the summer of 1837, after follow-up tours to Wisconsin and Missouri, he traveled to Georgia, where he talked with Cherokees, missionaries, tavern keepers, and militia officers less than one year before the forced removal of the Cherokees that became known as the Trail of Tears. Upon departing Cherokee land, Fenston met his friend John C. Calhoun, the senator and former vice president, in Dahlonega, Georgia, and the two men toured the gold mines of north Georgia together on horseback. Fenston returned to Washington in October 1837 after visiting Calhoun at his home in Fort Hill, South Carolina, and touring the Appalachians of North Carolina.

In 1838 Fenston was assigned to complete a survey along the disputed boundary between Maine and the Canadian province of New Brunswick. Given his English citizenship, Fenston balked at being involved in a political dispute between the United States and Britain. His refusal to participate in the project was not received well by the Van Buren administration, and Fenston concluded that he must resign his post as Geologist to the United States. Despite his aversion to serving as a representative of the United States for such a task, Fenston believed that a geological survey of the disputed territory was needed and could be useful in resolving the boundary controversy. Perhaps he could gain an appointment with the British government to conduct the survey. After consulting with contacts in England and visiting Quebec to meet with British officials in Canada, he sailed for England in early 1839. Fenston was appointed to the Foreign Office as a commissioner by Lord Palmerston and spent his first months in office studying the history of the boundary using maps and documents available in London and Paris.

In July 1839, Fenston returned to the United States in the employ of the British government. Along with a party of forty men, Fenston completed the diplomatically tricky and physically taxing boundary reconnaissance from August through October, during which he collected field data that supported the British boundary claim. Following diplomatic visits to the governor of Maine and officials in Boston and Washington, Fenston returned to England in early 1840 and spent that spring composing his official report.

The boundary negotiations were delayed by the United States presidential election of 1840 and the political uncertainty following the death of the newly elected president William Henry Harrison, so Fenston devoted much of 1841 to preparing for publication his "Historical Sketch of the Negotiations at Paris in 1782," which documented his detailed research into the history of the boundary. The dispute was finally resolved by the Webster-Ashburton Treaty of 1842. Fenston was bitter about the resolution because, although it kept the peace, he believed Lord Ashburton had surrendered too much of the British claim and that the Americans had been duplicitous throughout the negotiations. Despite Fenston's painstaking historical research and dangerous surveying expedition, for which he was praised in British political circles, he was told that his appointment to the Foreign Office would end effective March 1843.[49]

Left without government employment again, Fenston returned to writing and publishing his narrative of his *Excursion through the Slave States.* In a letter to John Murray in February 1844, Fenston submitted eight chapters of the book and described the manuscript he was preparing.

> Of the character of the work you will be able to form an opinion from reading what I now send, or even the first and eighth chapters. The tour narrated in it extends between 3,000 and 4,000 miles, going from the City of Washington, by unbeaten routes, to the frontiers of Mexico. You will find nothing hackneyed in the work, I have left New York, Philadelphia, Boston, etc, and all the wonderful things done by their inhabitants, to the overdone descriptions that have been given of them, so that in this work there will be a view of the manners and customs, the geology and natural history, of a part of America which had not been described. That which will be especially interesting to the man of science, I have endeavored to make agreeable to the general reader, and in the first chapter you will perceive my method of doing it, which is simply diminishing the ponderosity of such topics, by a lively manner of treating them. There will also be

> matter for the Statesman and Philanthropist treated in the same manner. In short I hope to have made the work sufficiently attractive to all classes of readers, without appealing to the prejudices of any; and there will not be found a thought or expression in it unfriendly to the Americans, though I hope there is a good deal in it to make people laugh at them. The only cure for that queer race is to shame them out of the absurd character they are making for themselves.[50]

Unlike Thomas Nuttall, Fenston had qualms neither about appealing to a popular audience nor about criticizing the cultural deficiencies that he perceived among Americans.

In late 1844, as his travel narrative was being praised outside of America and panned by Americans, Fenston received an appointment to the consulate at Havre, France as the British ambassador. Upon his arrival in France in December 1844, Fenston met King Louis Phillippe and was gratified to learn that the French king had read and enjoyed *Excursion through the Slave States*. As he settled into his office in Havre and began learning the delicate French-British diplomatic ropes, Fenston proposed another book to John Murray about his 1835 expedition to Wisconsin and Minnesota. Despite encouraging Fenston to pursue the work and send him a manuscript, Murray decided against publishing another book by Fenston when they disagreed over style and illustrations. Instead, the *Canoe Voyage up the Minnay Sotor* was published by Richard Bentley at the end of 1846 and received very positive reviews. In 1848, when the revolution began in France that led to the establishment of the Second Republic, Fenston personally arranged both the steamer and the ruse that allowed King Louis Phillippe and Queen Marie-Amélie to escape France to safe sanctuary in England. Despite his advancing years and the continuing political instability in France, Fenston remained at his consular post in Havre until his death in 1866 at the age of eighty-six.

Chapter Two

A Very Great Natural Curiosity

WILLIAM DUNBAR ON THE OUACHITA RIVER, 1804–1805

THE FIRST FEW DAYS of the expedition must have seemed easy. The Red River offered little resistance to the men as they made their way up its deep, winding, willow-lined channel. The weather was cool and pleasant, and few mosquitoes were on hand this late in the year to harass them. The men built a fire in the evening, ate fresh duck, and camped among the pecan trees on the shore. Perhaps it was a bit too relaxed. William Dunbar complained in his journal that the "soldiers do not exert themselves at the oar," and he was compelled to offer "a few words of advice and encouragement."[1] Although his words to them managed to improve their "activity and cheerfulness" for the time being, Dunbar continued to be annoyed by their slow progress and lack of effort. "More might be performed, but our Soldiers seem at certain times to be without vigour & now and then throw out hints that they can work only as they are paid."[2] Later in the expedition, Dunbar would reflect more deeply on the need for a commissioned officer to lead the soldiers and keep them motivated. Yet navigation upriver continued to be relatively easy for the next several days.

> No current to impede us, for altho' there be a feeble current along the principal thread of the stream, yet as this is deflected from bend to bend, we easily avoid its influence by directing our course from point to point or rather passing a little under the points, and in fact, where there is any current, a compensation is found by the counter current or eddy under the points.[3]

The challenges lay ahead.

William Dunbar, the Natchez, Mississippi, plantation owner, had been in correspondence with President Thomas Jefferson for the last few years. The plan to ascend the Red River to its source and return via the Arkansas River—the so-called Grand Expedition that would have rivaled the Lewis and Clark expedition in its scale and danger—had been abandoned. A more modest exploration of the Ouachita River and the hot springs of Arkansas was finally underway. Aboard a boat that William Dunbar doubted was suitable for the journey, the party of seventeen men departed from St. Catherine's Landing south of Natchez, Mississippi, on October 16, 1804. The party included Dr. George Hunter, a chemist from Philadelphia, Hunter's son, twelve enlisted men from the garrison at New Orleans, a sergeant Bundy in command of the men, and one of Dunbar's slaves.[4] After a rainy and windy night of camping along the banks of the Mississippi, they reached the mouth of the Red River the next day. The mouth of the river was impressive. It was about 550 yards wide with "no sensible current" and luxurious and fertile banks. Hunter was struck by the difference in the landscape and exclaimed, "Here at our first entrance the appearance of the face of the country seems changed, every vegetable puts on a fresher green."[5]

The expedition proceeded for three days without Dunbar or Hunter mentioning sight of another person, but excitement ensued on the fourth day when a black man with a canoe was spotted near the shore. The party suspected that he was a runaway slave, since the man fled when they approached him, and his canoe was empty. After lunch, two men stayed behind, hid in the bushes, and quickly apprehended the suspected slave. Harry was a "stout fellow" with nothing but the clothes on his back. He told the party that he was free, but Hunter doubted the man's story. Regardless, Harry was brought aboard and given ham and biscuits to eat, which he "devoured with a voracious appetite."[6] Harry stayed with the expedition for the next eleven days, but his luck ran out on October 30 when a man named Innes hailed the boat from the shore and claimed to be Harry's owner. Hunter noted, "We were relieved of the charge of him [Harry] to his Master's great satisfaction."[7]

On October 21 the party came upon a small settlement that impressed Dunbar to the point of double exclamation points in his journal: "How happy the contrast, when we compare the fortune of the new settler in the U.S. with the misery of the half starving, oppressed and degraded Peasant of Europe!!"[8] The possibility for additional settlement of this new portion of America is a running theme of Dunbar's journal. The notion of the self-sufficient American settling and civilizing the wild frontier was irresistible

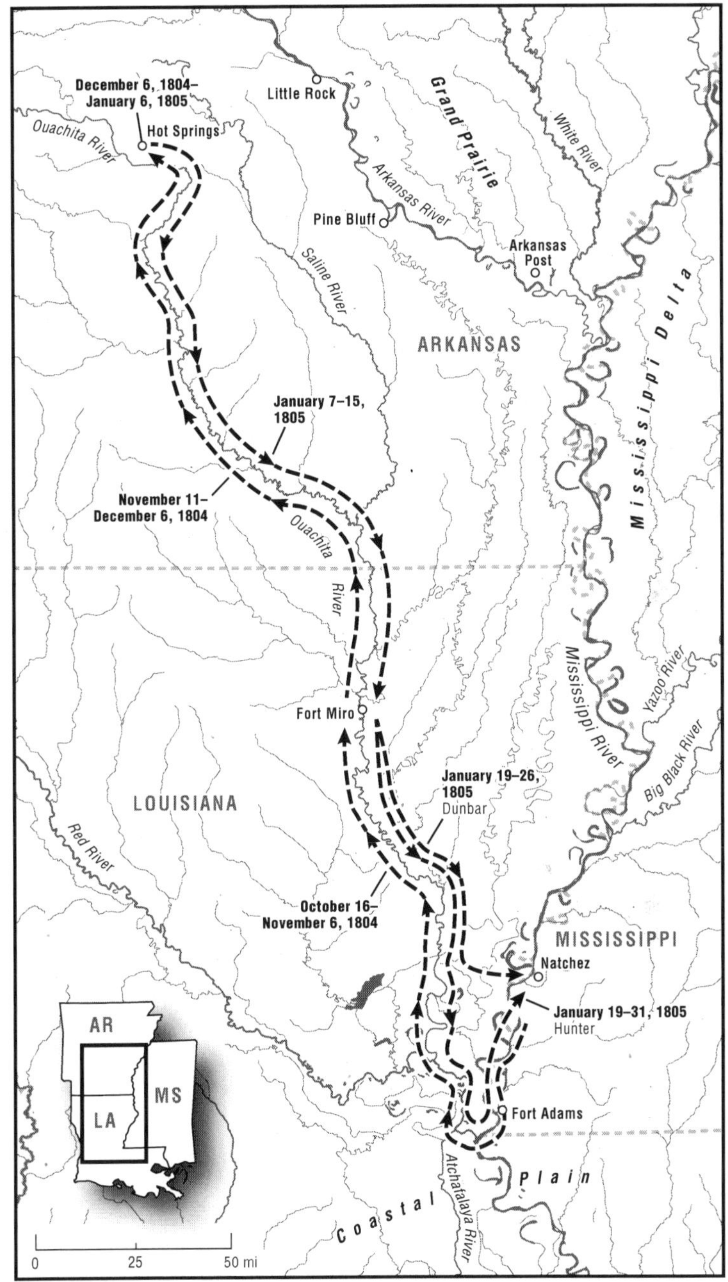

FIG. 2.1. Route of William Dunbar and George Hunter, 1804–1805.
Cartography by Erin Greb.

for some in Jeffersonian America. Dunbar describes the settlement as a case study for the future.

> A Covered frame of rough poles without walls serves for a house, and a Couple of acres of indian corn had been cultivated, which suffices to stock their little magazine with bread for the year; the forest supplies Venison, Bear, turkey &c, the river fowl and fish; the skins of wild animals and an abundance of the finest honey being carried to market enables the new settler to supply himself largely with all other necessary articles; in a year or two he arrives at a state of independence, he purchases horses, cows & other domestic animals, perhaps a slave also who shares with him the labours and the productions of his fields & of the adjoining forest.[9]

Perhaps what impressed Dunbar most was that these apparently independent settlers made their home in a location that posed challenges for agriculture, health, and transportation. The land was subject to frequent flooding. Dunbar explained that the land was "liable to inundation, not from the floods of this small river, but from the intrusion of its more powerful neighbour the Mississippi."[10] Life amid the cypress swamps of Louisiana could not have been easy. Overland transportation was difficult and unpredictable. "The nearest road to the high lands at the Rapid-settlement on the red river, nearly west is said to be 40 miles thro' an inundated alluvial country; it is probable the direct distance does not much exceed one half, the numerous lakes in the overflowed lands rendering the road very circuitous."[11] Moreover, the common belief at the time was that the miasma of the swamp lands was the cause of disease, and thus such land was deemed unhealthy. Yet, to Dunbar's eyes, the frontier people encountered here seemed to persist despite these impediments. The political need to settle Americans to secure claim to Louisiana was also pressing.[12] It is no surprise then that Dunbar expressed his double-exclamation point glee at this sight.

The Ouachita River of Louisiana

One week after the expedition departed from St. Catherine's Landing, they arrived at the mouth of the Ouachita River. Another small settlement that became the town of Jonesville, Louisiana, had formed here at the confluence of the Ouachita, Tensas, and Little River.[13] The possibility for settlement and agriculture here, too, seemed promising. The land was drained during the dry season from July to November and was covered in "luxuriant herbage" and "immense herds of Deer, of Turkeys, Geese, Ducks, Cranes &c &c feeding upon the grass and grain."[14] Hunter noted that, "the ground here is very rich & if it were to be defended by a dike or Bank would be inexhaustibly fertile."[15] The party met with a French man who received a Spanish land grant and who had "made a small settlement and [kept] a ferry boat for crossing men & horses traveling to or from Natchez and the settlements on red river and on the Washita river."[16] The man provided Dunbar and Hunter with information about distances upriver and nearby Indian mounds that are known today as the Troyville Earthworks.[17] The presence of indigenous populations for centuries in this region was a sign that settlement was promising. Dunbar later remarked that the Indians had modified the environment in a way that made it desirable.

> When a piece of ground is once got into this state in an indian country, it can have no opportunity of re-producing timber; it being an invariable rule to fire the dry grass in the Fall or winter, to obtain the advantage of attracting game when the young tender grass begins to spring; & thus the young timber is destroyed, & annually the prairie gains upon the wood land; it is probable that the immense plains known to exist in America may owe their origin to this practice.[18]

So far, the ascent of the deep and winding Red River and Black River had been relatively easy. The Ouachita River would prove to be much more exhausting.

The next two weeks revealed the inadequacy of their boat for the journey ahead. The vessel was unusual. Most ascents of rivers at this time would have been made in a keel boat or a flat boat. Instead, the party was aboard a "Chinese-style vessel" that George Hunter described as "somewhat in the form of a ferry flat, with a mast fixed to strike occasionally, & . . . a large sail. . . . [The boat] was 50 feet long & about 8 feet beam on deck at the mast which was her extreme breadth, tapering to the stern, had a cabbin [aft] & a pavilion amidships for the accommodation of the Officers and crew, with tarpaulins & curtains to keep off the weather."[19] Hunter had the boat constructed in Pittsburgh for his journey to Natchez. Dunbar was annoyed that Hunter did not consult him about the building of the boat and doubted its suitability for the expedition. He attempted to find another boat before the expedition departed but had to settle for adapting to Hunter's odd craft in hopes that it would be sufficient. Once the party began their ascent of the seasonally shallow waters of the Ouachita, it became quite clear that the boat

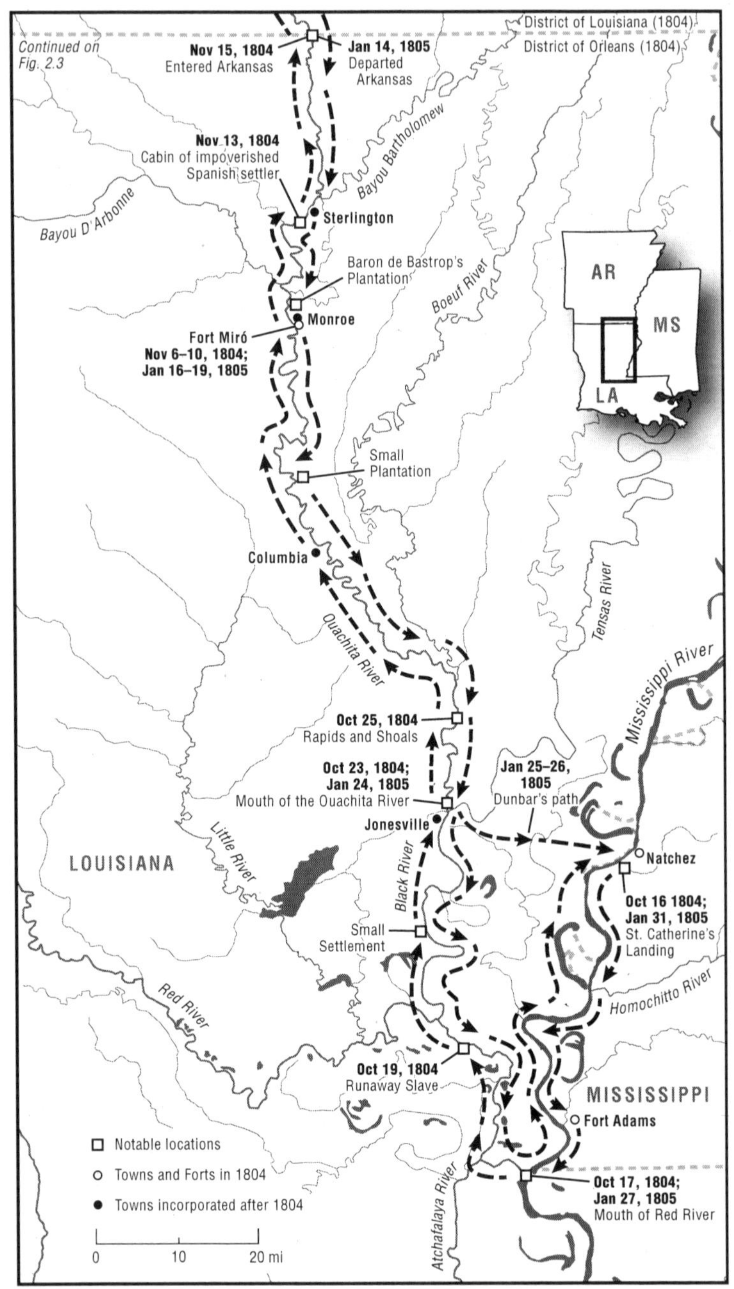

FIG. 2.2. William Dunbar and George Hunter in Louisiana, 1804–1805. Cartography by Erin Greb.

would not do. Dunbar complained that "a boat properly constructed for an expedition of this nature ought to advance with more than double our velocity."[20] Their progress was slowed by gravel and sandbars. The main problem was that the boat floated too deep in the water to move easily over these obstacles. Shortly after beginning their ascent of the Ouachita, they came to a gravel bar and had to dig a channel for the boat. Dunbar described the backbreaking work required.

> After breakfast commenced digging the canal which was required to be about an hundred feet long: this business went on heavily & slowly as usual, and it was not until noon that it was made barely of the depth which it was supposed might pass the boat. . . . After dinner the boat was moved into the channel, where she stuck fast. Cables, ropes, and pulies were got across and fixed to trees; handspokes were used to raise & push her along and we made some way thro' the bar, but evening coming on we were obliged to desist in hopes of being able to get over in the morning.[21]

They successfully navigated this obstacle the next day, but the slow and difficult work continued for the next week as the men alternately rowed, poled, pulled the boat with ropes, or waded in the river to drag the boat over incessant hazards. As Dunbar explained,

> the utmost care was necessary to keep clear of shoals and sunken logs. . . . We suffered much detention this day from those causes, being twice fast upon a sunken log under water, and our boat being so unwieldy & heavy, there was no getting her off by any exertion of poles &c which could be made on board, a rope was carried ashore from stern, & by that means she was hove backwards & cleared of the log; we lost 1½ hour each time by two such accidents, & several times upon shoals which delayed us greatly.[22]

Dunbar—and very likely the men doing the grueling work in the damp and cold weather—began to long for a proper boat. He imagined that a flat boat designed properly for such an expedition could make forty miles a day, yet they managed only four to six miles on some of the most difficult days. Dunbar recorded what was needed for future expeditions: "Light flat boats proper for the navigation of shallow waters would pass over all such obstacles without touching, & when they do touch, being light, they are easily pushed back."[23] The soldiers were understandably exhausted and impatient, yet Hunter was irritated by their lack of discipline and respect.

> The men, or rather some of them often grumbling & uttering execrations against me in particular for urging them on, in which they had the example of the sergeant who on many occasion of trifling difficulties frequently gave me very rude answers, & in several instances both now & formerly seemed to forget that it was his duty in such cases to urge on the men under his command to surmount them rather than to show a spirit of contradictions & backwardness.[24]

The expedition needed a break to recuperate. Better yet, the expedition needed a new boat.

Fort Miró and North Central Louisiana

Lieutenant Joseph Bowmar had been in command at Fort Miró, present-day Monroe, Louisiana, for less than seven months when Dunbar, Hunter, and the crew arrived on November 6, 1804. Bowmar had charted the river from its mouth to the fort and had collected information about the lands upstream from other sources. Hunter was complimentary of him: "He seems to be a plain, intelligent, active officer, is well liked here, has no affectation, treated us with civility & attention . . . did us all the services in his power, which we stood in need of."[25] One might imagine that one of the first conversations between Dunbar and Bowmar involved acquiring a new boat. Dunbar had concluded that their boat was "improper for the continuation of our voyage" and was determined to find a replacement.[26] After three days of inquiries, a boat was located that was about the same size as the old craft, but was "built tolerably flat, her bottom being still a little convex & being pretty well formed for running."[27] Dunbar acquired the boat for the rate of $1.25 per day.

Four days after arriving at Fort Miró, the men began loading the supplies and equipment onto the new vessel. The frustration must have been immense when the boat began to take on water. The night and following morning were spent unloading the boat, bailing it out, drying out what had become wet, hauling the barge ashore to be caulked, pushing the boat back into the water, and reloading it. The party was finally able to depart after lunch to continue their ascent of the Ouachita.

Although Lieutenant Bowmar and the men of the garrison had been helpful, Hunter had been impressed with neither the fort—because "the spaces between the stakes that compose the fort show the men in the inside"—nor the swampy surrounding lands that he described as "being habitable only here and there."[28] Yet Hunter saved his most biting critique for the settlers he encountered at this place.

> The old settlers chiefly Canadian French appear to have little ambition, few wants & as little industry. They live from hand to mouth & let tomorrow provide for itself. Some of them have from thirty to 100 cows, but no milk, butter, or Cheese; Their houses are cabins, afford but little protection against the winter. . . . As the woods afford pasturage for their cattle in the winter, they give themselves but little trouble to feed them; . . . They are supplied from the woods during the hunting season, with animal food, such as Venison, Bear meat, Buffaloe, &cc, wild ducks, Geese, Swans, Turkies, Brant in great abundance; But at other times they are often very badly off for provisions, both Animal & Vegetable; for altho the earth would produce very well, yet their want of forethought & industry leaves them in want of almost every comfort, except what is absolutely necessary for subsistence.[29]

Dunbar offered similar notes in his journal.

> A great part of the inhabitants still continue the old practice of hunting during the winter season. . . . In the summer these people content themselves with making corn barely sufficient for bread during the year; in this manner they always remain extremely poor; some few who have conquered their habits of indolence (which are always a consequence of the indian mode of life) and addicted themselves to agriculture, live more comfortably & taste a little the sweets of civilized life.[30]

A few days later, as they passed through the area of present-day Sterlington, Louisiana, Hunter offered these observations about a Spanish settler they encountered.

> Stopped at a Bark cabin inhabited by a Spaniard; it seemed to need no windows neither had it any, but what light passed thro the joints was fully sufficient for every purpose. It was one story high, about 15 feet square, an earthen floor, the chimney composed of mud & grass mixed; The furniture were, one bed for the whole family which consisted of the man & his wife, four Children, the eldest girl of about 16. The youngest at the breast, three short blocks of wood by way of stools, one of which was a trough to pound Indian corn in, a riffle & shot pouch; In short altho they said they had been settled these five years, there was no appearance of any crop or any store of any kind of vegetable produce, altho he had the winter before him already

> commenced, & a wife & 4 children to provide for.—Thus are indolence and poverty allied.[31]

Dunbar's and Hunter's language reveals how they interpreted the cultural landscape they encountered in Louisiana. Where they saw poverty, they concluded that the settlers were to blame for not making proper use of the environment.[32]

Before departing Fort Miró, Dunbar sent a letter to President Jefferson in which he remarked, "Hitherto we have not seen any thing interesting which is worthy of being particularly communicated to you at this moment." Dunbar did let the president know that they had experienced a "journey of trouble and retardment" but that he had made astronomical observations, had arranged for a new boat, and had hired a pilot to guide them up the Ouachita.[33] Dunbar was convinced of the need to hire someone who knew how to navigate the shoals and rapids upstream and who could hunt. The man they hired for thirty dollars per month, plus liquor and rations, was Samuel Blazier, who "resided about ten years in this country and had been several times to the hot Springs & thro that part of the Country on hunting expeditions."[34] With an experienced pilot on board, their lighter boat, and fresh beef and potatoes purchased from a Mr. Richards, the party appeared to be back on track.

Their standard day involved breaking camp and setting out around sunrise. Breakfast upstream would involve a one-hour break, and dinner would allow the men a two-hour break. Around sunset, the party would find a stopping place along the shore, so the men could pitch tents and collect firewood before dark. With about ten to eleven hours of daylight in November, the men were probably rowing, poling, and hunting for about seven to eight hours per day. Hunter noted that the men "row rather with more exertions than formerly when the weather was warmer," but he seemed to lament that the short days and long breaks for meals allowed them to make "but a short distance in a day."[35]

Arrival in Arkansas

The expedition arrived in Arkansas almost exactly one month after departing from St. Catherine's Landing. The boundary was a very new line at the time, but it remains on the map today. The border between Louisiana and Arkansas became effective about six weeks before Dunbar and Hunter crossed it on the

Ouachita River. Earlier that spring, the U.S. Congress approved the creation of the District of Orleans to the south and the District of Louisiana to the north with the division between the two set at thirty-three degrees latitude. The party was aware of the new boundary, but the name of the land they were entering was yet to be called Arkansas. The expedition would spend the next two months in Arkansas—or in what they would have called the District of Louisiana.

The observations of Dunbar and Hunter while in Arkansas were focused on the natural resources of the territory and their potential for beneficial use. The commercial landscape appeared promising. There were the salt licks that might produce potassium nitrate for gunpowder. There were the leaves on trees that might produce dyes. There was low-quality lignite coal and traces of iron that raised hopes for more high-quality varieties of both. There were the rumors of mines in the region that had been worked a few decades earlier for iron sulfide. There were the stones that might be used as oil stones for sharpening tools and others that might be useful as millstones. And there were the animals. Deer and bears, in particular, were abundant. Dunbar explained the value of bears as an economic commodity: "The hunters count much of their profits from the oil drawn from the Bear's fat, which at New Orleans is always of ready sale, and is much esteemed for its wholesomeness in cooking, being preferred to butter or hog's lard; it is found to keep longer than any other oil of the same nature, without turning rancid."[36]

Throughout the journals of Dunbar and Hunter, there is a hint of disappointment that the commercial landscapes they encountered in Arkansas were not complete with more immediately exploitable or valuable resources. Yet both men maintained optimism about the commercial potential for the natural resources of the territory. Regarding coal, Dunbar imagined that "the time may arrive when the Planter who shall be clearing his Plantation or farm of useless timber, will be enabled from the instructions of the Chemist to place the whole in a situation to be transmuted into an useful article capable of long preservation."[37] The bright side of the salt licks of the area was also pondered by Dunbar. He predicted "when this river comes to be settled" that "Salines or salt-licks exist which may be rendered very productive" and that "so necessary an article as marine salt will therefore be in sufficient abundance for the consumption of a full population."[38] At one point, Dunbar imagined south-central Arkansas as wine country when he noted that "some hills appear to be well adapted to the cultivation of the vine. . . . It is probable that a skillful Vigneron, who shall undertake the establishment of a Vineyard

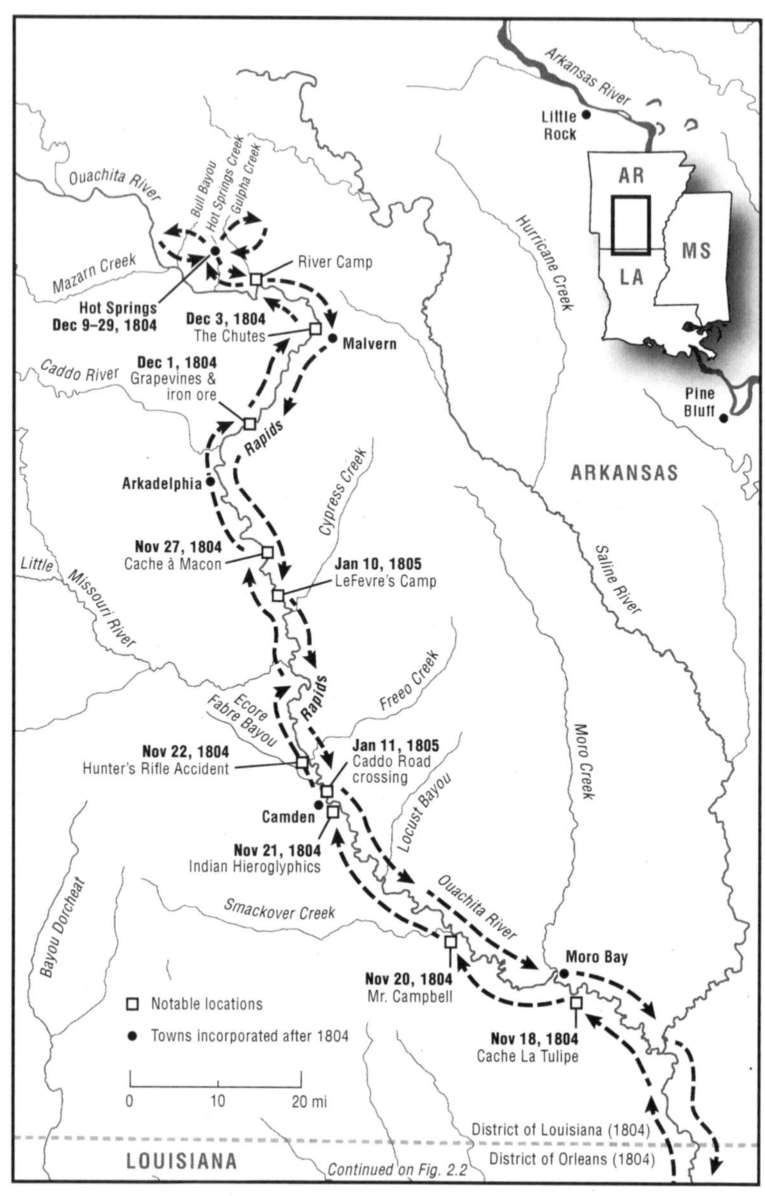

FIG. 2.3. William Dunbar and George Hunter in Arkansas, 1804–1805. Cartography by Erin Greb.

in a well-chosen position in this neighbourhood, will find his labors amply compensated; the market of New Orleans is at hand, where his wines (if good) may be immediately sold and paid for at a high price."[39] It is notable that Dunbar assumed that the land he was traversing would become more heavily settled, and therefore predicted the ways in which these new cultural landscapes and places could be supported.

Yet the land that would become Arkansas was not devoid of people. Despite the primary orientation of the expedition toward the prediction of commercial landscapes based on their scientific assessment of natural landscapes, several observations reveal Dunbar's and Hunter's exploration and perception of the cultural landscape of Arkansas in 1804. As they crossed into Arkansas, their pilot, Samuel Blazier, let the party know that they would not see any further settlements upstream. But the lack of settlements did not indicate a lack of people. The region was traversed by both white and Indian hunters, and the expedition happened to be crossing through the territory during hunting season. Dunbar remarked, "This is the season when the poor inhabitants . . . turn out to make their annual hunt; they carry no provision with them but a little indian corn, depending on their guns and ammunition for the rest."[40] The signs of hunting were evident in the caches that the party encountered along the shore. Many of the place names along the Ouachita River at the time, such as Cache la Tulipe and Cache a Macon, derived not from settlements in the area, but from the names of the hunters who camped and stored their caches along the banks. Dunbar explained,

> It continues to be a practice of both white and red hunters, to deposit their skins &c often suspended to poles or laid over a pole placed upon two forked posts in sight of the river, until their return from hunting; these deposits are considered as sacred and few examples exist of their being plundered.[41]

Yet not all who passed through the area appeared to respect the honor code of the hunters. Near present-day Smackover Creek, the expedition came across a canoe carrying a Mr. Campbell and a "consumptive person on board on his way to the hot Springs for the recovery of his health."[42] Campbell stuck close for the day and camped near the party that night. The next day near Locust Creek they came upon an old encampment with a cache of skins. Campbell claimed that these skins were his and began collecting them. Hunter insisted that these were not Campbell's property, yet Campbell seemed intent on stealing the cache. Thus, Hunter explained,

> we then concluded to take them into the boat & if we should come up with the Owner, who we concluded must be a Choctaw Indian, we should deliver them to him or some of his nation & in case we were disappointed in that, to take them back with us & leave them with the commandant at the Post or Garrison to be delivered to the true owner for we had no doubt that if we should leave them on the pole now Campbell was informed they were there, that he would take them & lay the blame on our boat.[43]

The party left Campbell and the sick man behind.

About a week later, south of present-day Arkadelphia, the party encountered a hunter named Paltz and his three grown sons. The man had lived in the area for forty years and had experience on the Arkansas, White, and St. Francis Rivers. Paltz provided them with a gold mine of geographical information. He explained that the White and St. Francis were "small rivers of difficult navigation" but that the Arkansas was "a river of great magnitude" with "a large and broad channel, and . . . long and great sand beaches like to the Mississippi."[44] Paltz must have raised Dunbar's hopes about the planned expedition on the Arkansas—particularly given their struggles with rapids and shoals on the Ouachita.

Although Dunbar and Hunter had few direct encounters with Indians in Arkansas, they described native landscapes based on information supplied by informants and the traces of the native presence that were evident in the natural landscape. For example, Hunter described what he called "Indian Hieroglyphics" near present-day Camden, Arkansas.

> The bark was taken off a cypress tree about breast high, for about 18 inches, & two thirds round it, & on the bare place was painted black in a rude manner, the figure of a person on horseback with one hand extended to the water & the other towards the woods, two other persons whose figures were a little defaced seemed to be shaking hands, one of whom had a round hat on; on both sides of these persons were the figures of about a dozen of large & small four footed animals apparently feeding, some thing like deer without horns.[45]

The Caddo are described by Dunbar based on information he received from an unknown source, perhaps Blazier or Paltz.

> The Cadadoquis (or Cadaux as the French who are fond of abbreviations generally pronounce the word) may be considered as Spanish Indians; They

> boast, I am told with truth, that they never have imbrued their hands in the blood of a white man: it is reported (perhaps falsely) that they are excited to enmity by the Spanish officers at Nacogdoches against the Americans.[46]

The "Nation of the aransas," or the Quapaws, are also described from second-hand sources. The group was reportedly fighting defensive wars with the Osages and was willing to make a treaty with the United States in which they would relinquish some of their territory in exchange for "the powerful arm of the U.S. [to] defend as their children in the possession of the remainder of our hunting ground lying between the Aransa & Washita rivers."[47]

While the Caddos and Quapaws were perceived to be peaceful, the fear and hatred of the Osages among Dunbar's informants is a recurring theme.[48] Dunbar explained,

> The tribe of Ozages live higher up than this position, but the hunters rarely go so high, being afraid of those savages who are at war with the world and destroy all strangers they can meet with. It is reported that the arcansa nation with a part of the Chactaws, Chicasaws, Shawnese &c have formed a league and are actually gone or going 800 strong against those depredators, with a view to destroy or drive them entirely off and possess themselves of their fine prairies which are most abundant hunting grounds, being plentifully stocked in Buffalo, Elk, Deer, Bear and every other beast of the chase, common to those Latitudes in America.[49]

Later, he noted that the group of Osages along the Arkansas River seemed to be "a lawless gang of robbers, making war with the whole world." Further into the journey, they are characterized as an "extremely faithless," "barbarous uncivilized race," and "no respecters of persons" who "rob, plunder, and even kill without any hesitation" and are held in "great abhorrence" by both old French hunters and other tribes.[50]

Rarely did either Hunter or Dunbar note any firsthand contact with Indians in the territory. One exception was near present-day Arkadelphia, where they met a "Delaware Indian" who called himself Captain Jacobs. The man is described as "painted with Vermillion round the eyes," and he provided information about a hunting party of Chickasaws and Choctaws on the Arkansas River.[51] Another exception to the lack of direct contact with Indians occurred toward the end of the expedition, when Hunter came across "some encampments of Pascagula Indians, who did not or would not understand,

English French or Spanish." He noted that he "could get no information from them."[52] Finally, Hunter described the following sad encounter toward the end of the expedition when he was back in Louisiana:

> I saw a small encampment with two fires & apparently two families of Choctaw Indians, I heard some melancholy mourning in a female voice, it seemed to come from the heart & was very expressive. I turned to the blanket, & leaning on a small heap of dead branches rudely piled together, to protect from the wild beasts of the wilderness, the remains of her first & only child, which I was informed died six months ago. Joy & Grief are the same in all languages.[53]

Despite these few personal encounters, Dunbar's and Hunter's exploration and perception of native landscapes is one that might be characterized as "Indians-in-the-distance."

On November 22, 1804, near present-day Camden, Arkansas, an accident occurred that could have brought an end to the expedition. Hunter was sitting on a trunk loading his pistol and, according to his account, was ramming the ball when the pistol slipped and discharged. The ball and ramrod tore through his right hand, his hat, and then out the roof of the boat. The force and proximity of the blast to his face caused black eyes, a bruised forehead, and scorched eye lashes, eye brows, and nose skin. The blast also burst his powder horn lying on a nearby table and spread gunpowder. If the nearly one pound of powder had gone up in flames, the boat would have been severely damaged or destroyed and casualties would have been likely. But it was only Hunter and his pride that were wounded. It would be about ten days before he recovered enough from his injuries to return to observations and writing journal entries.

The Ouachita River was reasonably gentle on the day the party entered Arkansas, but for the next two weeks, as the expedition traveled from the state line to current-day Arkadelphia, the river increasingly challenged the men. They began to encounter masses of driftwood, sandbars, gravel beaches, increasing currents, and rapids. In south-central Arkansas, the river seemed to be eating away at the banks.

> The river now and then running pretty strong, & in places so many trees carried bodily into the middle of the river some times almost opposite in both sides at the same time by the slipping in of the bank that it was with some considerable exertion the boat could be forced over the branches in

> such interstices as afforded the water sufficient to float it, for these trees with the bank that fell into the river with them often formed bars or shallows, rapids & difficult places.[54]

The men were at times forced toward the shore to catch hold of willows to haul the boat upstream because their oars and poles were useless against the strength of the current. Dunbar was impressed by the vigor and perseverance of the soldiers and noted that they "exceeded greatly my expectations."[55] Another challenge posed by the river was that it was frequently divided by islands into multiple channels. Here Blazier proved helpful in guiding the party up the best path. As they grew closer to the site of present-day Arkadelphia, Dunbar remarked that "the Country appears now to wear a new aspect; high lands and rocks frequently approach the river."[56]

Between the present-day cities of Arkadelphia and Malvern, the trials grew more severe. Each day involved fighting against the current and forcing the boat through increasingly violent rapids. Near present-day Rockport and Malvern, they reached a section of the river known as the Chutes. For approximately one mile, the river flowed over a series of rock outcroppings running diagonally across the river. The rushing water cut openings into the rocks and formed small waterfalls that the boat would be forced to ascend. The Chutes posed a set of exasperating dilemmas and grueling work for the men. The questions were numerous. Was the boat too wide to make it through these cascades? Was the water deep enough to allow the boat to pass over the sharp rocks? If the boat *could* make it through, which of the many falls in front of them would be the best to try? Their only option was trial and error. A couple of men were sent ahead along the shore in a canoe to tie a rope to a tree and repel back onto the boat. Using poles and the rope, the party attempted to pull and push the boat through one of the cascades. The first cascade they attempted proved to be too shallow and full of rocks, so they poled their way over to another fall. They pulled their way into the second chute and soon became stuck on the rocks. Four of the men jumped into the cold water and attempted to lift the boat. Despite their efforts, the boat remained jammed in the chute. As it grew dark, the men began to regret their attempt to ascend the Chutes so late in the afternoon. But they had no choice but to persevere. Most of the men were sent upstream to pull on the ropes while four were left behind to try to raise the boat. The dire situation became worse when the men on shore discovered that the rope was frayed and beginning to break. If the rope broke, the boat and everything onboard would be shattered on the rocks. While the men onboard quickly grabbed their poles to support the boat, another man splashed through the water with a new rope to secure to a tree upstream. The boat was finally hauled through this first cataract and the exhausted men pulled the boat to shore. Encamped that evening, Dunbar noted that the "incessant roar of the cataract" rapids reminded him of the "horrid din" of the hurricane that hit New Orleans in 1779.[57]

For the next three days, the party was confronted by rapids and cataracts. The day after ascending the Chutes, Dunbar recorded the drama of their encounter with another rapid:

> Arrived at the foot of a most tremendous rapid full of breakers, the passage being studded with pointed rocks of all magnitudes, which raising their rough heads above water, seemed to threaten with destruction the unwary voyager who should presume to attempt their passage; this place appeared to me much more difficult and dangerous than the Chutes, the water descended along a plane of considerable inclination with a most impetuous velocity, the spray & white foam dashing over the rocks, occasioned a very perceptible mist or vapor which spread about at a small elevation. . . . We stopped to contemplate this embarrassment & ordered out a rope, which was carried along shore by a certain part of the people, the rest using their poles on board; we made many fruitless essays to pass upwards by several openings near the shore; at length we attempted the center of the Cataract where the current was the most violent, but the water deeper, & by very great exertions we got over into moderate water, having consumed 1½ hour in making about ½ mile; 300 yards of this distance is difficult & perilous, the greatest prudence with unceasing exertion being indispensably necessary to the safety of such a barge as ours.[58]

Shortly thereafter they came to another rapid that Dunbar described as "more terrible than the last," with numerous fragments of rock peeking above the surface of the water.[59] They eventually pushed on and made it through at least three cataracts in one day. In what must be an understatement, Dunbar described the men camping that evening as "almost exhausted with fatigue."[60]

On day two above the Chutes, another hurdle presented itself. Dunbar estimated that the fall in front of them was about four-and-a-half feet vertical. Once again some of the men went forward to tie a rope to a tree. And once again the expedition was imperiled when the rope became entangled among sharp rocks. Eventually the rope was freed, and the men heaved, rested, and heaved some more. After about ninety minutes, the boat was lugged above the rapid and the party had advanced another 150 yards upstream. The next morning the men could not have been pleased to come upon more than four hundred yards of rapids. Once more they pulled on the rope and slowly ascended what Dunbar estimated to be "an inclined plane of 12 or 15 degrees."[61] After passing through the first portion of the rapids, the boat became caught on a rock. After unloading about a quarter of the cargo, the boat was lightened enough to proceed. Three hours later, the expedition conquered the final set of rapids and later that day arrived at their base camp near the hot springs. The ascent of the Ouachita was finally complete after seven weeks.

Hot Springs

On December 6, 1804, the expedition arrived at a landing near present-day Spencer Bay and Price, Arkansas. Blazier recommended that they stop here and transport their equipment overland about nine miles to the site of the hot springs. Dunbar was pleased with the "tolerably level" land upon which they encamped, along with the "good dark brown or blackish soil," the "large and handsome" timber, and the flowers and evergreen vines. Despite the aggravations posed by the rapids, Dunbar made regular reference along their ascent to the scenic beauty and quality of the land in central Arkansas. Just prior to their arrival at the Chutes, he waxed poetic about the natural landscape:

> This promontory presented some appearance at a distance, of the ancient ruined fortifications & Castles so frequent in Europe, the effect was greatly heightened by a flock of swans which had taken their stations under the Walls which rose out of the Water; as we approached the Birds floated about majestically upon the glassy surface, and in tremulous melancholy accents seemed to consult each other upon measures of safety, the ensemble produced a truly sublime picture.[62]

Further upstream, Dunbar again envisioned American settlement in the area as he noted "a high rocky hill . . . crowned with beautiful pine woods" that he deemed "a fine situation for building."[63] It appeared from their vantage point that all the nearby lands "lie very handsomely for cultivation."[64] Even the heavens appeared more radiant. Dunbar remarked that the stars in the Arkansas sky "shone with uncommon lustre."[65] The perceived quality of the land was matched by the quantity of wildlife in the area. They heard wolves howling in the night. They shot and ate the abundant wild turkeys almost every day. The numerous deer assured that there was plenty of venison to eat as well. They also encountered buffalo and learned the difficulty of killing one. At least three Arkansas buffalo were shot and wounded by the men of the expedition, but their attempts to catch up with their prey by following the tracks and the trail of blood were in vain.

The day after their arrival at the base camp, Dunbar sent Blazier and most of the men on the nine-mile hike to the hot springs. They carried their baggage and some of the provisions and were to return the next morning with a report. Despite temperatures that had dropped to the teens and twenties, the men returned the next day in high spirits, with "each giving his own account of the wonderful things he had seen."[66] Some of the men had tasted the water and compared it to spicewood tea. Others talked about how hot the water was as it discharged from the rock. The group had also discovered a cabin and a few sheds at the site. The men were sent back to the hot springs after lunch with another load of equipment and directions to return the next morning. The following day, Dunbar and Hunter joined the men on the third portage to the hot springs. Two of the men, Sergeant Bundy and a private, were left behind to guard the barge and the remaining provisions. The four-and-half-hour hike to the hot springs awoke Dunbar to the realities of portaging. Perhaps he also began to empathize with the exhausted men. "The people are much fatigued with this day's labor, altho' the road is by no means bad or hilly, but there is no doubt that a heavy load constantly bearing a man down must be very fatiguing upon the best of roads."[67]

Dunbar began to do the mental arithmetic as he thought about how this small portage compared to the ambitious plan of ascending the Red River and portaging across unknown land for an unknown distance to the unknown source of the Arkansas River. He recorded the results of his calculations in his journal.

> The provisions, instruments, arms & other baggage which may be deemed indispensable for 15 persons engaged on such an expedition, i.e. what must be transported from the head of one river to the commencement of navigation on the other, are certainly not over-rated at 3000 lib; of the whole party 10 carriers are the highest number we can calculate upon, some being necessary to guard the two camps while the scientific persons unattended would explore the environs: those 10 carriers from what we have seen could not be expected to carry for a number of days successively more than 50

> pounds each (several of our people were incapable of doing so much) and ten miles to go loaded & return empty day after day even on a tolerably level road, is perhaps beyond what we can flatter ourselves with accomplishing; thus it would require at least six days to transport the baggage 10 miles, and the seventh would be demanded as a day of repose: now if the heads of navigation should be only 50 miles apart, & the passage not rugged or mountainous, it would require at least 35 days to pass along the unknown region; and if allowance be made for such difficulties as ought to be expected including bad weather, we shall perhaps still flatter ourselves, if we expect to complete this portage in 50 days.[68]

Thus, Dunbar concluded, the portage between the sources of the Red and Arkansas Rivers might average only one mile per day. Imagine the horror of the men on such an expedition to discover that the sources of the two rivers are actually about five hundred miles apart.

Dunbar imagined that a better strategy would be to ascend one river at a time. Once the expedition reached the headwaters of a river, several short scientific excursions of thirty to fifty miles each could be launched in every direction from a base camp and specimens could be transported back downriver. If the original plan to ascend the Red and descend the Arkansas was to be followed, Dunbar estimated that it would require "two young men of science of robust constitutions attended by four Canadian or other woodsmen inured to fatigue and who can depend altogether on their guns for subsistence."[69] In addition to men who could handle the heavy workload, Dunbar thought the next expedition must include men who could do without their "execrable whiskey."[70] The men of future expeditions should be capable of transporting all their supplies at once, thus eliminating the need to travel back and forth to two camps to move supplies forward. Dunbar suggested that these supplies include "their blankets, their arms and ammunition, a little parched meal, very light instruments . . . and 3 or 4 days provisions in case of disappointment in finding game."[71] All in all, Dunbar had concluded that none of the current party—himself included—was up to the challenge of the planned Grand Expedition.

When they finally arrived at the hot springs, they found a cabin about twelve feet square with no chimney and a few huts that had been built for use during the summer and for "persons resorting to the Springs for the recovery of their health."[72] They were eager to feel and drink the water from the hot spring. Dunbar and Hunter failed to notice any special taste or "cathartic properties" in the water despite what some of the men appeared to believe.[73] Perhaps the exhausted men were eager for relief of any kind. The soldiers had spent the better part of the past three weeks fighting rapids and then transporting gear over nine miles in cold and damp weather. Dunbar agreed due to the "complaints of great fatigue by the people" to allow the men to rest—briefly.[74] He sent them back to the base camp on the river and told them to remain there overnight and then return the next day with lighter loads. One of the tasks that needed to be completed at the hot springs camp was repairs to the cabin and huts. The nights were cold, and they were unable to keep a fire in the cabin without a chimney. During the first few days at the hot springs, some of the men were tasked with building a chimney for the cabin and shutting up the cracks and openings between the logs to buffer against the cold and deteriorating weather.

The "dark, damp, and disagreeably cold" weather descended into rain and sleet a few days after their arrival.[75] As the temperatures dropped, the party was greeted one morning with a blanket of four inches of snow and continuing accumulation. Yet Dunbar remained sanguine: "The eves of our Cabin hang with beautiful icicles, which we have the pleasure of admiring thro' the logs as we sit by the fire side: outdoor business being out of the question, I continue to augment my list of vegetables from memory."[76] The temperatures remained below freezing at night and scarcely reached the forties during the day while the snow continued intermittently. The snow pack remained on the ground and a layer of freezing rain caused branches to fall from surrounding trees. To make matters more miserable, the valley location of the hot springs is prone to a wind-tunnel effect—forcing strong, cold winds through their camp. The physical discomfort was intensified as Dunbar, Hunter, and some of the men battled various illnesses. On one day, Dunbar's brief entry in his journal noted that he and Hunter were "both a little indisposed, probably from cold and wet feet & the inclemency of the weather."[77] Hunter was continuing to recover from the gunshot wounds that made his hand tender and spent a few days in "pain & griping" with kidney stones, or as he put it, "a severe attack of the gravel."[78]

Despite the uncomfortable weather and physical ailments, Dunbar and Hunter must have been eager to engage in their scientific observations, excursions, and experiments. For the next three weeks, they gathered data and proposed hypotheses about the source of the hot springs, the surrounding geology, the vegetation in the water and on the land, the organisms in the water, the height and characteristics of the surrounding hills, the wildlife, the weather patterns, the equipment needed for proper observations, and the commercial and agricultural potential of the area. Perhaps the first order of business was to study the hot springs. Hunter and Dunbar collected readings on the temperature of the water issuing from different locations, estimated the flow of the springs, and offered hypotheses about the possible sources of the springs. After tasting, smelling, and touching the spring water, they noted that it did not have "any other taste except that of very good water rendered hot by culinary fire," that the water was "so hot as to make it impossible for a person to hold his hand half a minute in it," that there was "nothing particular to the smell," and that drinking the water caused one to belch.[79] Hunter, the chemist, conducted a variety of chemical tests on the water. He concluded that the water "appears to be pure water containing only a small proportion of Carbonic Acid."[80] He also estimated the flow of one of the springs at 165 gallons a minute.

On their first day at the hot springs, Hunter and Dunbar explored the immediate area and found six springs issuing from the surrounding rocks. They recorded that the highest temperature reading was approximately 148 to 150 degrees Fahrenheit. Hunter and Dunbar were reduced to speculation about the cause of the heated water, and admitted that the answer to this important question "will require some reflection, & perhaps a knowledge of more facts than we are at present possessed of."[81] The hypothesis that Hunter offered was that the water was heated by "some chemical mixture" that forced vapor into the cavities of the mountain leading to condensation. The condensed water would then "issue throu such apertures as present themselves very hot yet still many degrees below boiling water." He acknowledged that this hypothesis was "mere conjecture." After additional study of the water, the deposits of rock and material in and around the springs, and the surrounding geography, Dunbar was similarly stumped about the source of the heat for the springs.

> It may be proper to pause for a moment and enquire what may be the cause of the perpetual fire which keeps up without change the high temperature of so many springs flowing from this hill at considerable distances from each other. Upon looking around us no data present themselves sufficient for the situation of the problem.[82]

He noted that there was no evidence of volcanic activity in the area and ventured that the heat could be created by the chemical decomposition of an underground stratum of minerals or metamorphic rock. He also postulated that the "springs may be supplied by the vapor of heated water ascending from the caverns where the heat is generated or the heat may be immediately applied to the bottom of an immense natural Cauldron of rock contained in the bowels of the hill, from which a reservoir of springs may be supplied."[83] Dunbar concluded that the mystery would have to be resolved by a future "ingenious observer of Nature."[84]

Short excursions were also launched to explore the surrounding environmental landscape. One of the first orders of business was to climb the surrounding hills. The hikes up present-day West Mountain and Hot Springs Mountain yielded estimates of the height of the peaks, observations of the rocks, soil, and vegetation, water temperature samples, and a view of the valley and distant hills. Hunter and a small group of men also embarked on lengthier explorations of the lands to the northeast and southwest. On December 16, 1804, Hunter, a few of the men, and Blazier set out to the northeast to the area near present-day Gulpha Creek with a spade, a mattock, and their rifles. They crossed "high cragy mountains" and found only "poor, thin stoney pine lands."[85] Hunter declared the land "not the country for metals, at least as far as we have gone" and returned having discovered nothing that he deemed of importance.[86] The following day, Hunter ventured with a small party to the southwest near the present-day community of Piney, Arkansas. He again returned with apparent disappointment that they "observed no essential difference between the soil, trees, mountains, stones &cc now & yesterday" and noted that he deemed it "unnecessary to trouble the men to carry any sample to camp."[87] Toward the end of their time at the hot springs, Hunter and a few men trekked further to the northeast over three days through sleet and cold weather. They returned once more with a note of dissatisfaction that there were "no appearances of minerals or metals in this part of the country worth further search" and that the "face of the country was like that we had seen."[88]

Notwithstanding the absence of sensational discoveries in the surrounding area, Dunbar satisfied his scientific inquisitiveness by investigating the springs and imagining the prospects for future scientific investigation and commercial development. He examined the plants, organisms, and "green matter" living in the water and was delighted by what appeared to be new discoveries. At times, Dunbar remarked on the novelty of the findings and the risk that others might not believe his report.

> It is surprising to see plants, shrubs & trees with their roots absolutely in the hot water . . . we found some branches of the wax-myrtle thrust into the

> bottom of a spring-run, the water being 130 of Fahrenheit thermometer, the foliage & fruit of the branch were not only sound and healthy, but at the very surface of the water fresh roots were actually sprouting from the branch; the whole being pulled up for examination, it was found that the part which had penetrated into the hot mud was decayed: this phenomenon is so new & singular, that few persons will at first be disposed to believe, judging that deception or want of accuracy has led us into error; it is however in the power of every curious person who will give himself the necessary trouble to try the experiments himself.[89]

Dunbar also observed that when the green matter was no longer submerged in water, it is "speedily converted into a rich vegetable earth & becomes the food of plants . . . [which] now vegetate luxuriantly upon this soil."[90] Hunter examined some of the moss from the water under a microscope and noted the presence of "many microscopic shell animals resembling clams of the size of a pin point or about the 50th part of a inch in length. It shows four legs & a double tail."[91] Dunbar was also captivated by the process of rock formation around the water and deemed it "worthy of the attention of the mineralogist."[92] He described this curious phenomenon:

> Any spring enjoying a freedom of position proceeds with great regularity in depositing its solid contents, the borders or rim of its basin forms an elevated ridge, from whence proceeds a glacis all around; when the waters have flowed for some time over one part of the brim, this becomes more elevated & the water can no longer escape on that side, but is compelled to seek a passage where the resistance is least, thus it proceeds with the greatest regularity forming in miniature a Crater resembling in shape the conical summit of a volcano; the hill being steep above, the progress of petrification is at length stopped on that side, & the waters continue to flow and spread abroad, encrusting the whole face of the hill below. I am persuaded that the accumulations and extent of the calcareous matter would have been vastly greater, perhaps the whole valley might have been filled up with it, did not the continual running of the creek put a stop to its progression on that side.[93]

The men collected a variety of samples for additional analysis and Dunbar concluded that the hot springs were ripe for future scientific study.

The prospects for commercial and agricultural development of the area were also chronicled. Both men were impressed by the "great deal of excellent black vegetable earth" in the area.[94] Dunbar again imagined vineyards producing Arkansas wine: "Nature has bestowed a soil which will reward the future labors of the industrious Vigneron: Nature herself indeed unaided by man has already planted on them three or four species of vines, which are said to produce annually an exuberance of excellent grapes."[95] He found what he supposed to be a wild species of cabbage, predicted that wheat would grow well in the area, and collected samples of native plants that he was told had medicinal qualities "in hopes of procuring in due time seeds from which the curious may be furnished."[96] Similarly, Hunter advised that cement could be manufactured from limestone deposits and that bituminous oil was evident in the water high on one of the hills. But the most creative moment of commercial fantasy came from Dunbar as the party endured below-freezing temperatures and a blanket of snow on the ground. Dunbar noticed a patch of ground where the plants remained green and the snow appeared to melt on contact. In the midst of his intrigue, he envisioned "what a fine situation for a green or hot house, where at small expense all the tropical fruits may be propagated."[97] In his optimism, Dunbar imagined a productive commercial landscape and place despite the miserable weather.

The only break for the soldiers during the three weeks of camp at the hot springs was Christmas. Dunbar agreed to "indulge the men with a holy day for which purpose they had hoarded up their ration whiskey to be expended on this day."[98] Hunter described the celebration that ensued for the weary men:

> They had made a reserve of their liquor for the occasion, with which & a Saddle of Venison they made themselves very merry, dancing, Hooping in the Indian Manner & singing alternately, not forgetting to serenade us from time to time with a volley from their riffle, wishing us an happy Christmas with all the compliments of the season &cc. The night came at length with the heavy rain which put a period to their mirth, & sleep closed their joys for the day.[99]

Dunbar judged the "great deal of frolick" to be "perfectly innocent."[100]

Return to Natchez

As 1804 drew to a close, the expedition departed the hot springs and returned to the river camp and their boat with plans to begin their descent of the river. But along with the New Year arrived a foot of snow, single-digit temperatures at night, and little water in the almost frozen river. On January 4, 1805, Dunbar remarked with exasperation, "We continue here as prisoners, waiting for what is usually called bad weather [rain], to bear us away from this place."[101] Two days later, a light rain began to fall, and the river began to rise. By January 7, the midday temperature had risen to 75 degrees "producing the sensation of a summer's sun of 90 degrees."[102] The boat had been repaired and outfitted with a better cabin and new poles, and the hunting parties had returned over the past few days with a supply of venison, turkey, rabbit, and a young bear cub, though some of the provisions—notably flour and whiskey—had been expended. "To the no small joy of all hands," it was time to go home.[103]

The rapids that had caused so much strife as they ascended the river were much less troublesome on the descent. Although the party had to stop above each rapid to determine the best path, Dunbar and Hunter did not record any major problems as they passed over the Chutes and the other rapids between Hot Springs and present-day Arkadelphia. In cold temperatures, with hail and snow, the party was able in two days to descend the river a distance that took five days to ascend. On the third day of the descent, the men reached a point near present-day Camden—a distance that had taken almost two weeks to cover on their way to the hot springs. Here, they came upon a hunting party of ten Indians and the French-Canadian trader Pierre LeFevre.[104] Dunbar was impressed that LeFevre possessed a "considerable knowledge of the interior of the Country," and he recorded a substantial journal entry of geographical information about the land, rivers, Indians, animals, and mountains to the west.[105] The prairies are described in terms that reveal the enthusiasm that Dunbar must have felt about the potential for American settlement of the West. Here, Dunbar forecast a landscape of the future that far exceeded the extant conditions and was not based on firsthand knowledge.

> The whole of those prairies is represented to be composed of the richest and most fertile soil, the most luxuriant and succulent herbage covers the surface of the Earth interspersed with millions of flowers and flowering Shrubs of the most ornamental and adorning kinds: Those who have viewed only a Skirt of those prairies, speak of them with a degree of enthusiasm as if it was only there that Nature was to be found in a state truly perfect; they declare that the fertility and beauty of the rising grounds, the extreme richness of the valleys, the coolness and excellent quality of the water found in every valley, the Salubrity of the atmosphere and above all the grandeur and Majesty of the enchanting landscape which this country presents, inspires the Soul with sensations not to be felt in any other

> region of the globe. This Paradise is now very thinly inhabited by a few tribes of Savages and by immense herds of Wild Cattle which people those countries. . . . Should it be found that of this rich and desirable country there is 500 miles square, and from report, there is probably much more, the whole of it being cultivated, it will admit of the fullest population, and will at a future day vie with the best cultivated & most populous countries on the Globe . . . It will be capable of subsisting a nation composed of twenty six million of souls.[106]

For Dunbar, this paradise clearly needed to be explored, settled, and made commercially productive. In addition to bison, the immense prairies were said to be home to "vast numbers of a species of wild goat" and "great flocks of an wool-bearing animal larger than common sheep," yet according to Dunbar the Canadian who supplied information about the animals to the west, presumably Pierre LeFevre, also "pretends to have seen a unicorn."[107]

Dunbar also recorded a comparison of the Arkansas and Red Rivers based on the information supplied by his sources. He learned that both rivers were long, passed through the prairies, were not potable, and were navigable to an unknown distance, but that the Arkansas was preferable for navigation. According to Dunbar's informants, the Arkansas River was fed by springs of fresh water, lacked the raft of debris that blocked the Red River near present-day Shreveport, and flowed near immense deposits of salt that "may be raked up into large heaps" in some places and "dug out with the Crow-bar" in other places.[108] Regarding the Platte River, Dunbar referred to this "neighborhood" of river sources: "a branch of the Missouri called the river platte or shallow river takes its rise so far south, as to derive its first waters from the neighborhood of the sources of the Red and arcansa river."[109] In the distance to the west were the mysterious Rocky Mountains. According to Dunbar's informant,

> The great dividing mountain is so lofty that it requires two days to ascend from its base to its top, other ranges of inferior mountains lie before and behind it; they are all very rocky & sandy, large lakes and valleys lie between the mountains; some lakes are so long as to contain considerable islands, and rivers flow from some of them. . . . From the top of the high mountain, the view is bounded by a curve as upon the ocean and extends over the most beautiful prairies which seem to be unbounded.[110]

There was much that was unknown, misunderstood, or doubted in the geographical information that Dunbar recorded. Regarding the great prairies to the west, he admitted that the "breadth of this great plain is not well ascertained," but was "said by some to be at certain parts or in certain directions to be not less than two hundred leagues, but I believe it is agreed by all that have a knowledge of the Western Country, that the mean breadth is at least two thirds of this quantity."[111] Regarding coal in Arkansas, Dunbar doubted an informant he called "fond of the marvelous" who "pretends to have been up among the sources of the Washita 100 leagues higher than the hot springs" and who claimed to have "found true mineral coal, which burns with a strong heat and bright flame without the aid of other fuel."[112] Later Dunbar met "an American who pretends to have been up the Arcansa river 300 leagues," yet again Dunbar doubts the information received about silver on three of the rivers in Arkansas.

> I do not give implicit faith to this man, when he speaks largely of the silver which he pretends to have himself collected upon that river [Arkansas], and even says that on the Washita 30 leagues above the hot springs he has found silver ore. . . . He asserts also that the ore of the mine upon the little Missouri was carried to Kentucky by a certain Boon, where was found to yield largely in silver.[113]

On January 15, 1805, the expedition crossed the boundary line between Arkansas and Louisiana. They had spent two months in Arkansas. The following day, they arrived at Fort Miró, where they parted with Blazier and LeFevre and returned their borrowed boat. Two days at Fort Miró were needed to resupply, to make repairs to their first boat, and—perhaps as a bonus—to allow one soldier suffering from dysentery some time to recover. Hunter remarked that their original vessel

> looked more weather beaten than if we had used her all the time. The men were set to clean her out, cut & make six more oars to replace as many broken on the journey, to cut & form a new mast in the woods, to bend the sail & put all the rigging in order, & to take back again from the Garrison all our spare articles which on account of their weight we had found it necessary to leave behind.[114]

Dunbar and Hunter separated at Fort Miró. Dunbar received letters from home when he arrived at Fort Miró and determined that he should "get to Natchez as soon as possible."[115] He departed the fort by canoe on January 19, 1805, with his slave and a soldier, obtained horses at Catahoula from a French ferry operator named Hebrard, and was home for breakfast one week later on

January 26.[116] The journey could have been faster if not for delays in obtaining horses and in crossing the swampy territory between Jonesville, Louisiana, and Natchez, Mississippi. Along the overland journey, Dunbar recorded the difficulty, unpredictability, apprehension, and serendipity involved in such travel.

> We pushed on but the roads proved extremely bad being under water for leagues together, it became dark, & we expected to be obliged to spend the nig't in the woods without fire, perhaps without a spot of dry land to rest upon; it was difficult to keep the path, by the sagacity of our horses we had the good fortune about 9 hours in the evening to get to a house four miles short of the river, where we were hospitably entertained with good homely fare.[117]

Despite the hindrances of the physical landscape, Dunbar recorded that the territory had experienced settlement in the brief period since the Louisiana Purchase.

> A large lake called St. John's lake occupied a considerable part of this passage between the Mississippi and the Tenza . . . it has been in some former period the bed of the Mississippi . . . has lately occupied & improved; many similar possessions and improvements have been made since the first news of the cession of Louisiana by the French to the American government.[118]

Dunbar also predicted a bright future for the site of present-day Jonesville, Louisiana: "There is no doubt that as the country augments in population and riches, this place will become the site of a commercial inland town, which will hold pace with the progress and prosperity of the country."[119]

For Hunter and the remainder of the men, the journey back to St. Catherine's Landing ended three weeks after departing the hot springs. Still hopeful of finding additional commercial resources, Hunter slowed the return on January 21 to search for rumored deposits of gypsum, but found none: "Altho I landed now & then to search, I was not more fortunate than we were going up, for I could not find the place of either one or the other."[120] Hunter also noted an encounter with a boat carrying an emaciated, elderly French man from Baton Rouge who was "on his way to the hot springs for the recovery of his health." Despite his firsthand scientific observations, Hunter wished not to dash the hopes of the old man: "I thought it best to give him hopes of recovery, he was very eager to know if the waters were salutary which [I] assured him they were."[121]

For the final ten days, Hunter and the men met a few ultimate obstacles before their journey came to an end. Near the confluence of the Red and Black Rivers, the men fought against a current that seemed to be running the wrong way. Although they were heading downstream, Hunter recorded a "running back of the water" in which a tributary is overtaken near its confluence with a backflow from a larger river.[122] There was also the "unusually severe" winter weather that happened to plague southern Louisiana that month. The days during which "the wind blew fresh in our teeth" and the "cold & stormy & very uncomfortable" nights became more wearisome when they encountered ice near the mouth of the Red River.[123] The half-inch-thick ice across the river required "four men at the Bow breaking ice as we went."[124] The hardships overcome, the Ouachita River Expedition came to an end on January 31, 1805, when the "Chinese Vessel" arrived back at St. Catherine's Landing with George Hunter, his son, and a crew of soldiers who were probably exhausted but who had great tales to tell their companions in New Orleans.

Chapter Three

A Greenhorn in the Ozarks

HENRY ROWE SCHOOLCRAFT, 1818–1819

PERHAPS HENRY ROWE SCHOOLCRAFT intended for his journal to open with a literary flourish that would catch his reader's attention and foreshadow a tale of danger and intrigue. In this moment of rhetorical zeal, he stated boldly, "I begin my tour where other travellers have ended theirs, on the confines of the wilderness, and at the last village of white inhabitants, between the Mississippi River and the Pacific Ocean."[1] If some readers extended poetic license to the young man for his exaggeration, others surely read such a statement as naive braggadocio. He was certainly naive. On the second day of the journey, he admitted that he and Levi Pettibone ". . . shall necessarily encounter some difficulties from our want of experience."[2] Incredibly, his list of lessons-to-be-learned included how to hobble a horse properly, how to build a campfire, how to cook a piece of venison, and how to boil a pot of coffee. Thus, two men proudly "clothed and equipped in the manner of the hunter" with few of the skills needed to survive in the backwoods, set out into unknown and dangerous territory in November 1818 with only a general idea of the direction they should travel.[3] The twenty-five-year-old New Yorker who had failed in the New England glassmaking business attempted to swallow his fear after the first day of the journey.

> We turned to pursue our way with such feelings as many travellers have experienced on turning their backs upon the comforts and endearments of life, to encounter fatigue, hard fare, and danger.[4]

Thus, Schoolcraft heightened the drama of his journey by drawing a line between a cultural landscape of civilization and one of savagery—and then proclaiming that he was about to cross that line.

Potosi, Missouri, to Bennetts Bayou, Arkansas

Henry Schoolcraft had been in southeastern Missouri touring the mining operations in the area and befriending Stephen F. Austin for the last several months. He had convinced fellow Yankee Levi Pettibone, the brother of his lawyer, to accompany him on a trek to the Southwest, where they would survey the mining opportunities near present-day Springfield, Missouri. Henry enjoyed the "pleasing and picturesque appearance" of Potosi, Missouri, and its "delightful valley," meandering stream of "the purest water," hills of "primitive limestone," "cultivated farms," and "furnaces smoking through the trees."[5] The village included "seventy buildings, exclusive of a court-house, a jail, an academy, a post-office, one saw, and two grist mills, and a number of temporary buildings necessary in the smelting of lead."[6] Lead was king in Potosi, and Henry noted that it was "the medium of exchange, as furs and peltries formerly were in certain parts of the Atlantic states" and that "very great quantities of lead are annually made at this place, and waggoned across the country to the banks of the Mississippi, a distance of forty miles, for shipment."[7] The effects of two decades of heavy mining on the landscape was severe. As they departed Potosi, Henry noted the "heaps of gravel and . . . other rubbish" that impeded their path, as well as the danger of falling into pits twenty to thirty feet deep.[8] Nevertheless, Henry admired the "beautiful prospect" of Potosi as he and Levi departed over the hills to the southwest on November 6, 1818.[9]

After spending the night in an uninhabited cabin, the second day of their journey began with the inconvenience of searching for the horse they had not hobbled properly the night before. Once the horse was located and packed, Henry and Levi continued the journey toward the west-southwest for fourteen more miles. Schoolcraft noted that the current inhabitants of this territory engaged in both hunting and farming, but he expected agriculture to take hold in the future when more settlers arrived. He explained that the banks of today's Courtois Creek, a tributary of the Meramec River, "afford some very rich lands, but they do not extend far, consisting merely of a strip of alluvion running parallel with the river, and bordered by hills, whose stony aspect forbids the approach of the farmer. . . . The district of tillable land is much more extensive, however, than has generally been supposed."[10] It was in this area, on their third day of travel, that Henry and Levi met the first of several Ozark settlers who would assist them.

The barking of the Robertses' dogs announced their arrival. As Henry and Levi awaited the return of Mr. Roberts, they were given a lesson by Mrs.

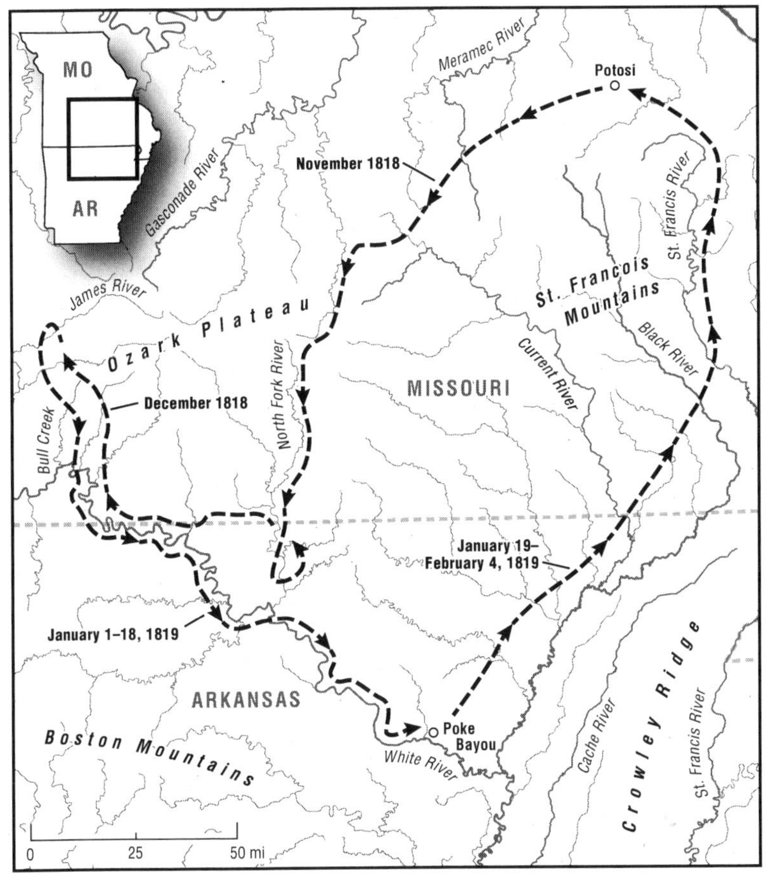

FIG. 3.1. Route of Henry Rowe Schoolcraft, 1818–1819. Cartography by Erin Greb.

Roberts on several aspects of Ozark geography and travel.[11] Though the men were somewhat surprised to be lectured about these matters by a woman, Mrs. Roberts proceeded to advise the men that their guns, clothing, and equipment were not appropriate for the journey ahead. She also explained the direction of the trace they should follow, the streams they would cross, and the game they would find along the way. Mrs. Roberts was also the first of many white settlers to warn them of the dangers of traveling near the territory of the Osages. She told them stories of robberies and murders and explained "that it was dangerous travelling in that quarter on account of the Osages, who never failed to rob and plunder those who fell in their way, and often carried them in captivity to their villages, on the Grand Osage river."[12] Mr. Roberts had become fearful of hunting alone and running into a party of Osages. Yet not all of the Indians in the region were considered dangerous by white inhabitants. In the next valley to the west, and approximately four to five miles from the Roberts's cabin, were two small villages of Delaware Indians and a larger village of Shawnees settled on today's Huzzah Creek.[13]

When Mr. Roberts returned home, he agreed to accompany Henry and Levi for a short distance. Schoolcraft, Pettibone, and Roberts traveled southwest through current-day Crawford County, Missouri, along the Osage Trace. On their first night with Roberts, Henry explained that hunters had a difficult time sleeping at night.

> The sleep of the hunter is not sound, neither is his vigilance to be eluded; and the anxiety he is kept in, from the fear of the Indian on the one hand, and the approach of wild animals on the other, produces constant wakefulness during the night. His horse and baggage also demand occasional notice during the darkness of the night, and he lies down with his rifle in his arms, to be prepared for emergencies.[14]

Henry seemed to have no trouble sleeping after the long days of hiking. In fact, Roberts had to awake Henry in the middle of the night to let him know that their pack horse had strayed from camp. Once again, the horse was found about three miles away and was led back to camp before daylight. Roberts's alertness for deer and elk paid dividends when he shot a doe and brought her back on his shoulders for a breakfast feast of roasted venison. The sleep of the hunter could also be disturbed by howling wolves, but Henry noted with confidence, "We had already been long enough in the woods, and were sufficiently conversant with the hunter life, to know that this animal will only attack men in cases of the most extreme hunger; and as we knew their common prey, the deer, was abundant in that quarter, we had little apprehension for our safety."[15] Roberts decided after a day with Henry and Levi that he would go off on his own to hunt. He told the men that he would catch up with them later, but they never saw him again. Henry and Levi were left to wonder whether he had been captured by the Osages or had simply become lost. They learned when they returned home that Roberts had become lost in the woods while hunting deer. Whether Mr. Roberts was truly lost or had simply decided to bow out of the greenhorn expedition remains a mystery.

The environmental landscape through much of south-central Missouri did not impress Schoolcraft. Over a period of three days and fifty miles of travel, he repeatedly referred to the land and soil as "poor," "barren," "stony," and lacking in timber and water.[16] But Schoolcraft's language changed when he and Levi reached the valley of the Current River.[17] Here the soil was "rich," the valley was "deep and romantic," the walls of limestone were "majestic" and "stupendous," the forest was "lofty," and the views were "sublime" and "picturesque."[18] Schoolcraft noted that artists might find inspiration here: "[the] views which are presented are commanding and delightful, and to the painter who wishes to depict the face of nature in its wildest aspect of rocky grandeur, I could recommend this valley, and the adjacent country, as one of unrivalled attractions."[19] Even the food seemed to be better in this place: "We partook of [supper] with that keen appetite, and that feeling of lordly independence, which are alone felt by the wild Indian, and the half-starved Missouri hunter."[20]

In addition to taking in the beautiful scenery, their primary purpose for visiting this area was to explore the caves. During the War of 1812, William Henry Ashley manufactured gunpowder in Potosi and mined saltpeter from a cave in this area.[21] Schoolcraft observed that the mining works were idle at this time and that "large quantities of crude salt-petre are lying in the fore part of the cave."[22] Given the volatility of this substance—several miners had been killed in explosions in recent years—it is fortunate that the journey and their lives did not end when Henry and Levi foolishly built a fire in the cave. Fortunately, the potassium nitrate surrounding them did not explode and Henry and Levi survived to explore seven different caves, examine the stalactites and stalagmites, and collect samples of the saltpeter.

For the next two days, a rainstorm kept the men confined to Ashley Cave. This delay gave Schoolcraft time to reflect on the scientific curiosities and commercial opportunities that awaited further investigation. He noted that "the earth found in this cave, and which is now so highly charged with nitrous salts, presents an extraordinary circumstance for the consideration of the geologist, and one which must be conclusive in regard to the antiquity of the cave itself."[23] He speculated on the geological processes that led to the formation of the valleys and caves, the purification of potassium nitrate, and the mineral deposits evident such as quartz, slate, granite, hornstone, flint, iron ore, manganese, and pyrite. Yet, the young man was also swept up in spiritual reflections as he and his companion awaited clear weather. After exploring Ashley Cave, Henry noted:

> We did not return from our examination without feeling impressions in regard to our own origin, nature, and end, and the mysterious connection between the Creator of these stupendous works and ourselves, which many have before felt, but none have yet been satisfied about. In contemplating this connection, we feel humiliated; human reason has no clue by which the mystery may be solved, and we imperceptibly became silent, absorbed in our own reflections.[24]

Yet after a second day confined to the cave, Schoolcraft and Pettibone became less enamored by their surroundings.

> Thus situated, beyond the boundaries of the civilized world, shut up in a dreary cavern, without books to amuse the mind, or labour to occupy the body, we have had ample leisure to reflect upon the solitude of our condition, and in reverting to the scenes of polished life, to contrast its comforts, attractions, and enjoyments, with the privations and danger by which we are surrounded.[25]

On November 15, 1818, the weather finally cleared, and Henry and Levi resumed their journey. For the next two days, and approximately thirty miles of travel, Henry again was impressed neither by the environmental landscape nor with the difficulties of traveling by foot in the region. The path they chose for this leg of the journey involved ascending and descending a series of ridges, crossing a highland prairie, and then fording a series of streams. Henry explained that for six miles they encountered ridges running at right angles to their course so that they were "continually climbing up slowly to the tops of these lofty heights or descending with cautious tread into the intervening gulfs."[26] This was understandably perilous and arduous to the men. The thick underbrush through which they trudged took a toll on their skin and clothing. He described the highland landscape as "a level woodless barren covered with wild grass and resembling the natural meadows or prairies of the western country in appearance, but lacks their fertility, their wood, and their remarkable equality of surface."[27] He also observed, "In travelling across such a district of country, we have found little to interest. There are no prominent features in the physiognomy of the country to catch the eye. There is no landmark in perspective, to which, by travelling, we seem to approach. The unvaried aspect of the country produces satiety."[28] As he had done earlier, Henry resorted to language such as "rough," "barren," and "wholly uninteresting" to explain his sense of the environmental landscape.[29]

The silent march and vacant scenery was occasionally interrupted by a deer, a startled rabbit, or the eruption of a brood of quail from the bushes, but Henry found little else to disturb the monotony. The final leg of this two-day trek involved crossing three streams. They spent most of the day attempting to cross one stream and emerged with a "handsome wetting."[30] Perhaps it is understandable that Schoolcraft's mood after thirty miles of difficult travel led him to insert into his journal the following snide remark about this portion of the Ozarks.

> When the Edinburgh Reviewer estimated that Louisiana only cost three cents per acre, on the average of the whole number of square miles in the territory, he probably had no idea that there was any part of it which could be considered dear at that price. Yet, I think it would be money dearly expended in the purchase of such lands as we have this day traversed.[31]

As Henry and Levi trudged over ridges and through streams for two days, they were crossing a drainage divide that runs through south-central Missouri. To the north and west of this divide, rivers and streams flow northerly and empty into the Missouri River. To the south and east of this divide, waters flow southerly toward the Mississippi. Thus far, they had traveled in two river systems that were fairly well-known. They began their journey in the watershed of the Meramec River that flows easterly to the Mississippi River and empties just south of St. Louis. Their visit to Ashley Cave brought them into the valley of the Current River that flows to the southeast and is a tributary of the White River that flows to the Mississippi River as well. In crossing the divide, the men were now splashing through streams of the Missouri River system. On November 17 Henry admitted, "We have been at a loss to know what river the streams we passed yesterday are tributary."[32] They deduced correctly that the streams flowed north toward the Missouri River, but they incorrectly believed that they had passed the headwaters of the Gasconade River and had entered the Osage River system.[33] They determined that they were too far north and decided to alter their course to a more southerly bearing. They selected a stream to follow, but it curved off to the west; they ended up in the highlands again. Regardless of the exact geography of the watersheds, the two men were becoming disoriented.

After setting another new course, Henry and Levi spotted four bears in trees along their path. Reflecting on the trip so far, Henry remarked, "[We] have not . . . sought to go out of our way for the purpose of hunting, but this was . . . too fine an opportunity to exercise our skill in hunter sport to be neglected."[34] The men decided to give the bears "battle." After tying their horse to a sapling and loading their guns, they approached their prey. The bears quickly spotted Henry and Levi, and began to climb down from the trees. Henry and Levi decided to charge toward the bears in a clumsy attempt to keep them in place, but while running across the rugged ground Levi sprained his ankle and fell. As the last of the bears hopped to the ground, Henry fired his gun from fifty yards away and missed. The bears loped away over a ridge and into a field of tall grass. Henry and Levi spent an hour trying to sight the bears again, but succeeded only in becoming exhausted and aggravating the injury to Levi's ankle. Henry confessed that the "bears certainly were victorious."[35] Thus far, the day involved a growing trepidation regarding their whereabouts and an ankle injury. By mid-afternoon, Levi was in severe pain and unable to put weight on his ankle, so they found a place to camp in a nearby valley.

Henry began to worry. What if Levi's condition worsened? Was his life in danger? All they had packed for medicine was "a box of Lee's pills and some healing salve."[36] The pills were for indigestion or nausea, and the salve was for scratches and cuts. Neither would do much for the pain of an ankle injury or worse. Henry prepared a warm saltwater bath for Levi's ankle, wrapped it in flannel and buffalo skin, and assembled a bed of skins and grass. Henry's anxiety grew as he began to gauge their circumstances. They were without sufficient medicine. They were not sure of their location. They did not know if there were other people in the vicinity. There was not enough forage for the horse nearby. The wood close to the camp would not last very long. And what about food? Their provisions might not last for a week, and there did not seem to be many deer or turkeys in the area. Regardless of the presence of wildlife, though, Henry and Levi had just experienced a rude lesson in how ineffective they could be at hunting. With these thoughts racing through his mind, Henry sauntered with his gun through the grass within earshot of the camp and looked for small birds that he might be able to shoot for supper. He came back to camp emptyhanded and fed Levi a meal of coffee and biscuits.

The dawn brightened the scene immensely. Levi could stand, and his pain had subsided. He suggested that they rearrange the packs on the horse so that he could ride until his ankle improved. "We bid adieu to our camp," Henry recorded, "with spirits as much exhilarated above the common tune, as they had, the evening before, been depressed below it."[37] Having escaped disaster, Schoolcraft and Pettibone headed south toward Arkansas. Their path took them between the present-day communities of Cabool and Mountain Grove, Missouri, where they crossed the river divide again, leaving the Missouri

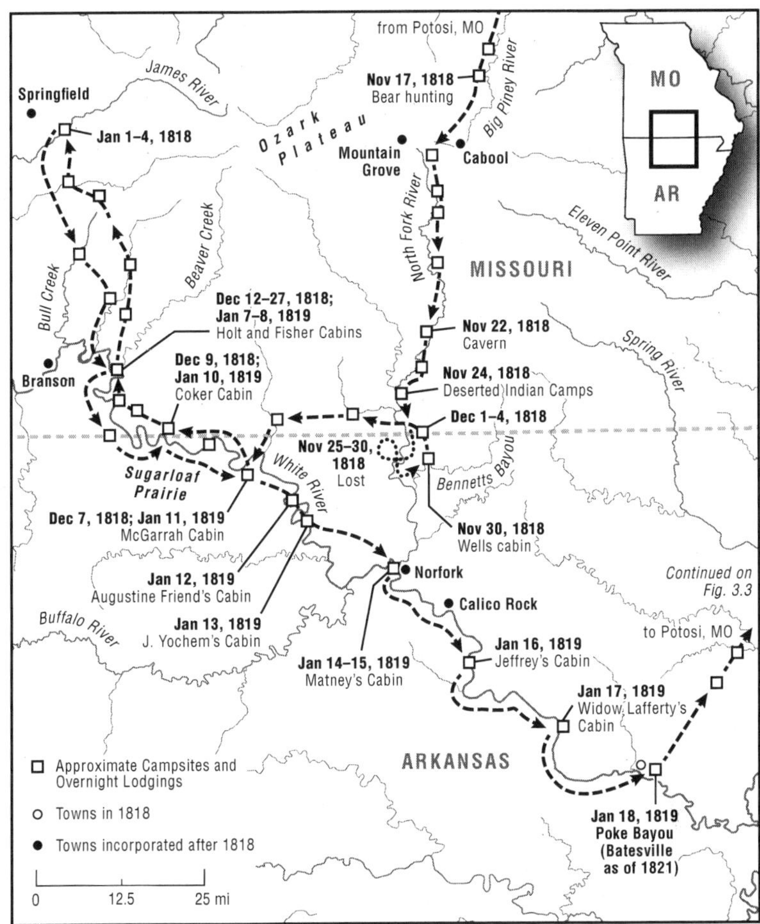

FIG. 3.2. Western Portion of Henry Rowe Schoolcraft's route, 1818–1819. Cartography by Erin Greb.

River system and entering the White River watershed of Arkansas. As they descended from a ridge, they entered a valley containing a stream running south and reasoned correctly that they had reached a tributary of the White River. Over the next three and a half days, the men followed the course of the stream south for approximately forty miles.

Although Henry found the "mineralogical character of the country" to be "quite uninteresting," the waters of the Ozarks merited attention and praise in his journal.[38] He described the water of the North Fork of the White River as "very pure, cold, and transparent." The volume and source of the water was also impressive. He noted that the stream "is wholly composed of springs which gush at almost every step from its calcareous banks, and it rapidly assumes the character of a considerable river."[39] The men thought it intriguing that they did not find any tributary streams flowing into the river, but instead observed that the stream was fed completely by very pure and often large springs. Henry exclaimed that one spring "deserves to be ranked among the natural phenomena of this region." The spring "rushes out of an aperture in a lime-stone rock, at least fifty yards across, and where it joins the main river, about 1000 yards below, is equal to it, both in width and depth, the waters possessing the purity of crystal." Henry found a large elk horn near the water and hung it on an oak tree "to advertise [to] the future traveller that he had been preceded by human footsteps in his visit to the Elkhorn Spring."[40]

The next day, Henry noted that the depth of the river could be deceiving. The water is "so clear, white, and transparent, that the stones and pebbles in its bottom, at a depth of eight or ten feet, are reflected through it with the most perfect accuracy as to colour, size, and position, and at the same time appear as if within two or three feet of the surface of the water."[41] This illusion proved nearly disastrous when Henry, Levi, and their horse attempted to ford the river at one point. The horse stepped into the stream expecting to land his hoof on the pebbles below when he suddenly plunged into the cold water. He swam to safety, but their supplies—tea, meal, salt, sugar, skins, blankets, clothes, and some of their gunpowder—were soaked. It was near the end of the day, so the men set up camp and attempted to save any supplies that had not been ruined by the plunge into the illusory river.

In addition to the crystal-clear water, the country was also teeming with wildlife and thick with greenery. Henry noted that wild turkey, duck, and grey squirrels were "almost constantly in sight," and that "we have been continually breaking in upon the retreats of those natural possessors of the soil, the bear and the deer."[42] Despite their earlier misadventures in bear hunting, Henry and Levi decided to test their skills once more when they came upon two bears playing. "[We] each put an additional ball in our guns," Henry recorded, "and examined our priming; then taking a deliberate aim, both fired at the same moment," but "neither shot took effect, or if wounded, they ran with their usual clumsiness over an adjoining hill, leaving us the satisfaction of having shot at a bear."[43] Schoolcraft also recorded that the rich bottom lands along the stream were covered with elm, beech, oak, maple, sycamore, and ash. As they proceeded along the North Fork of the White River, he described a "luxuriant growth of forest-timber, shrubs, vines, cane, and greenbriar."[44] They also sighted plants that were still green despite the late autumn season, including black haw. Although the greenery made for scenic territory, it slowed their travel considerably. Henry, Levi, and their horse became entangled repeatedly in thickets of greenbrier and grapevine: "so wound around our bodies that we are obliged to use a knife in cutting through."[45] While bushwhacking through one thicket, Henry lost his mineral hammer; "a misfortune I shall have frequent cause to regret."[46]

Given their struggles with the underbrush and vines in the valley of the river, the men decided to alter their course and proceed through the highlands. They marched about two miles due west before they escaped the ravines, forests, and brush that followed the course of the river. Travel became much easier here. Schoolcraft described the landscape as "an open barren, with very little timber, or under-brush, and generally level."[47] They easily made another fourteen miles heading to the south-southeast. Henry, Levi, and their horse must have been relieved to march along with such ease across "sterile soil, destitute of woods, with gentle elevations."[48] There was one major disadvantage to this mode of travel: no water. By late afternoon, the lack of water was becoming a problem. They again altered their course—this time to the southeast—in hopes of finding a valley with a spring or stream. For two miles, they followed the course of a rocky valley with no signs of wood, water, or grass. The sun set and the wind began to blow and still there was no sign of water. About the time they were ready to give up and camp without water or a fire, they spotted a small spring and the entrance to a cave. The cave was spacious, so they kindled a fire, ate a small meal of dried venison, bread, and water, and admired the reflection of the firelight on the rugged roof of the cave. Schoolcraft remarked that the illumination of the cave "produced an effect of aweful grandeur which it is impossible to describe."[49] The combination of the serene setting and the drama of their search for water carried the men into a reflective conversation about their journey, the hunter's life, the differences between "savage" and "civilized" society, and home. As the light faded and they prepared for sleep, Henry carved the date of their visit and a few lines of a poem into the wall of the cave.

While Henry and Levi were enjoying the tranquility of the cave, they turned their horse loose to search for food. Henry expected that the horse would have the "poorest prospect of picking up a meal than he has yet experienced."[50] The men spent most of the morning searching before reuniting with their horse. After tying up the horse at camp, Henry and Levi hiked back up the river for several miles. They believed that a tributary stream must have entered the river somewhere to the north since the river was now flowing so full. Failing to find any tributary, they trekked back to their horse and made a few more miles to the south before camping for the night. Henry noted that "a considerable change in the face of the country has taken place."[51] The "rich bottoms" and "perpendicular bluffs" were replaced in the environmental landscape by "high oak-prairie" and "long, sloping hills, covered by oaks."[52] The North Fork of the White River had also increased in size and, Henry estimated, was probably deep enough to "float a keel-boat of twenty tons."[53] Schoolcraft noted that the numerous bear, deer, elk, and beaver he spotted heralded opportunities for large quantities of skins to be collected. They also passed through several abandoned Indian camps that suggested that human habitation was feasible. Henry explained that "several causes have induced the Indians to relinquish hunting in this quarter, and principally their wars among themselves, which have kept them in mutual fear of each other" and that the "Indian title has been extinguished by purchase by the United States, and this stream will no longer be included in their hunting grounds" though it was "claimed by the Osages."[54] In addition to these other commercial features of the Ozark landscape, agriculture was not out of the question. Near the current state line between Arkansas and Missouri, Henry recorded, "The climate we are in is adapted to the growth of cotton, several stalks of which were found growing spontaneously among the weeds encircling our camp. The bowls were handsomely filled with cotton of a fine quality, and we picked some of it, for the purpose of kindling a fire."[55]

Approximately three weeks after departing from Potosi, Schoolcraft and Pettibone entered Arkansas. Their situation was dire. They had been without bread for more than a week. There was only enough corn meal to last another day. Their supply of dried meat was gone. Even if they had had the skill to hunt for fresh game, they had run out of shot. This was not the original plan. They expected to have made it to the White River in about half the time they had been traveling. Running low on supplies and unsure whether or not they had reached the White River, they hoped to find a hunter's cabin soon. So far, they had only stumbled upon deserted camps and an empty cabin. A glimmer of hope emerged when Henry discovered three pumpkins growing on a vine at an abandoned camp. One had been partially eaten by a wild animal, so Henry fed the remainder to his horse. The other two he returned triumphantly to their camp where Levi congratulated him on his bounty. The men dined that evening on a soup of pumpkin, water, and salt. Henry quipped, "Some epicures would not have relished the entertainment. Nevertheless, we enjoyed a most hearty and social repast."[56]

The pumpkin soup proved to be the last positive note in what was otherwise a very dismal period of the journey. Determined to find another human before they starved to death, Henry and Levi left their baggage and horse at an abandoned camp and set out in search of some sign of civilization. Their pulses must have quickened when they heard a gun fired in the distance, but after an hour or two spent trying to catch up with the hunter they gave up the search. To make matters worse, the weather was turning colder, and a dense fog settled. Neither did the environmental landscape help. Henry complained, "Nothing can exceed the roughness and sterility of the country we have to-day traversed; the endless succession of steep declivities, and broken, rocky precipices surmounted, added to a languor consequent to our situation has rendered the day's march unusually fatiguing."[57] Thirsty, hungry, fatigued, and lost, Henry and Levi dined on acorns and managed little sleep while trying to stay warm.[58]

On the morning of November 30, 1818, Schoolcraft and Pettibone broke camp early in the morning and renewed their search for a settlement in the Ozark backcountry. Their elation must have been immense when they stumbled upon a horse path with fresh tracks. It appeared that the path was used to travel between two settlements, but they were unsure which direction might lead to the nearest cabins. After traveling to the northeast for a few miles, they changed their minds and headed back in the other direction. Before long, their day grew even brighter when they met a man on horseback. Henry exclaimed in his journal: "He was the first human being we had encountered for twenty days, and I do not know that I have ever received a greater pleasure at the sight of a man."[59] The stranger informed Henry and Levi that they had been following the North Fork of the White River and that they were within ten miles of the confluence with the White River. He agreed to lead them to a hunter's cabin that was about seven miles away on Bennetts Bayou.

The cabin belonged to a Mr. Wells who was known to be a skilled hunter.[60] His talent was on display around his cabin in the form of bear skins, deer hides, and other trophies hung on trees and poles around his property. The Wellses' dogs raised a cacophony of incessant barking to make sure that everyone within earshot knew that strangers were approaching. The one-room log cabin of the Wells family was newly constructed to replace an older cabin that the family had outgrown. Henry was not impressed with the décor.

> Its interior would disappoint any person who has never had an opportunity of witnessing the abode of a man beyond the pale of the civilized world. Nothing could be more remote from the ideas we have attached to domestic comfort, neatness, or conveniency, without allusion to cleanliness, order, and the concomitant train of household attributes, which make up the sum of human felicity in refined society.[61]

The interior walls were adorned with deer and buffalo horns, rifles and shot pouches, dried meats, and leather coats. Thus, remarked Henry, the one-room house served as the "wardrobe, smoke-house, and magazine" of the family.[62] The clothing of the Wells children caught Henry's attention. He recorded that the "boys were clothed in a particular kind of garment made of deer-skin, which served the purposes of shirt and jacket," and the "girls had buck-skin frocks, which it was evident, by the careless manner in which they were clothed, were intended to combine the utility both of linen and calico." Both the boys and the girls were "abundantly greasy and dirty."[63]

As Mrs. Wells prepared a meal of cornbread, butter, honey, and milk, Henry and Levi described the land they had crossed and the timber and game they had encountered. Intrigued by the information Henry and Levi shared, Mr. Wells decided to set off on a bear hunt the following day. In return, Mr. and Mrs. Wells answered Henry's questions about the nearest settlements, the quality of the soils in the region, the presence of minerals, and the types of vegetation to be found. In the course of their conversation, Henry and Levi explained the saga of their journey thus far. They told Wells they had been out for twenty-four days, had run short of shot, and had been without meat or bread for several days. Mr. Wells took hold of Pettibone's shotgun and said, "I reckon stranger you have not been used much to travelling in the woods."[64] After dinner, Henry and Levi attempted to make small talk with Mrs. Wells and the daughters of the house, but the women "could only talk of bears, hunting, and the like. The rude pursuits and the coarse enjoyments of the hunter state were all they knew."[65] A day that began with anxiety and hunger ended in comfort as Henry and Levi drifted to sleep on a skin in front of the fire in the Arkansas cabin of the Wells family.

Henry and Levi needed provisions to continue their journey. In addition to food and bullets, they needed new shoes for their sore feet. Henry explained, "Our shoes were literally cut to pieces by the stony region we had crossed, and we had purchased a deer skin for the purpose of making ourselves a pair of mockasons a piece."[66] They bought corn, wild honey, lead, and a deerskin from Mr. Wells at what Henry described as "very liberal, if not exorbitant prices."[67] Henry and Levi planned to spend the first day of December pounding their newly purchased corn into meal, stitching their deerskin into new moccasins, molding bullets from lead, and otherwise preparing their provisions and resting their bodies for the journey ahead. Mr. Wells and his sons had other ideas. They were eager to go hunting for the bears that Henry and Levi had told them about the previous night, and perhaps wished to be rid of the travelers. Mr. Wells told Henry and Levi that he could guide them back to the camp where they left their horse and other baggage—for a price. This was a difficult offer to refuse since Schoolcraft and Pettibone did not know exactly where their horse and baggage were located and probably dreaded the thought of wasting more time, energy, and provisions trekking aimlessly in search of the camp. The men compromised. Henry and Levi would have a few morning hours to pound their cornmeal using the Wells's wooden mortar and pestle and they would pay Mr. Wells to guide them to their camp. In return, Mr. Wells would escort Henry and Levi back to their horse and baggage before the end of the day and would shoot a deer for them.

Mr. Wells, the Wells boys, a neighbor, Schoolcraft, and Pettibone set off before noon, loaded with knapsacks, hunting gear, and "a troop of hungry dogs, who made the woods re-echo with their cries."[68] Lacking horses and still fighting fatigue and soreness, Henry and Levi could not keep pace with the hunters. The repeated stops to allow Henry and Levi to catch up must have irritated Mr. Wells and the others eager to get on with the thrill of the hunt. At their slow pace, they would not complete the twenty-mile journey before the end of the day. The men began to alternate riding on their horses and allowing Henry and Levi a turn to ride. Two of the men separated from the rest of the party in hopes of killing a deer for Henry and Levi but returned only with two turkeys. At ten o' clock that night, the party finally reached the camp, where the horse and baggage were found unharmed. A few of the hunters set out early the next morning in search of a deer for Henry and Levi but came back empty-handed. So far, only two turkeys had been killed by the Wells party, and, having eaten one for dinner, the other was roasted for breakfast. After dining on the last of the food, Wells and his sons jumped on their horses and bid the greenhorn travelers farewell.

Henry was outraged. He described the scene and recorded a lengthy diatribe in his journal that reveals much about his underlying disdain of hunters at this stage of the journey.

So abrupt a movement took us rather by surprise, and as they trotted off through an adjoining forest, we stood surveying the singular procession, and the singular beings of whom it was composed, and which, taken altogether, bore no comparison with any thing human or divine, savage or civilized, which we had ever before witnessed, but was rather characterised in partaking of whatever was disgusting, terrific, rude, and outré in all. It was, indeed, a novel and striking spectacle, such as we had never before experienced, and when they had passed out of sight we could not forbear an expression of joy at the departure of men, in whose presence we felt rather like prisoners than associates. From their generosity we had received nothing; they had neglected to fulfil one of the most essential engagements, and departed without even an apology for it; their manner and conversation were altogether rough and obscene, and their conduct such as to make us every moment feel that we were in their power. Nothing could more illy correspond with the ideas we had formed of our reception among white hunters, than the conduct we had experienced from these men. Their avarice, their insensibility to our wants, not to call them sufferings, and their flagrant violations of engagements, had served to sink them in our estimation to a very low standard; for, deprived of its generosity, its open frankness, and hospitality, there is nothing in the hunter-character left to admire.[69]

Westward through the Ozarks

After recovering from the shock of the hasty departure of the Wells party, Henry and Levi pondered their circumstances. Their lack of experience with wilderness travel was weighing heavily. They were back at the same spot they had left five days earlier. The only food they had to eat was cornmeal and honey. Such fare would hardly satiate their hunger or provide them with the sustenance they needed for long days of hiking. They had enough lead to make five bullets, but this was precious little ammunition for men who were not skilled hunters with guns not well-suited to hunting. If this were not enough to stress the weary men, they doubted the directions given to them by Mr. Wells. They were lost again. The day was spent making moccasins and contemplating what was needed to continue the tour.

Over the next few days, the men would experience another emotional roller-coaster ride of despair and delight. The morning after the departure of Mr. Wells, Henry "sallied into the adjoining woods with [his] gun, with a determination to kill something."[70] He spent several hours and three of their five bullets chasing game and came back to camp empty-handed. Levi took a turn hunting and spent the fourth bullet without luck. The men decided to wait until dark to try again. Henry cleaned his gun carefully and replaced the flint. The final ball was cut into thirty-two pieces to make shot. After nightfall, Henry and Levi carried a torch and their gun into a group of trees where a flock of turkeys had taken roost. While Henry held the torch, Levi took careful aim at a large bird sitting low and fired their last bit of lead. The turkey dropped from the tree. At last they would dine that evening on meat instead of cornmeal and honey.

The nights had turned cold and the day after their turkey feast they were confined to camp by constant rain. When they were able to resume the journey after two days in camp, they headed west as directed by Mr. Wells in search of a settlement on the sugarloaf prairie along the White River. As they had experienced earlier in the journey, traveling near a river was not pleasant. The hills and thickets were exhausting enough, but the rain had also turned the land swampy. Again, their journey could have come to a tragic end when their horse became mired while attempting to cross a boggy cane brake. Henry and Levi struggled to free their horse from the muck, but their "exertions only served to sink him deeper in the mire."[71] They managed to free their baggage from the horse's back, but after two hours of struggle they could not free the horse. Henry and Levi rested with their baggage on a spot of dry ground and thought about the situation. Without a horse, they could not carry much of their gear and their supplies. Without their supplies, the journey would be much more difficult, if not impossible. With mounting desperation, they returned to the horse to find him sunk to his neck in the black mud. Once again though, Henry and Levi—and their horse—managed to escape disaster. After another hour of toil, they succeeded in freeing the horse from the morass, cleaned the mud from his body, and repacked him.

Luck had been on their side through two serious trials. Would it hold for another familiar complication? Henry and Levi were lost again. They had traveled west for two days expecting to encounter the river and a settlement but had traveled twice the expected distance and had come across neither. Once again, they surveyed the scene and considered their options. Perhaps if they continued west just a bit farther they would find the river. Then again, maybe they had passed the settlement and should alter their course. Luck was on their side for a third time. After heading south for about a mile they stumbled upon a faint horse path and followed it to a better path that led to the river. On the opposite bank of the White River, they spotted a house.[72]

The McGarrah family welcomed the travelers into their home.[73] Henry was impressed by what he saw.

> [McGarrah] had a field of several acres under cultivation, where he raised corn, with several horses, cows, and hogs. The house was of logs, built after the manner of the new settlers in the interior of Ohio, Indiana, and Illinois. He was provided with a hand-mill for grinding corn, a smoke-house filled with bear and other meats, and the interior of the house, though very far from being either neat or comfortable, bore some evidence that the occupant had once resided in civilized society. I noticed a couple of odd volumes of books upon a shelf. Some part of the wearing-apparel of himself and family was of foreign manufacture. Upon the whole, he appeared to live in great ease and independence, surrounded by a numerous family of sons and daughters, all grown up; received us with cordiality, gave us plenty to eat, and bid us welcome as long as we pleased to stay.[74]

Henry and Levi were treated to a wealth of geographical information. McGarrah explained that the White River was navigable by keelboat from their location to the Mississippi River and that several settlements had sprung up along the course. Traders used large canoes to bring supplies to their area and to a settlement upstream. As they had heard before from Mr. and Mrs. Roberts, their intended journey into Osage territory was considered dangerous. McGarrah told Henry and Levi that the Osages would rob or take into captivity white hunters or travelers who crossed their path. The Osages had robbed the McGarrah house twice, and took horses, clothes, and other household items. A neighbor was robbed of eight beaver traps and was taken prisoner. Schoolcraft noted in his journal that "numerous other instances were related, all tending to prove that the Osage Indians felt hostile to the white settlements along that river, and that they were habitual robbers and plunderers, not only of them, but of every person who happened to fall defenseless into their hands."[75] Henry was surprised to learn that there was little recourse for the white settlers of Arkansas. He was under the impression that "the United States have enjoyed an uninterrupted peace with this tribe of Indians ever since the acquisition of Louisiana."[76] Henry suggested to Mr. McGarrah that perhaps the U.S. government was unaware of the situation and that the Indian agent in St. Louis should be notified. McGarrah told him that the long trip to St. Louis would be more expensive than what was lost. Henry was also surprised to learn of continuing hostilities between the Cherokees and the Osages since he had "witnessed the conclusion of a treaty of peace between these two tribes, made at St. Louis under the auspices of Governor Clark."[77] Mr. McGarrah informed Henry that such treaties had little value and explained that as soon as "the Cherokees returned from the council which concluded that treaty, they pursued a party of Osages near the banks of White River, and stole, unperceived, twenty horses, and carried them safely off."[78]

Mr. McGarrah proved to be generous not only with geographical information, but also with supplies. The following morning, as Henry and Levi prepared for their journey upstream toward the Sugar Loaf Prairie settlement, McGarrah took Henry to his smokehouse, gave him a knife, and told him to go in and cut what he wanted. Henry entered the smokehouse and found it "well filled with dried buffaloe's beef, and bear's meat, both smoked and fresh."[79] McGarrah also refused payment for the food and lodging he provided the men the evening prior and agreed that Henry and Levi could leave their horse and some of their baggage at the McGarrah house until they returned. Although there is no note in Schoolcraft's journal, one can imagine that his experience with the McGarrah family began to complicate his views toward hunters. The experience of the McGarrah place was as sweet as the experience with Mr. Wells was sour.[80]

The horse path to the west from the McGarrah house along the White River through present-day Marion County, Arkansas, was faint, but they were able to follow it for at least sixteen miles. Following a night of camping, Henry and Levi lost track of the path the next day and were forced to follow the course of the river through cane and briar. While trudging through a thicket of cane, the men encountered a small clearing and a family who had recently migrated from downriver. Henry remarked that "nothing could present a more striking picture of the hardships encountered by the backwoods settler, than this poor, friendless, and forlorn family."[81] The distressing situation of the woman and her small children left to wait while her husband searched for game led Henry and Levi to put their own discomforts into perspective. Early that afternoon, Henry and Levi came to the Sugar Loaf Prairie settlement. Henry noted that the settlement, consisting of four families within eight miles of one another, was so new that "a horse-path has not yet been worn from one cabin to another."[82] As they approached one of the houses, their arrival was once again broadcast by the barking and yelping of Mr. Coker's dogs.[83] They made their way past the skins drying on poles and trees around the house and were greeted by Mr. Coker with "frankness and blunt hospitality" as he attempted to pacify his dogs.[84]

Schoolcraft took time at this stage in the journey to record a lengthy set of observations about the culture of the white settlers in the Ozarks. This was the fourth family with whom he had interacted, but this settlement was the most remote location he had yet visited. Henry recorded that the diet of the Ozark settlers in Arkansas consisted primarily of bear meat, other wild meats, and corn. They did not grow surplus corn for trading but grew enough to make bread and provide feed for their horses. And corn was the only crop they appeared to grow. Henry remarked that "no cabbages, beets, onions, potatoes, turnips, or other garden vegetables are raised. Gardens are unknown."[85] Houses were temporary structures since the people moved regularly to find more plentiful game. Henry suggested that this lack of permanence in residence also reflected a rootlessness and lack of attachment to places and objects. While the settlers were not engaged in agricultural trade, Henry explained that there existed a system of trade centered on furs and skins in exchange for household necessities.

> Vast quantities of beaver, otter, raccoon, deer, and bear skins, are annually caught. These skins are carefully collected and preserved during the summer and fall, and taken down the river in canoes to the mouth of the Great North Fork of White River, or to the mouth of Black River, where traders regularly come up with large boats to receive them. They also take down some wild honey, bear's bacon, and buffaloe-beef, and receive in return, salt, iron-pots, axes, blankets, knives, rifles, and other articles of first importance in their mode of life.[86]

The primary threat to the white settlers was a familiar story to Henry and Levi by this point in their journey. The Osages were feared and to be avoided. Mr. Coker cautioned Henry and Levi about entering the Osage territory at this time of year and suggested that they arm themselves with rifles and as little baggage as possible. In sum, Henry judged the Ozark settlers to be "hardy, brave, independent people" and though "rude in appearance" were "frank and generous."[87] Moreover, Henry thought this mode of life prepared the men well for frontier warfare since they were "ready trained, . . . require no discipline, [are] inured to danger, and perfect in the use of the rifle" and "their system of life is . . . one continued scene of camp-service."[88] Despite these positive traits, Henry found fault with the culture of the settlers and noted with contempt that "in manners, morals, customs, dress, contempt of labor and hospitality, the state of society is not essentially different from that which exists among the savages. Schools, religion, and learning, are alike unknown."[89] Mr. Coker would not accept payment for the accommodations provided to Henry and Levi, but he did attempt to sell them an old rifle for "double the worth of it."[90] In addition to a rifle, Henry and Levi had been in search of someone willing to serve as a guide. Mr. Coker, Henry explained, "wished us to engage an idle hypochondriac, who hung about him, as a guide."[91] The men could not come to an agreement on a price for the rifle, and the idle man could not be convinced to go.

As they left the Sugar Loaf Prairie Settlement, Henry and Levi hoped to reach Beaver Creek and then to follow its course to its confluence with the White River where there was another small settlement. Once again, Henry and Levi departed with directions to their next destination, but without a guide who had traveled the path. And once again what appeared to be simple directions proved to be difficult for Henry and Levi to follow. The weather was beginning to "assume a wintery character," and Henry noted, "This is the first day we have been troubled with cold fingers."[92] On the second day out from Mr. Coker's house, they forded a river that they mistook for Beaver Creek and soaked themselves to their waists. After traveling a few more miles in the wrong direction, they realized their error, turned around, and forded the river again at a location that was three-hundred yards wide and about four to five feet deep. In the windy and cold weather, Henry and Levi were deeply chilled and uncertain of their exact location. They managed little sleep in their shivering state and set out the next morning amidst a thick frost. While attempting to locate Beaver Creek, they came across a cavern that Henry explored.

> All was dark within, but by throwing down stones, it appeared evident from the noise, that there was a large cavity, and thinking it might repay the risk and trouble of going down, I determined to descend; or, at least, to make the attempt. There was just room enough at the mouth to squeeze myself against the rocks, carefully feeling my way down, and as I descended, could see the light from above. At the distance of twenty feet, this orifice, which had increased gradually, though irregularly, in size, opened into a spacious chamber, terrific in appearance from its rugged walls, viewed by the feeble light transmitted from above. In three several directions, passages of nearly equal size diverged, as from a centre, descending gradually into the earth, and appearing like rents caused by some mighty convulsion. I followed down one of these as far as the least glimmering of light could be discerned, and groped along some distance further, but as this was rather a dangerous

business, and I had no light for exploring with any degree of satisfaction, I gave up the attempt, bringing out a fragment of the rock, which appeared, on inspection, to be similar in every respect to the rock on the surface, viz. secondary limestone.[93]

BEAVER CREEK, MISSOURI

The men continued to follow the winding course of the White River, and this ultimately led them to Beaver Creek. Henry described the creek as "a beautiful, clear stream of sixty yards wide, with an average depth of about two feet, and a handsome gravelly bottom."[94] Fortune shined on the men again as they located a horse path along the creek that led to a small settlement at the confluence of Beaver Creek and the White River that consisted of two families who lived about one-half mile apart. The Holts and the Fishers had been at this site for only four months and had not cleared land or finished their houses when Henry and Levi arrived.[95] Schoolcraft claimed, "We are now at the last hunter-settlement on the river, which is also, the most remote bound to which the white hunter has penetrated in a south-west direction from the Mississippi River toward the rocky mountains."[96]

Near the settlement was a large bottom land at the bend of the river that was heavily forested with a variety of hardwood trees including oak, ash, maple, walnut, mulberry, and sycamore. The opposite bank of the river was an impressive three-hundred-foot limestone bluff capped with cedar. Schoolcraft exclaimed that "the bold and imposing effect of this scene is much heightened by beholding two natural pyramids, or towers of rock, ascending with a surprising regularity from the highest wall of the bluff, to a height of fifty or sixty feet."[97] Henry and Levi talked with Mr. Holt and Mr. Fisher about serving as guides for their journey to the James River. The hunters declined and explained that their houses were not finished, they did not have enough corn for their families, and they were not keen to risk being robbed by the Osages. Henry realized that the most important impediment was money. After some discussion, Henry and Levi came to an agreement with Holt and Fisher. Mr. Holt would serve as their guide and in exchange would receive their horse, ten dollars, and all the furs or skins he could collect during the excursion. Before departing though, Holt and Fisher would go downstream to purchase corn for the women and children. During the hunter's absence, Henry and Levi would build a canoe, help with construction of the houses, and generally look after the women and children. It would be two weeks before Henry and Levi would continue their journey. The hunters departed with three horses and one of the sons on December 16, 1818, and did not return until December 23. This interlude provided Henry and Levi a firsthand experience of frontier life.[98]

A typical day at the Beaver Creek Settlement consisted of rising at or before dawn and building "a large cabin-fire of logs eight feet long." Next, they would "pound the corn which is to serve the family during the day . . . with a wooden mortar with a pestle attached to a spring pole" and work at tasks such as "patching mockasons, &c." After breakfast, Henry and Levi would "sally out into the forest with [their] axes, and chop and clear away cane and brush until dinner [at] about five o'clock."[99] Although the daily work whetted their appetites, their meals were repetitive and monotonous plates of boiled corn and bear's bacon. They ended the day by "building a large night fire and packing up, from the adjoining forest, wood enough to replenish it during the night, and succeeding day." Henry noted that they enjoyed a "sweet repose" at the end of each day "on a bear-skin before the fire."[100]

The warmth of the evening fire must have been a pleasant relief for Henry and Levi, who endured icy temperatures carrying out their daily work. Pounding corn in the morning required pouring water on it, but one frigid morning the water froze in the bowl before it could be carried to the mortar thirty yards away. The late December weather caused the creek to freeze. Henry and Levi took advantage of the frozen sheet covering the creek to cross it and investigate the limestone bluff. The water was remarkably pure, Henry noted, and "the ice, too, is so clear, that, in walking across, it appeared as if we were walking on a pane of glass, reflecting every inequality of bottom, pebble, &c. with as much accuracy in this depth, as if covered by a pane of glass in a merchant's case."[101]

Schoolcraft recorded several observations on the cultural landscape that he witnessed among the Holts and the Fishers in the Ozarks. He was frequently acerbic in his critiques. Regarding the lack of religion and observance of the Sabbath, he complained,

> To him all days are equally unhallowed, and the first and the last day of the week find him alike sunk in unconcerned sloth, and stupid ignorance. He neither thinks for himself, nor reads the thoughts of others, and if he ever acknowledges his dependence upon the Supreme Being, it must be in that silent awe produced by the furious tempest, when the earth trembles with concussive thunders, and lightning shatters the oaks around his cottage, that cottage which certainly never echoed the voice of human prayer.[102]

Henry found time to talk about religion with one of the men. Either Holt or Fisher told Henry that he had occasionally attended a Methodist meeting when he lived on the Mississippi River, but that he found there to be "as many rogues there as anywhere else" and decided not to attend again. He also remarked that it was a "useless expense to be paying preachers for telling us a string of falsehoods."[103] While organized religion was missing, Henry recorded with disapproval that "superstition" was widespread. Mr. Fisher told them that he was forced to sell a rifle of his because he was unable to kill anything with it after a neighbor had cast a spell on it. Mrs. Holt wore a brass ring that she believed to be "an infallible remedy for the cramp."[104] Henry concluded with contempt that "witchcraft, and a belief in the sovereign virtue of certain metals . . . which reflect disgrace upon our species, have still their advocates here."[105]

Along with a lack of religion, there were also no schools and "no species of learning [was] cultivated." Henry lamented that the "children are wholly ignorant of the knowledge of books and have not learned even the rudiments of their own tongue."[106] Instead of books, the boys were schooled in the survival skills needed for life in the backcountry. Henry explained that boys are encouraged to "begin to assert their independence as soon as they can walk."

> By the time they reach the age of fourteen, [boys] have completely learned the use of the rifle, the arts of trapping beaver and otter, killing the bear, deer, and buffalo, and dressing skins and making mockasons and leather clothes. They are then accomplished in all customary things, and are, therefore, capable of supporting themselves and a family, and accordingly enter into marriage very early in life.[107]

Girls, on the other hand, were "brought up with little care" and were trained in "servile employments." Henry did not paint a very flattering portrait of the Ozark country girls that he encountered.

> They have ruddy complexions, but, in other respects, are rather gross, as they live chiefly on animal food. Being deprived of all the advantages of dress, possessed by our fair country-women in the east, they are by no means calculated to inspire admiration, but on the contrary disgust; their whole wardrobe, until the age of twelve, consisting of one greasy buckskin frock, which is renewed whenever worn out.[108]

Life did not improve much for the girls as they became women. Infant mortality was painfully high. Four of Mrs. Holt's children had died before the age of two. Henry speculated that women had few surviving children due to the lack of medical aid and the fact that pregnant women were "being frequently exposed to the inclemency of the weather, always to unusual hardships and fatigues, doing in many instances the man's work, living in camps on the wet ground without shoes, &c."[109] In sum, Henry did not see a bright future for the white settlers of the Ozarks. He concluded, "Thus situated, without moral restraint, brought up in the uncontrolled indulgence of every passion, and without a regard of religion, the state of society among the rising generation in this region is truly deplorable."[110]

Mr. Holt and Mr. Fisher returned on December 23, 1818, under a clear, blue sky and milder temperatures. The men spent Christmas Eve "hewing out a table, daubing and chinking the house. &c."[111] On Christmas, Henry and Levi convinced Holt and Fisher "to kill some turkeys, as [they] wished one for a Christmas dinner," and "prevailed on Mrs. H. to undertake a turkey-pie with Indian meal crust," which they "partook of under a shady tree on the banks of the river, the weather being warm and pleasant."[112]

JAMES RIVER, MISSOURI

On December 28, 1818, Henry and Levi departed with Mr. Holt and Mr. Fisher to conclude the final leg of their outbound journey. Henry felt optimistic that guides would prevent them from getting lost or needing to worry about food during this portion of the excursion. For the next four days, the men hiked to the northwest toward their destination on the James River just east of current-day Springfield, Missouri. Their path took them through the territory of the Osages where they encountered three deserted camps. Henry noted that the camps were large and well-ordered, and was fascinated by what he found: "Both the method of building camps, and the order of encampment observed by this singular nation of savages, are different from any thing of the kind I have noticed among the various tribes of aboriginal Americans, through whose territories I have had occasion to travel."[113] Schoolcraft was intrigued not only by the contrast between the Osages and other Indian groups he had observed, but also by the contrast between the cultural ecology of the Osages and that of the white hunters. He explained that the conflict between the two groups could be understood in part by the different ways of interacting with and shaping the environmental landscape.

> The white hunter, on encamping in his journeys, cuts down green-trees, and builds a large fire of long logs, sitting at some distance from it. The

> Indian hunts up a few dry limbs, cracks them into little pieces a foot in length, builds a small fire, and sits close by it. He gets as much warmth as the white hunter, without half the labour, and does not burn more than a fiftieth part of the wood. The Indian considers the forest his own, and is careful in using and preserving every thing which it affords. He never kills more meat than he has occasion for. The white hunter destroys all before him, and cannot resist the opportunity of killing game, although he neither wants the meat, nor can carry the skins.[114]

The winter weather slowed their journey, and they were occasionally forced to stop and build a fire to warm themselves. Henry and Levi also took time, to the likely annoyance of Holt and Fisher, to explore the dimensions, water, and deposits of a cave they stumbled upon. Henry remarked that "the first appearance of this stupendous cavern struck us with astonishment, succeeded by a curiosity to explore its hidden recesses. . . . We spent an hour in it, the hunters being satisfied after gazing a few minutes, and anxious to continue the journey."[115] On January 1, 1819, the party finally reached the James River and constructed a camp near the shore. The James River was a "large, clear, and beautiful stream" surrounded by a landscape of "extensive bodies of the choicest land, covered by a large growth of forest-trees and cane, interspersed with prairies."[116] The men dined on prairie hen and goose that evening. A snowstorm kept the party confined to the camp one afternoon, but for most of three days Henry and Levi examined lead mines, collected ore samples, explored the adjacent country, and built a small furnace to smelt lead for bullets.[117]

Henry was very impressed by the environmental landscape he witnessed.

> It is an assemblage of beautiful groves, and level prairies, of river alluvion, and high-land precipice, diversified by the devious course of the river, and the distant promontory, forming a scene so novel, yet so harmonious, as to strike the beholder with admiration; and the effect must be greatly heightened, when viewed under the influence of a mild clear atmosphere, and an invigorating sun.[118]

The prairies to the west were, Henry noted, "the most extensive, rich, and beautiful, of any which I have ever seen west of the Mississippi river," and were "covered by a coarse wild grass, which attains so great a height that it completely hides a man on horseback."[119] The river was bordered for a mile or two in each direction by "a vigorous growth of forest-trees, some of which attain an almost incredible size."[120] The "rich black alluvial soil" seemed well-suited for corn, flax, and hemp, while the highlands that sloped from the river appeared to have soil appropriate for wheat, rye, oats, and potatoes.[121] In addition to the advantages of soil, timber, and lead, there was plentiful deer and buffalo, as well as bears, to provide food and skins. Schoolcraft predicted that a profitable fur trade could be established too. Commercial mining, agriculture, fur trading, and other endeavors could be supported by river transportation to the Mississippi River via the James and White Rivers. Additionally, the area was situated well to serve as a post for Indian trade with the Osages, Cherokees, Pawnees, Delawares, and Shawnees in the region. In short, this was a perfect location, in Schoolcraft's view, for the extension of white settlement and commerce.

> Taking these circumstances into view, with the fertility and extent of soil, its advantages for water-carriage, and other objects, among which its mines deserve to be noticed, it offers great attractions to enterprising emigrants, and particularly to such as may consider great prospective advantages an equivalent for the dangers and privations of a frontier settlement.[122]

In his four days on the James River, Henry grew so fond of the surroundings that he was wistful about departing. He recorded in his journal that the country had become "so familiar to [them] as to appear, in some measure, a home."[123]

Two to three inches of moist snow crunched under their feet as they began the trip back to the Beaver Creek settlement on January 5, 1819. Henry remarked that they were surprised by the "innumerable tracks of the deer, wolf, elk, bear, and turkey, [in] the snow . . . affording a perfect map of their movements."[124] The highlight of this leg of the journey though was the discovery of an oak "bee-tree" containing a hollow limb with several gallons of wild honey. Henry learned that it was customary among the white hunters, and perhaps also among the Indians, to gather around the tree where honey was discovered and binge on the treat. Henry and Levi chopped the limb down, and the men indulged in the frontier ritual.

> Each stood with a long comb of honey, elevated with both hands, in front of the mouth, and at every bite left the semi-circular dented impression of a capacious jaw, while the exterior muscles of the throat and face were swelled by their incessant exertions to force down the unmasticated lumps of honey. . . . When this scene of gluttony was ended, the dog also received

> his share, as the joint co-partner and sharer of the fatigues, dangers, and enjoyments of the chase.[125]

The remainder of the honey that they were unable to eat was tied up in a wet deer skin and carried with them.

In addition to their initiation into the custom of devouring wild honey, Henry and Levi learned about the strategies used by the hunters to kill their prey. Mr. Holt explained that deer have a "fatal curiosity" that cause them to stop and turn around to look at the hunter chasing them. The hunter simply startled the deer and chased it until it turned around to look at him. At this moment, the hunter fired. Bear hunting required a different strategy. Hunters tracked bears to their dens using dogs to follow their scent or tracks in the snow to follow their paths. Bears in large caves would be shot easily. When the bear was hidden, the dogs were sent in to "provoke him to battle" and "while engaged with the dogs, the hunter walks up deliberately to within a few feet, and pierces him through the heart."[126] If the shot hit the bear in the shoulder, thigh, flank, or other part of the body, the bear became further enraged and multiple shots were needed before the bear was killed. The beaver, by contrast, "has wisdom enough to cut down trees and form dams, and elude the vigilance of its enemies, both man and beast, in an hundred ways, yet falls a sacrifice to its passion for high sweet-scented herbs and spicy barks."[127] The secret recipe for baiting beaver traps involved some combination of musk taken from the beaver stomach, sassafras, and other barks and herbs. The white hunters shared a sense of pride in the knowledge and skills associated with their craft. Despite his disgust with many aspects of the white Ozark hunter culture, Henry seemed to appreciate the allure of this way of life.

> When seated around his cabin-fire, the old hunter excites the wonder of his credulous children, gathered into a group, to listen to the recital of his youthful deeds, and thus creates in their breasts a desire to follow the same pursuits, and to excel in those hunting exploits which command the universal applause of their companions, and crown with fancied glory the life of the transalleganian hunter, whether red or white.[128]

Two animals were particularly important in the culture and lore of the hunter. One was the faithful dog. Dogs were guards, companions, and instrumental in the success of the hunt. Dogs who were killed in the line of duty were honored and mourned. A good hunting dog became a story for the generations.

> [A good dog's] achievements in the chase, his deep-mouthed cry, his agility and fleetness, his daring attack, and desperate gnash, and his dexterity in avoiding the fatal paw of his antagonist, these long continue to be the theme of admiration.[129]

The other significant animal was the horse. Henry recorded that although the horse with them was "a most sorry jade," Mr. Holt "lavished great encomiums on the sagacity and faithfulness of his horse, whose pedigree and biography we were now entertained with."[130] The horse did perform well at one task when called upon. The trail had become obscured by several inches of snow and a fog had settled. Despite the skills of Mr. Holt as a guide, the men had become lost on the final leg of the journey back to the Beaver Creek settlement. Holt told Henry and Levi that he had let the horse take his own path in similar situations in the past, and that the horse had guided him back to his house or to a familiar campsite. Henry described the outcome of the "very novel experiment."

> Throwing the reins loose upon its neck, the animal took its own course, sometimes climbing up hills, then descending into valleys, or crossing over streams, and at last, to the infinite satisfaction of all, and to the surprise of myself and co-travellers, led us to the top of a commanding precipice which overlooked the valley of White River, with its heavy-wooded forest, the towering bluffs on its southwestern verge, with the river winding along at their base, and the hunters' cottages, indicated by the curling smoke among the trees, in plain perspective. Joy sparkled in every eye.[131]

THE WHITE RIVER OF ARKANSAS

Henry and Levi had planned for the entire excursion to the James River and back to Potosi to be completed in less than sixty days, yet they had already been gone that long and had hardly crossed the halfway point of their journey. Henry noted morbidly, "Our friends would be ready to conclude we had fallen a sacrifice to the dangers of a tour, which few had approbated as advisable in the outset, and all united in considering as very hazardous."[132] They decided to descend the White River to Poke Bayou, Arkansas, and then to take a different overland path back to Potosi, Missouri. This route would allow them to see a different part of the country and would expedite their return and avoid the wilderness that had almost cost them their lives in the first month of the tour.

A day was spent readying provisions. Henry and Levi purchased a canoe from Holt and Fisher and loaded it with smoked bear's meat, dried venison, cornbread, salt, and other necessities such as lead and bullets. Early on the morning of January 9, 1819, the Holt and Fisher families followed Henry and Levi to the riverbank to wish them well and to repeat directions and precautions. The nine-day journey on the White River from the Beaver Creek settlement to Poke Bayou was the most pleasant of the entire tour. Henry remarked, "We . . . found ourselves, with a little exertion of paddles, flowing at the rate of from three to four miles per hour down one of the most beautiful and enchanting rivers which discharge their waters into the Mississippi."[133] Henry heaped praise upon the environmental landscape of the White River.

> It unites a current which possesses the purity of crystal, with a smooth and gentle flow, and the most imposing, diversified, and delightful scenery. Its shores are composed of smooth spherical and angular pieces of opaque, red, and white gravel, consisting of water-worn fragments of carbonate of lime, hornstone, quartz, and jasper. Every pebble, rock, fish, or floating body, either animate or inanimate, which occupies the bottom of the stream, is seen while passing over it with the most perfect accuracy; and our canoe often seemed as if suspended in air, such is the remarkable transparency of the water.[134]

Schoolcraft and Pettibone were welcomed along the river at the cabins of hunters who were both new and old acquaintances. At the end of their first day on the river, they stayed at the cabin of Mr. Yocum and were treated to a roasted beaver tail feast.[135] Henry explained that beaver tail was "one of the greatest dainties known to the Missouri hunter," and was "cooked by roasting before the fire, when the skin peels off, and it is eaten simply with salt." He described the taste as "mellow" and "luscious" and "something intermediate between [marrow] and a boiled perch." Unfortunately, there was also "a slight disagreeable smell of oil." Henry imaged that if the oily smell could be removed or covered "by some culinary process," that beaver tail "would undoubtedly be received on the table of the epicure with great éclat."[136] The following day, Henry and Levi reunited with Mr. Coker, who was pleased by the success of their journey to the James River. Another day on the White River brought them to Mr. McGarrah's cabin. McGarrah was happy to see them and congratulated them on completing the dangerous journey "with so much hazard from Indian hostility," but he thought that Holt and Fisher had taken "unmanly advantage" of Henry and Levi by making them spend "two weeks' probation . . . employed upon their habitations, and in chopping wood, &c."[137]

At the confluence of Big Creek and the White River in present-day Marion County, Henry and Levi encountered a "petty trader" in a large canoe who was carrying the "remains of a barrel of whiskey, and a few other articles intended to be bartered off for skins among the hunters."[138] Henry was hopeful that the trader might share news of "how the civilized world was progressing," but was disturbed to discover both the political obliviousness and apathy of the Ozark resident.

> [We] were disappointed to learn that he . . . knew nothing of those political occurrences in our own country, about which we felt solicitous to be informed. He evinced, indeed, a perfect indifference to those things, and hardly comprehended the import of such inquiries. He knew, forsooth, that he was living under the United States' government, and had some indefinite ideas about St. Louis, New Orleans, and Washington; but who filled the presidential chair, what Congress were deliberating upon, whether the people of Missouri had been admitted to form a state, constitution, and government, and other analogous matters, these were subjects which, to use his own phraseology, 'he had never troubled his head about.' Such a total ignorance of the affairs of his own country, and indifference to passing events . . . surprised us.[139]

The river had posed no problems for them during this part of the journey, but Henry and Levi faced dangerous rapids after departing the McGarrah house. There was a fast-moving "fall of fifteen or twenty feet" that was full of rocks and "a hundred channels" where the risk was high of "being dashed upon the rocks, or sunk beneath the waves." Their thirty-foot canoe was "drawn rapidly into the suction of the falls" and the "conflicting eddies drove [them] against a rock" upon which they were "instantly thrown broadside upon the rugged peaks" and into the cold January water.[140] Fortunately, their canoe did not fill with water and they were eventually able to right it. Twice more, Henry and Levi fought to navigate through rapids and managed to survive.

At the end of the harrowing day, they stopped at the cabin of Mr. Friend, who shared his geographical knowledge of the region with them.[141] Friend had explored the area extensively and was familiar with the James River lead mines, rock salt deposits between the White River and the Arkansas River, and marble to be found near the Grand Osage River. Before arriving at Mr. Friend's, Henry and Levi had spotted evidence of the "remains of ancient works, which appear to indicate that it has been the seat of metallurgical operations in former ages, and previous to the deposition of the alluvial soil upon its banks."[142] Henry collected specimens of a metallic alloy that appeared to be lead mixed with tin or silver, as well as fragments of pottery and arrowheads made of flint, hornstone, and jasper. Mr. Friend was aware of other ancient sites nearby and guided Henry and Levi on a tour the following day, during which Henry collected additional specimens of flint, bones, and arrowheads. They spent so much time exploring the sites with Mr. Friend that it was late in the day before they continued their trip down the river.

A few miles downstream from Mr. Friend, they encountered and dined with a fellow Yankee named Mr. Lee. After dinner, they continued a few miles further where they met and stayed with another Mr. Yocum.[143] The river downstream from Yocum's followed a winding path and included at least two difficult shoals formed by confluence of the White River with Crooked Creek and the Buffalo River, respectively. Mr. Yocum needed to carry bear's bacon and pork to a trader at the confluence of the White River with the Great North Fork. While the river path to the confluence was estimated to be thirty-five miles of challenging navigation, the overland horse-and-foot path was about fifteen miles. Henry and Levi were reluctant to test their navigation skills once more on a rough section of the river. The men agreed to lend their canoe to Yocum to carry his goods and their baggage downstream. Henry and Levi would take the overland route and meet Yocum at the mouth of the Great North Fork River. Their meeting spot, present-day Norfork, Arkansas, was a significant trading location at the time. Schoolcraft explained that navigation of the White River from the Mississippi River to Norfork was possible for the largest boats, including steamboats. Flour, salt, whiskey, coffee, and other small goods were brought upstream and exchanged for bear's bacon, pork, buffalo beef, beeswax, honey, skins, and furs. Henry noted, "From the rates of exchange noticed, I concluded a trading-voyage on this stream is attended with immense profit."[144]

Henry and Levi made the journey by foot to Mr. Matney's at the mouth of the Great North Fork in one day, but Yocum and their canoe had not arrived yet.[145] They decided to spend the next day exploring the nearby territory. Henry was impressed by what he witnessed.

A diligent search of the whole river could not in all probability have afforded a point uniting, in the circle of a few miles, so many objects calculated to

> please the eye, or to instruct the understanding. To a geographical situation, the most important in the whole course of the river, it united scenery the most bold and enchanting, and embracing so many objects calculated to awaken and invite attention, that the inquiring traveller could scarcely be disappointed, be his studies or pursuits what they might. Here were beautiful views for the landscape-painter, rocks for the geologist, minerals and fossils for the mineralogist, trees and plants for the botanist, soil for the agriculturalists, an advantageous situation for the man of business, and a gratifying view for the patriot, who contemplates with pleasure the increasing settlement, and prospective improvements of our country.[146]

Yocum and their canoe arrived late in the day, so Henry and Levi spent another night at Matney's. The night proved to be a firsthand lesson in Ozark partying. Yocum was accompanied by a dozen neighbors and friends who arrived in their canoes to trade. Henry described the scene that commenced.

> Whiskey soon began to circulate freely, and by the time they had unloaded their canoes, we began plainly to discover that a scene of riot and drinking was to follow. Of all this, we were destined to be unwilling witnesses; for as there was but one house, and that a very small one, necessity compelled us to pass the night together; but sleep was not obtained. Every mouth, hand, and foot, were in motion. Some drank, some sang, some danced, a considerable proportion attempted all three together, and a scene of undistinguishable bawling and riot ensued. An occasional quarrel gave variety to the scene, and now and then, one drunker than the rest, fell sprawling upon the floor, and for a while remained quiet. We alone remained listeners to this grand exhibition of human noises, beastly intoxication, and mental and physical nastiness. We did not lie down to sleep, for that was dangerous. Thus the night rolled heavily on, and as soon as light could be discerned in the morning. We joyfully embarked in our canoe, happy in having escaped bodily disfiguration, and leaving such as could yet stand, vociferating with all their might like some delirious man upon his dying bed who makes one desperate effort to arise, and then falls back in death.[147]

After another two days canoeing down the White River, Henry and Levi arrived at Poke Bayou on the afternoon of January 18.[148] Along the way, they passed Calico Rock, which Henry dubbed "one of those rare and fanciful works of nature which are seldom met with."[149] They also encountered a Mr. Jones who showed them a sample of what was believed to be tin and discussed with him a rumor of natural tin to be found in the area. Henry recognized that it was not tin and quipped that "this incident seems to show how readily persons who have devoted little attention to the subject are deceived in the appearances of a mineral, and how prone they are to ascribe to it a value which it does not possess."[150]

Poke Bayou, Arkansas to Potosi, Missouri

The night before their arrival at Poke Bayou was spent with Mrs. Lafferty.[151] The white settlers in the area had recently learned of an agreement with the Cherokees to abandon lands in Tennessee in exchange for land between the Arkansas and White Rivers. The white settlers who had settled on the south bank of the White River were expected to move to the north bank, which Henry noted was "considered a piece of injustice" by those in the area.[152]

Henry described the town of Poke Bayou as a "village of a dozen houses situated on the north bank of the river" and "advantageous as a commercial and agricultural depot."[153] The emerging town was certainly situated well. There were at least two ferries that crossed the White River nearby and the "Arkansaw Road" that had emerged as an overland path from southeast Missouri to Arkansas came through Poke Bayou. The change in the environmental landscape of Arkansas that emerged near present-day Batesville was noted by Henry in his journal.

> A gradual change in the face of the country . . . is observable. The bottom lands, as you descend, increase in width; the bluffs become more remote, and decrease in height, and finally disappear . . . where that extensive alluvial formation, which reaches to the banks of the Mississippi commences. From this fork, the scenery is unvaried. A rich level plain, covered with heavy forest-trees and canebrake, extends as far as the eye can reach, on both banks of the river, gradually depressed toward the Mississippi, where it is subject to semi-annual inundation.[154]

At Poke Bayou, Henry and Levi sold or traded their canoe, skins, and other items in exchange for knapsacks for the overland journey and were "entertained with hospitality" by Robert Bean.[155] Six weeks earlier, after being abandoned by Mr. Wells, Henry had seen little to admire in the character of the white hunters of the Ozarks. Before departing Poke Bayou, though, he recorded an encomium to the Arkansas and Missouri hunters who had made their journey a success.

> It is due to the hardy, frank, and independent hunters, through whose territories we have travelled, and with whom we have from time to time sojourned, to say, that we have been uniformly received at their cabins with a blunt welcome and experienced the most hospitable and generous treatment. This conduct, which we were not prepared to expect, is the more remarkable, in being wholly disinterested, for no remuneration in money for such entertainment (with a very few exceptions) was ever demanded; but, when presented, uniformly refused, on the principle of its not being customary to accept pay of the traveller, for any thing necessary to his sustenance. Nor can we quit the house at which we have here been made to feel our return to the land of civilization, after an absence of several months, without a grateful expression of our sense of the kind civilities and generous attention with which we have been treated.[156]

The two-week journey from Poke Bayou, Arkansas, to Potosi, Missouri, was slowed by a sprained ankle suffered by Henry on their first day on foot and a late January rainstorm that swelled the streams and muddied the road.[157] Levi Pettibone was anxious to return to St. Louis. After seventy-five days together, Levi left Henry to recover at a farmer's house in Arkansas and set out alone. Henry managed to return to traveling within a day, but his pace was slow and painful. His path led him through a region of northeast Arkansas and southeast Missouri that was becoming settled by white Americans. The rich soil formed from the deposits of the five rivers flowing from the northwest to the southeast into the Black River provided land that was ripe for farming. The junctions of the road with the rivers also provided locations for ferries and trading. Henry noted that within ninety miles he had crossed five rivers—Strawberry, Spring, Eleven Point, Fourche à Thomas, and Current—that were "entitled to the particular notice of the future geographers of Missouri and Arkansaw."[158]

Henry crossed from Arkansas into Missouri at Hick's Ferry, south of present-day Doniphan, Missouri, on January 25, 1819. He observed that the site of the town was "dry, airy, and eligible, and will command many advantages for mercantile purposes."[159] The valley of the Little Black River in present-day Ripley County, Missouri, was showing recent signs of white American settlement. Henry observed that "some improvements are . . . made, and the newness of the buildings, fences, and clearings, indicate here, as at every other inhabited part of the road for the last 100 miles, a recent and augmenting population."[160] He also noted that these recent migrants

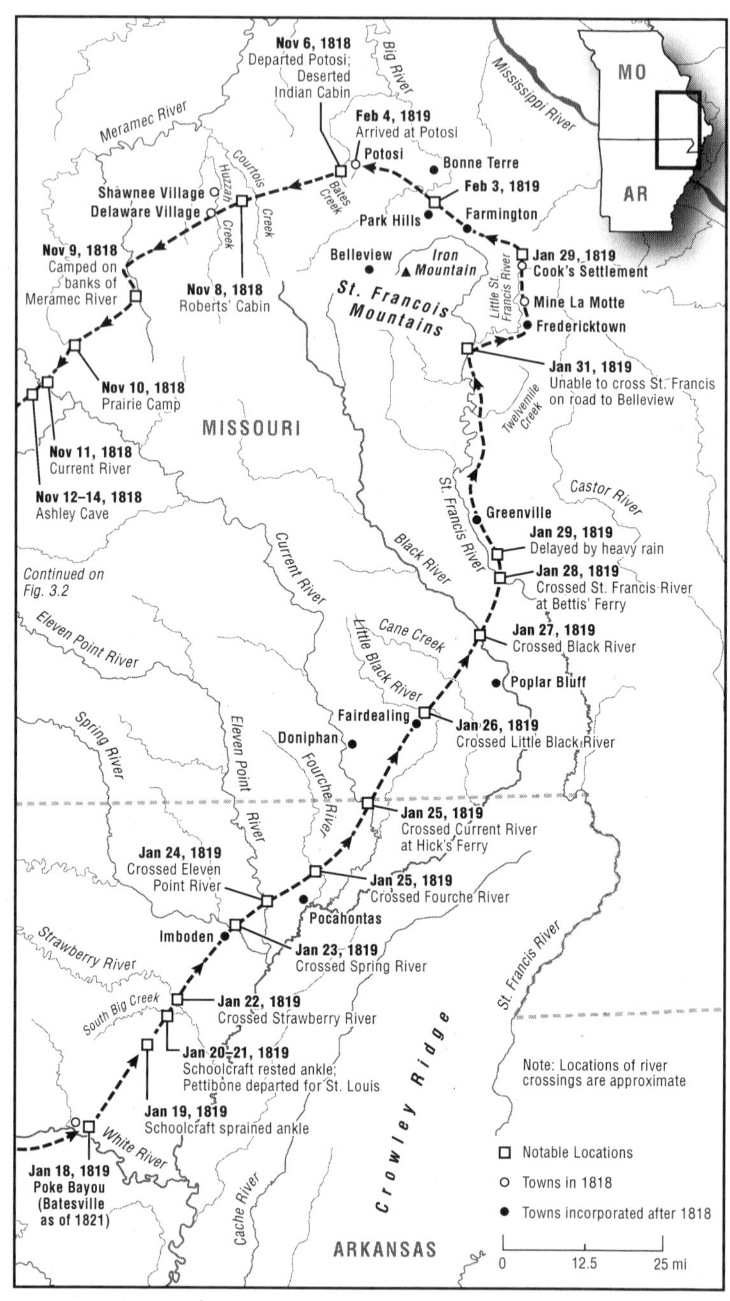

FIG. 3.3. Eastern Portion of Henry Rowe Schoolcraft's route, 1818–1819. Cartography by Erin Greb.

were mostly from Pennsylvania, the Carolinas, Kentucky, and Tennessee. Similarly, Henry found an emerging American agricultural industry along the Black River near present-day Hendrickson, Missouri.

> Agriculture forms the principal employment of the inhabitants along this stream, and its tributaries. A small proportion are mechanics, less merchants, and very few professional men. The soil and climate are considered favourable for different species of our domesticated graminea. Wheat and corn are the surest, and most advantageous crops. Rye, oats, flax, and tobacco, are also cultivated, the latter partially; and cotton is also grown, but not as a market crop, merely for family convenience, and domestic consumption. The raising of cattle has also engrossed considerable attention in this section of the country, and graziers have been well remunerated.[161]

At present-day Fredericktown, Missouri, Henry found

> a village of sixty houses, and the county seat of Madison, according to a recent act of the legislature. It has three stores and a post-office. This village was originally settled by the French, and has for many years been in a state of decline; but since its selection as the seat of justice for the new county, has received what is called a start, that is, has rapidly improved in appearance.[162]

Nearby, Henry passed through Mine la Motte and commented that the road traversed ongoing excavations.

> These mines have been worked with little interruption for a century, and are not yet exhausted; but on the contrary, yield as much as formerly. Large piles of the ore, crystallized in shining facets, were lying near the road as I passed, and a number of workmen engaged either in the excavations, or smelting.[163]

Henry knew he had returned to his version of civilization as he passed through the final settlement before returning to Potosi. He recorded the flourishing status of present-day Farmington, Missouri.

> Murphy's Settlement . . . is already a large and flourishing neighborhood of industrious farmers, and presents many well-cultivated fields, fenced in a neat and substantial manner, with young apple and peach-orchards, and framed dwelling-houses, clap-boarded in the eastern style. There is also

> a post-office in this settlement, where a mail is received once a-week, a school-house, and a physician resident. All these things indicate the wealth, the industry, and the intelligence of the inhabitants.[164]

Henry Schoolcraft finally arrived back at Potosi on February 4, 1819. He observed, "The first man I met . . . expressed surprise at seeing me, as he had heard from the hunters . . . that I had been killed by the Indians."[165]

Chapter Four

A View from the Banks of the Arkansas River

THOMAS NUTTALL, 1818–1820

THE FIRST DAY on the Mississippi River was coming to a close, and as the sun set it was time to find a good landing spot. The men spotted a sandbar with two other boats that had landed and decided to follow the lead of these fellow navigators. Good fortune had been with the travelers to this point in the day. They successfully dodged the ice that floated haphazardly in the December river and avoided the perils of the pervasive sunken trees that threatened to capsize their craft at any moment. Their luck came to an end, though, as they attempted to land on the sandbar for the night. The boat drifted beyond their desired landing spot and became mired on a shallow bar downstream. Thomas Nuttall plunged into the frigid water and tried in vain for nearly an hour to free their boat. Cold, wet, and exhausted, Nuttall and his companions sat down to contemplate their predicament. They must have been relieved and pleased when two boatmen appeared and offered to assist. Yet relief may have turned to wariness when they learned that assistance would come at a price. Nuttall paid the men five dollars and their boat was soon floating.

As dawn broke the next day, Nuttall discovered that the new landing spot the boatmen had guided them to in the dark left their boat grounded. The river had fallen overnight and all of their efforts could not get the boat loose. The boatmen who assisted the prior evening sailed passed them in the morning and ignored their calls for help. Nuttall and his companions began to unload the boat in hopes of lightening it enough to free it from the sand. As they worked, the owner of a neighboring boat arrived, expressed disgust at the treatment they received from the boatmen, and offered his assistance—for free. Another helper arrived who maintained that the boat was far too mired in the sand to be able to pry it loose until the river rose again. After some negotiation, the boat owner and his men agreed that for eight dollars they would engage in what they claimed would be the difficult and likely hopeless work of freeing the boat. Nuttall reluctantly paid the men and, despite their claims of the severity of the situation, the boat was pried loose and set afloat within a minute. The boatmen must have been amused at how easily they had conned the traveler out of his money and, to add further insult to injury, they brashly refused to help reload the boat as promised. Perhaps it was fitting that Wolf's Island was the name for this spot near the confluence of the Ohio and Mississippi Rivers.

Descent of the Mississippi River

Thomas Nuttall, the English botanist who had toured most of the eastern United States in the previous ten years, was two months into his planned expedition to the Rocky Mountains when he began his trip down the Mississippi River in mid-December 1818. Despite his experience as a traveler, this river posed many new challenges. More dangerous than the scoundrels of Wolf's Island were the numerous snags, sawyers, sandbars, and shifting channels that plagued anyone who dared to travel on the Mississippi River. Travelers had some help in navigating the channels and sandbars of the meandering river from guidebooks such as the *Pittsburgh Navigator*. When faced with an island in the middle of the river, the traveler had to determine which channel to follow. Selecting the wrong channel could mean becoming mired in sand, wrecked on floating tree trunks, slammed by a rapid current or eddy, or floating in a stagnant pool. Yet Nuttall found that the guidebook was frequently out-of-date with the realities of the powerful and volatile river. Near present-day Osceola, Arkansas, Nuttall noted, "We . . . could not ascertain our situation any longer by the vague trifling of the *Navigator*."[1] Nuttall explained one such incident that illustrated how the *Navigator* could prove to be out-of-date and the best plans for steering a boat could sometimes go awry.

> On approaching the . . . island . . . nearly in the middle of the river, we had at first determined to take the left-hand side, set down by the *Navigator*

as the channel, but finding ourselves to float very slowly, we rowed a little, and then submitted to the current. It was soon observable, that we drifted towards the right-hand channel, though much the narrowest, and my companion advised that we should keep the left, especially as it was the nearest, and as the wind accompanied by rain blew strongly up the river. However, on finding still that the current drew to the right, even against the wind, and having arrived at the commencement of the bar of the island, I determined, at all events, to keep to the right. At length, after considerable labour, we landed at a neighboring cabin, and were informed that the left channel had not in places more than 12 inches of water, being nearly dry, and almost destitute of current. Here, again, we made a fortunate escape.[2]

If the guidebooks proved less than helpful in providing advice on the best channels to follow, they were quite useless in predicting the presence of the ever-shifting trees and debris that floated and bobbed in the river. Trees that were submerged in the river and whose branches would bob up and down with the current in a sawing motion were known as sawyers. Other forms of dangerous snags included upturned tree roots that floated just beneath the surface, shards of dead and dying logs and branches that became entangled into rafts, and submerged living vegetation lurking under floodwaters or near the bank. Nuttall described a day full of such river hazards between present-day Osceola, Arkansas, and Fort Pillow State Park in Tennessee.

We observed the river contracted within a narrow space by a spreading sandbar (or island), and planted almost across with large and dangerous trunks, some with the tops, and others with the roots uppermost, in a perpendicular posture. The water broke upon them with a noise which I had heard distinctly for two miles, like the cascade of a mill-race, in consequence of the velocity of the current; with all our caution to avoid them, the boat grazed on one, which was almost entirely submerged, and we received a terrific jar. . . . I counted, in the space of a minute, about 100 huge trees fixed in all postures, nearly across the whole river, so as scarcely to leave room for passage. . . . With all our exertions in rowing off, we but narrowly escaped from being drawn into the impassable channel of a sand island which spread out into the river, presenting a portion of water resembling a sunken forest. The only course which we had left appeared no less a labyrinth of danger, so horribly filled with black and gigantic trunks of trees, along which the current foamed with terrific velocity.[3]

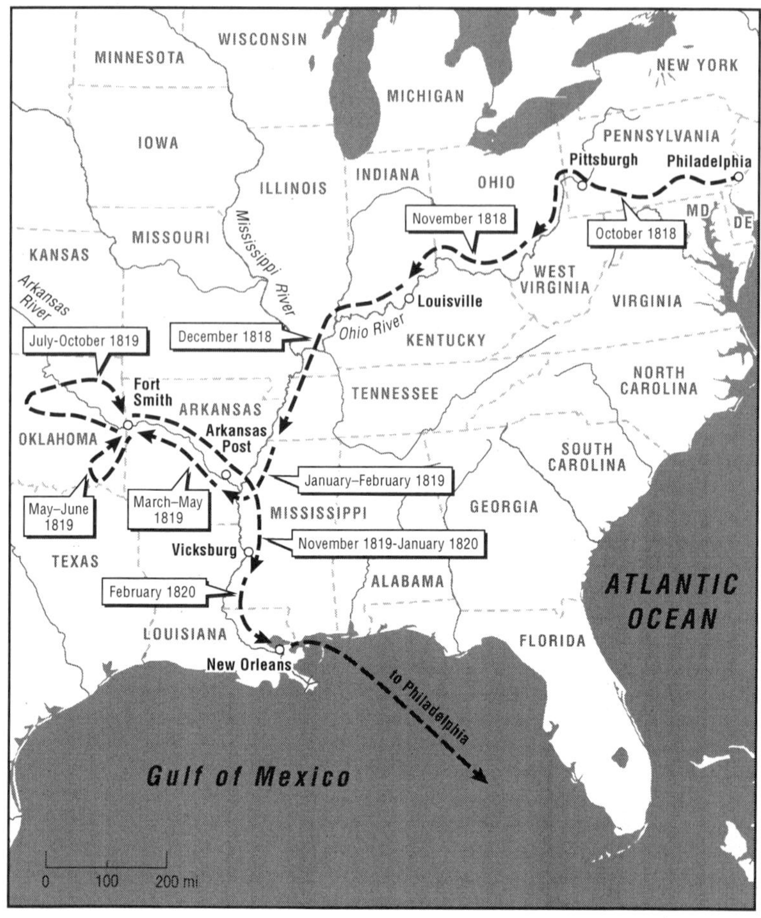

FIG. 4.1. Route of Thomas Nuttall, 1818–1820.
Cartography by Erin Greb.

Nuttall encountered very few settlements along the Mississippi River between the mouth of the Ohio River and the mouth of the White River. Near present-day Cairo, Illinois, Nuttall explained that "the whole country here, on both sides of the Mississippi and the Ohio, remains uninhabited in consequence of inundation."[4] Yet, the area was teeming with wildlife such as bears, deer, turkeys, and geese and consequently attracted hunting parties. Nuttall described the following experience with the Indians hunting in the area.

> We were visited by a couple of Delaware Indians, and shortly after by a hunting party of Shawnees, who reside some miles west of St. Louis. I invited one of them into our cabin, and prevailed upon him to take supper, with which he appeared to be well satisfied and grateful. On the following day, a number of the Shawnees came with our evening guest, and desired to purchase gun powder. They behaved with civility, and almost refused to taste of spirits, but their reluctance was at length overcome by some of our neighbors, and the night was passed at their camp with yells and riot.[5]

As they descended the Mississippi River, the environmental landscape was formidable and discouraged settlement. Nuttall noted shortly after his unfortunate experience near Wolf Island, Missouri, that "the river here appears truly magnificent, though generally bordered by the most gloomy solitudes, in which there are no visible traces of the abode of man. It is indeed a sublime contrast to the busy hum of a city, and not altogether destitute of interest."[6] One settlement that had begun to take root in the late eighteenth century was New Madrid, but the effects of the powerful earthquakes that devastated the region in 1811 and 1812 were still visible when Nuttall passed through in 1818.

> New Madrid is an insignificant French hamlet, containing little more than about 20 log houses and stores miserably supplied, the goods of which are retailed at exorbitant prices. . . . Still the neighboring land appears to be of a good quality, but people have been discouraged from settling in consequence of the earthquakes, which besides the memorable one of 1811, are very frequently experienced, two or three oscillations being sometimes felt in a day.[7]

The devastation was not confined to New Madrid. Nuttall noted that settlements downstream at Point Pleasant and Little Prairie, between New Madrid and present-day Caruthersville, Missouri, had also been abandoned or swept away and that tremors continued to be felt for miles.

Along the banks of current-day Mississippi County, Arkansas, Nuttall began to observe the presence of small encampments of white hunters and Indians. Following their nearly disastrous encounters with sawyers and conflicting channels in the river south of current-day Osceola, Nuttall recorded that they, "met with two or three families of hunters, with whom were living some individuals of the Shawnees and Delawares. They had lately caught an unusual abundance of beaver in the neighbourhood, and were anxious to barter it for whiskey, though scarcely possessed either of bread or vegetables."[8]

The presence of hunters also meant the presence of dogs. In one sad tale, Nuttall relates the story of a lost and starving dog they encountered along the banks of the river.

> A dog lost in the forest, and perishing with hunger, came up to the bank of the river, yelling most piteously; but would not enter our skiff, which was sent for it, and continued to follow us for some distance, but the danger of the shore, and the rapidity of the current, rendered our endeavors to assist the miserable animal perfectly useless, and, after some time, he fell back, stopped and yelled, till he reluctantly disappeared.[9]

The largest settlement along the river was Fort Pickering at present-day Memphis, Tennessee. Nuttall observed that the supply store engaged in unfair trade with the local Indians.

> The advance upon articles sold to the natives is very exorbitant: for example, a coarse Indian duffell blanket four dollars, whiskey, well watered, which is sold almost without restraint, in spite of the law, two dollars per gallon, and every thing else in the same proportion. Yet the Indians get no more than 25 cents for a ham of venison, a goose, or a large turkey.[10]

Although Nuttall found the Chickasaws in the area to be "in a state of intoxication," he remarked with approval that "they are generally well dressed, extravagantly ornamented, and, from the fairness of many of their complexions, and agreeable features, appear to have profited by their intercourse with the whites. Several of them possessed some knowledge of English, and a considerable number are making advances towards civilization."[11] South of Fort Pickering, Nuttall observed a land with great potential for settlement but with few settlers. Although he encountered a few inhabitants living in log cabins, he recorded that more substantial settlements had not arisen or had been abandoned after the earthquakes.

Near the mouth of the St. Francis River in the present-day Arkansas counties of Lee and Phillips, Nuttall envisioned a future landscape of American culture and commerce. A hike of a few miles from the river into the forest revealed land that Nuttall estimated was elevated above inundation levels and possessed quality soil. He observed that some of these lands had been previously occupied by Indians, and thus should prove to be fruitful locations for future settlers. There was also scrub grass that Nuttall expected would be readily available winter fodder for cattle. What appeared to be prime surroundings led Nuttall to exclaim, "How many ages may yet elapse before these luxuriant wilds of the Mississippi can enumerate a population equal to the Tartarian deserts! At present all is irksome silence and gloomy solitude, such as to inspire the mind with horror."[12]

The Mississippi River could be a violent and merciless neighbor though. The New Madrid earthquakes had proven to be a dramatic force that would reshape the cultural and environmental landscape for years to come. And the daily action of the river was even more insidious. Nuttall observed that the river meandered in wide elliptical arcs. Some of these curves reached six to eight miles in length as the river snaked in both directions. Nuttall explained how the current constantly exerted force on the surrounding banks.

> The principal current pressing against the centre of the bend, at the rate of about five miles per hour, gradually diminishes in force as it approaches the extremity of the curve. Having attained the point of promontory, the current proceeds with accumulating velocity to the opposite bank, leaving, consequently, to the eddy water, an extensive deposition in the form of a vast bed of sand, nearly destitute of vegetation, but flanked commonly by an island or peninsula of willows. These beds of sand, for the most part of the year under water, are what the boatmen term bars. The river, as it sweeps along the curve, according to its force and magnitude, produces excavations in the banks; which, consisting of friable materials, are perpetually washing away and leaving broken and perpendicular ledges, often lined with fallen trees, so as to be very dangerous to the approach of boats, which would be dashed to pieces by the velocity of the current. These slips in the banks are almost perpetual, and by the undermining of eddies often remarkable in their extent. To-day we witnessed two horrid sinkings of the bank, by which not less than an acre of land had fallen a day or two ago, with all the trees and cane upon them, down to the present level of the river, a depth of 30 or 40 feet perpendicular. These masses now formed projecting points, upon which the floating drift was arrested, and over which the current broke along with more than ordinary velocity. Just after passing one of these foaming drifts, we narrowly escaped being drawn into a corresponding eddy and vortex that rushed up the stream, with a fearful violence, and from which we should not have been easily extricated.[13]

Thus, those who dared to settle along the banks of the river could find their land suddenly sucked into the voracious Mississippi.

Arkansas Post

The journey on the Mississippi River was a meandering obstacle course of sandbars and snags. To add interest to the already challenging navigational feat, Nuttall and his companions experienced two days of heavy rain and fog that forced them to delay their descent of the river. On January 12, 1819, they finally arrived at a "house of entertainment" run by a Mr. M'Lane at the mouth of the White River.[14] South of this point, a peninsula is formed as the nearby Arkansas River flows almost parallel with the Mississippi River for several miles before the confluence of the two rivers. The journey around the peninsula today is about thirty-six miles, while the distance across the top of the peninsula from the mouth of the White River to the Arkansas River is about five miles. Rather than navigate further down the Mississippi River to the mouth of the Arkansas River in order to then ascend the Arkansas, someone at M'Lane's tavern advised Nuttall to cut through the inundated land that connected the mouth of the White River with the Arkansas River. Nuttall was eager to get into Arkansas. He had already become impatient with delays on the Ohio River and the Mississippi River and noted in his journal: "The idea of so soon arriving on the ground which I more immediately intended to explore, did not fail to inspire me with hope and satisfaction."[15] The shortcut appeared to be a great idea, but Nuttall needed the assistance of a boatman to help him navigate the bayou. Once they reached the Arkansas River, he would also need assistance going upstream for several miles to the settlement at Arkansas Post.

Over the next few days, Nuttall discovered that the man he had hired was "one of the most worthless and drunken scoundrels imaginable."[16] The original agreement between Nuttall and the boatman was five dollars plus another hand if needed, but within a few hours the boatman demanded ten dollars and the boat. The trek up the White River was slow and difficult. The boat had to be pushed and pulled upstream using oars and a cordelle, or towrope, but the hired boatman refused to do anything but steer while Nuttall and another man he hired performed the hard labor. They made about three miles the first day and decided to leave the boat and hike back to Mr. M'Lane's for the evening. Nuttall learned that the scoundrel he had hired planned to return to the boat that night to rob him. He thwarted the thief by hiring a young man who helped Nuttall repair the boat that evening and then waited with him, armed, to confront the rogue. The danger passed, though, as the would-be robber could not find a getaway boat, and thus abandoned his larcenous plan. The following day Nuttall and his new assistants completed the difficult ascent of the White River and traversed the bayou on a small current that guided them toward the Arkansas River. Nuttall estimated that the distance across the bayou was eight or nine miles. On January 16, 1819, Nuttall entered the Arkansas River. He would spend almost all of the next year near its banks.[17]

The Arkansas River was low, muddy, meandering, and gentle. All of these factors made for a difficult journey upstream. Nuttall and his hired hands managed to pull the boat only six and a half miles on their first day on the Arkansas. The second day was also filled with "exceedingly tiresome" labor with little distance covered.[18] Unfortunately, Nuttall discovered that his hired hands were "scarcely willing to wet their feet, although I had to pay them exorbitant wages."[19] Despite the gentle winter current, the river exerted transformative effects on the environmental landscape. Nuttall observed:

> As in the Mississippi, the current sets with the greatest force against the centre of the curves; the banks of which are nearly perpendicular, and subject to a perpetual state of dislocation. In such situations we frequently see brakes of cane; while on the opposite side, a naked beach of sand, thinly strewed with succulent and maritime plants, considerably wider than the river, appears to imitate the aridity of the desert, though contrasted at a little distance by skirting groves of willows and poplars.[20]

Also in common with the Mississippi, the volatile river discouraged settlement. Nuttall noted that there was potential for agriculture in the area on land that appeared to be elevated enough to be safe from inundation, but that this region had been mostly neglected by settlers. In a cutting assessment of the Arkansas delta, Nuttall declared that the region was "almost destitute of every thing which is agreeable to human nature." He continued:

> Nothing yet appears but one vast trackless wilderness of trees, a dead solemnity, where the human voice is never heard to echo, where not even ruins of the humblest kind recall its history to mind, or prove the past dominion of man. All is rude nature as it sprang into existence, still preserving its primeval type, its unreclaimed exuberance.[21]

After three days of hard labor dragging his boat up the muddy and winding Arkansas River, Nuttall arrived at Arkansas Post. Nuttall described the place as a dispersed settlement of thirty to forty houses on elevated prairie land. A cultured reception from several of the inhabitants and merchants in

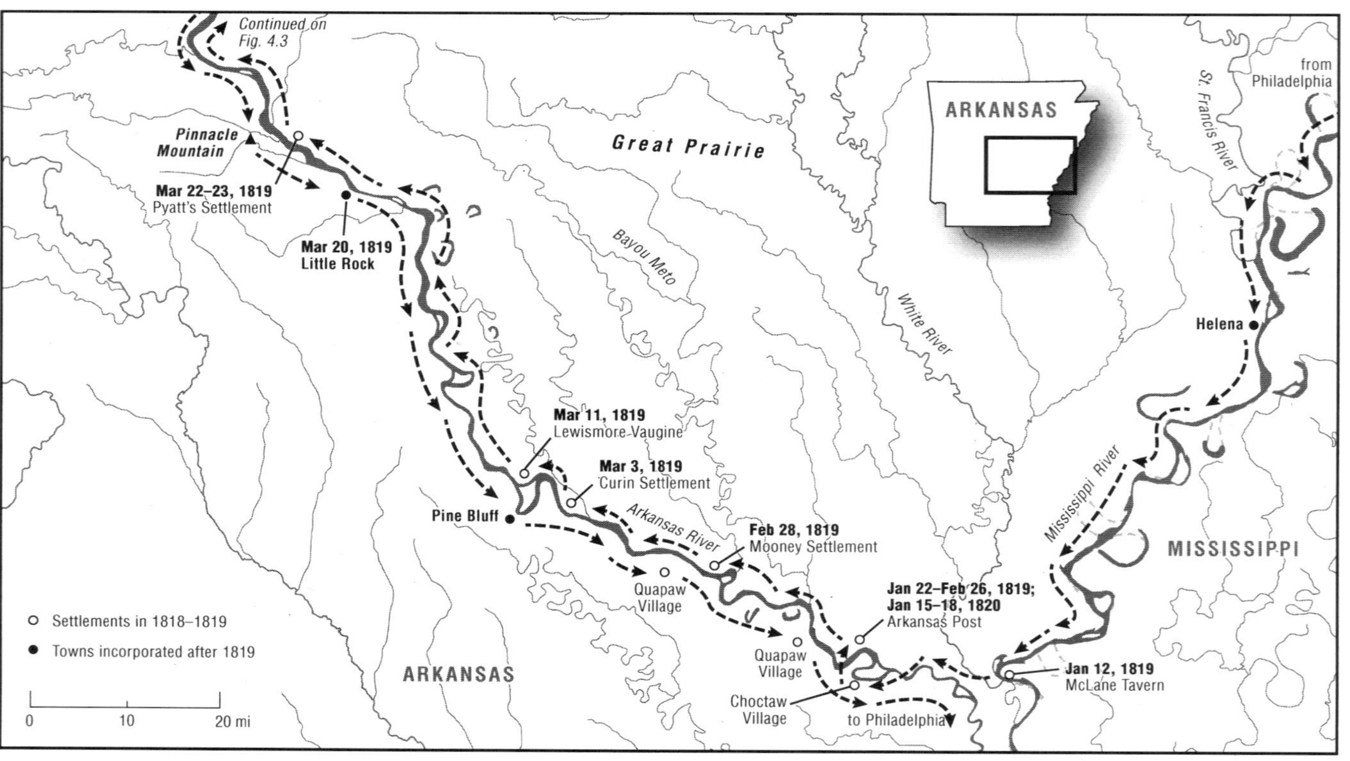

FIG. 4.2. Thomas Nuttall in Southeast Arkansas, 1819–1820. Cartography by Erin Greb.

the area, perhaps combined with the mild weather and his respite from the river, led Nuttall to record a series of positive observations about the idyllic surroundings. His botanical interest was piqued by the flowering plants that were "doubly interesting, as the first fruits of a harvest never before reaped by any botanist."[22] As Nuttall hiked and hunted in the area, he was greeted by blooming white and blue flowers and the songs of red birds and blue sparrows from the branches of pecan, oak, poplar, and walnut trees. The Great Prairie that stretches to the north and west "like a shorn desert, but well covered with grass and herbaceous plants" was also intriguing to the botanist.[23]

Beyond the beauty and fascination of the environmental landscape, Nuttall predicted a great commercial future for southeast Arkansas once the area was settled by a cultural group willing and able to transform it.

> Nature has here done so much, and man so little, that we are yet totally unable to appreciate the value and resources of the soil. . . . Under the influence of a climate mild as the south of Europe, and a soil equal to that of Kentucky, wealth will ere long flow, no doubt, to the banks of the Arkansa.[24]

Cotton and rice would certainly thrive here, but neither crop had thus far been cultivated at the scale that Nuttall thought possible. Similarly, the great prairie was "an invaluable body of land, and, where sufficiently drained . . . would produce most species of grain in abundance. As pasture it is truly inexhaustible, though in the hottest months of summer occasionally deprived of water."[25] Yet, much of the best land had been granted in large parcels by the Spanish and, despite the efforts of the U.S. Congress to limit the size of claims, the uncertainty over land titles persisted.

Nuttall was mostly complimentary of the people he encountered near Arkansas Post. One of the early Arkansans in this area with whom Nuttall spent time was Monsieur Bougie.[26] Nuttall credited Bougie with much of the success of the settlement and noted that, although Bougie "disguised himself in the garb of a Canadian boatman," he greeted Nuttall with "great politeness and respect" and "appeared to take a generous and active interest in my favor." Bougie, who was in his late sixties at this time, also impressed Nuttall with his "vigour and agility of youth."[27] In addition to Bougie, Nuttall approved of the other merchants in the area at the time, such as "Messrs. Braham and Drope, Mr. Lewis, and Monsieur Notrebe."[28] When introduced to Drope, Nuttall exclaimed that he "could not but for a while consider myself as once more introduced into the circle of civilization."[29] But Nuttall was not universally impressed by the settlers of French Canadian descent whom he labeled as "ignorant" and whose "habits . . . are generally opposed to improvement and regular industry."[30] He recorded that the "love of amusements, here, as in most of the French colonies, is carried to extravagance, particularly gambling, and dancing parties or balls" and that the "Canadian descendants, so long nurtured amidst savages, have become strangers to civilized comforts and regular industry." He predicted that these settlers would in time "give way to the introduction of more enterprising inhabitants."[31]

Evidence that the area had been settled for centuries was apparent in the multiple mounds holding native remains and pottery. Nuttall noted that there were only about two hundred "warriors" remaining among the "aborigines of this territory, now commonly called Arkansas or Quapaws and Osarks," and offered the following assessment of them:

> They bear an unexceptionally mild character, both amongst the French and Americans, having always abstained, as they say, from offering any injury to whites. . . . As hunters, they are industrious, but pay little attention to agriculture; and pleased by intercourse with the whites, they are not unwilling to engage as boatmen and hunters. . . . They say, that in consequence of their mildness and love of peace, they have been overlooked by the Americans; that [Americans] are ready enough to conciliate by presents those who are in danger of becoming their enemies, but neglect those who are their unchangeable friends.[32]

Nuttall did not intend to spend a full month exploring the surroundings of Arkansas Post. His plan was to find a boat to take the bulk of his supplies up river to the Cadron Settlement near present-day Conway, Arkansas, so that he could explore on foot the Great Prairie and the northeastern bank of the river. The land speculators and traders with whom Nuttall negotiated were not willing to take on his baggage—at least not for a price that Nuttall was willing to pay. According to Nuttall, the "illiterate" speculators were "incapable of appreciating the value of science" and would offer him passage only if he agreed to provide for himself and work as a boatman.[33] Eager to continue his botanical explorations in the interior of Arkansas territory, Nuttall ultimately abandoned his plan for an overland trek and eventually arranged passage on a boat that was proceeding upstream. Yet the boat was slow to depart since "most of our company were fond of whiskey" and "it was difficult to get them parted from their companions and conversation."[34] The river route would afford Nuttall with a view of the "considerable line of settlements along the north border of the river" that existed along the three hundred river miles from Arkansas Post to the Cadron settlement. Nuttall remarked that "the greatest uninhabited interval did not exceed 30 miles."[35] Thus, on February 26, 1819, Nuttall departed Arkansas Post for what would turn out to be a two-month journey up the Arkansas River to Fort Smith.

The Arkansas River from Arkansas Post to Little Rock

The late February weather was mild during the day and, despite slight frosts overnight, Nuttall observed peach trees and redbud trees in bloom along the banks of the Arkansas River. On the first two nights out from Arkansas Post, Nuttall and his companions camped on sandbars surrounded by willows where they could "avoid the attacks of musquitoes."[36] He proclaimed the beach encampments "by no means interesting, yet far from disagreeable to him who can enjoy the simple fare of the hunter, and the calm and unsullied pleasures of nature."[37] Yet the men were hardly alone on the river. For the next two weeks, as he traveled through current-day Jefferson County, Nuttall encountered a growing and transforming cultural landscape and sequence of places. Within twenty-five miles of Arkansas Post, there were two Indian villages on the south bank of the river. One was the "periodical residence of a handful of Choctaws" and the second a Quapaw village.[38] Nuttall noted that "on this side of the river there appeared to be considerable bodies of very fertile land elevated above inundation."[39] On the second day on the river, Nuttall came to a small settlement of three or four families.[40] The surrounding land impressed Nuttall.

> Near this house [of Mr. Davison], and about 200 yards from the river, there was a fine lake of clear water, of considerable extent, communicating with the river by a bayou, which enters a few miles below. Its bed appeared to be firm and sandy. The neighboring land was of a superior quality, either for corn or cotton. . . . The climate was considered unusually healthy, and the soil, with but little labour, capable of insuring a comfortable independence to the cultivator.[41]

With the temperature at seventy degrees by noon the next day, Nuttall decided to take a walk in the woods. He was surprised when he emerged at the Quapaw village they had passed the day before. The river meandered in a six-to-seven-mile arc around a peninsula of land that was less than a mile across. Nuttall decided to take a different path back to the river that he thought would be shorter. Instead, he became tangled in a canebrake: "horrid . . . interlaced with brambles, through which I had to make my way as it were by inches." The delay, he noted, "created alarm among my companions, who fired three guns to direct me to the spot where they waited, and where I soon arrived, pretty well tired of my excursion."[42] On the following evening, Nuttall and his companions encamped on a beach opposite another Quapaw village with about fifteen cabins. He noted that the village was on the edge of a forest surrounded by good land and that the French referred to the village as Ville de Grand Barbe due a former Quapaw chief who wore a long beard.

Five days after departing Arkansas Post, the boat arrived at Curran's settlement near the present-day city of Pine Bluff, Arkansas. Here Nuttall found six families living on "a body of very superior land" where "1000 to 1500 pounds of cotton have been produced upon the acre" and the corn was "as luxuriant as possible." He remarked, "What most recommended this settlement, in my estimation, was the unequivocal appearance of health and plenty."[43] The next day, the party arrived at the farm of Joseph Kirkendale, where Nuttall enjoyed fresh milk and butter, as well as an interview with the Quapaw chief Heckaton, or Dry Man. The chief had recently signed a treaty with the United States that ceded Quapaw land to the United States and defined a boundary for the Quapaws in southeastern Arkansas. Heckaton carefully unfolded a copy of the treaty and survey for Nuttall, who was impressed by the "negotiating conquests of the American republic, made almost without the expense of either blood or treasure!"[44] Heckaton warned Nuttall of the dangers posed by the Osages who would "strip [him] naked, and leave [him] to perish for want," but assured him that among the Quapaws "the stranger was always welcome."[45] Nuttall was unable to learn much about the origins of the Quapaws from Heckaton, but the chief did tell Nuttall about the various Quapaw ceremonies performed to ensure successful harvests, including the Green-corn dance and, to Nuttall's horror, the sacrifice and consumption of a lean dog. Nuttall was complimentary of Heckaton's appearance, hospitality, and intellect, but also proclaimed him to be "much too fond of whiskey" and the Quapaws in general "slaves to superstition."[46] Nuttall remained in the vicinity downstream of present-day Pine Bluff for approximately five days.

On March 8, 1819, William Drope, whom Nuttall met in Arkansas Post, arrived with "his large and commodious trading boat of 25 tons burthen . . . on his way to the garrison," and Nuttall joined him for the journey to Fort Smith.[47] The river itself was active with people. Near Pine Bluff, Nuttall met Nathaniel Pryor, a member of the Lewis and Clark expedition and a veteran of the War of 1812, who was descending the river "with cargoes of furs and peltries, collected among the Osages."[48] Nuttall continued to be impressed by the extensive, rich, and elevated land upon which farms and small settlements had been established, as well as the adjoining woods that were in bloom with buttercups. Nuttall was not complimentary, however, of the cultural landscape of Quapaw villages that were often across the river from Euro-American farms.

> The Indians, unfortunately, are here, as usual, both poor and indolent, and alive to wants which they have not the power of gratifying. The younger ones are extremely foppish in their dress; covered with feathers, blazing calicoes, scarlet blankets, and silver pendants. Their houses, sufficiently convenient with their habits, are oblong square, and without any other furniture than baskets and benches, spread with skins for the purpose of rest and repose. The fire, as usual, is in the middle of the hut, which is constructed of strips of bark and cane, with doors also of the latter split and plaited together.[49]

Nuttall was similarly dismissive of the métis families near Pine Bluff with whom Drope traded. The métis, according to Nuttall, "are very little removed in their habits from the savages, with whose language and manners they are quite familiar."[50] The remnants of French settlement in Arkansas also did not impress Nuttall. He speculated that the few French hunters remaining in the area were "in all probability the descendants of those ten Frenchmen whom de Tonti left with the Arkansas, on his way up the Mississippi in the year 1685."[51] He characterized the French hunters as "Indians in habits" who "pay no attention to the cultivation of the soil."[52] Despite his disdainful remarks and smug sense of superiority, Nuttall remained interested in interacting with and learning from and about the Indians he encountered along the river. On one occasion, for example, Nuttall and Drope walked along the river before departing the Pine Bluff area. Nuttall observed, "a canoe of Quapaws coming in sight, we prevailed on them to land, and . . . I amused myself with learning some of their names for the forest trees. While thus engaged, I observed, that many of their sounds were dental and guttural, and that they could not pronounce the *th*."[53]

As he continued his journey by boat up the Arkansas River, Nuttall saw great commercial potential in the places and landscapes that are now northeastern Jefferson County. The "extensive bodies of fertile land" combined with a "comparatively healthy climate" boded well for the "cultivation of cotton, rice, maize, wheat, tobacco, indigo, hemp, and wine, together with the finest fruits of moderate climates." Nuttall observed that such crops could be grown "without the aid of artificial soils or manures" and that the location on the river made these lands "all sufficiently contiguous to a market." Additionally, peaches were already growing in abundance and the "spontaneous mulberry" suggested opportunities for silk production.[54] On the "Indian side" of the river, Nuttall observed "thickets of Chicasaw plum-trees, which appear to have overgrown the sites of Indian huts and field."[55] He concluded that "the territory watered by the Arkansa is scarcely less fertile than Kentucky, and it owes its luxuriance to the same source of alluvial deposition." In addition to agriculture, Nuttall imagined the possibilities for ranching due to the abundance of "pasturage" that could allow "some of our domestic animals [to] become naturalized, as in Paraguay and Mexico."[56] Better yet, the "forests every where abound with wild turkeys" awaiting the hunter's rifle, and the lack of roads "is scarcely felt in a level country meandered by rivers." He also noted that "the privations of an infant settlement are already beginning to disappear, grist and saw-mills, now commenced, only wait for support."[57] Here, Nuttall envisioned a transformed and improved cultural and commercial landscape that capitalized on the endowments of the environmental landscape. The future for Arkansas appeared to be bright.

Little Rock to Dardanelle, Arkansas

The mild weather that Nuttall had enjoyed so far in Arkansas changed dramatically as he approached Little Rock. Freezing temperatures, ice, and strong winds slowed their progress up the river. Nuttall remarked, "This sudden transition, after such a long continuance of mild weather, felt extremely disagreeable, and forboded the destruction of all the fruit in the territory."[58] In addition to the wind and the ice, the boat was slowed by low water levels. Thus, the party managed to proceed only eighteen to twenty miles per day. Despite these poor conditions, Nuttall praised the navigability of the Arkansas River.

> The almost uninterrupted alternation of sand-bars in the wide alluvial plain of the Arkansa afford, as on the Mississippi, great facilities to navigation, either in propelling the boat by poles, or towing with the cordelles.

> As the bars or beaches advance, so they continually change the common level of the river, and driving the current into the bend with augmenting velocity, the curve becomes at length intersected, and the sand barring up the entrances of the former bed of the river, thus produces the lakes which we find interspersed over the alluvial lands.[59]

In current-day southeastern Pulaski County near Little Rock, Nuttall recorded that they "were again gratified with the sight of a human habitation."[60] The place where a Mr. Twiner had settled was a mixture of desirable and less desirable environmental features. On the west bank, there were hills approximately six to eight miles from the river. These "Indian reservation" lands included pine lands that Nuttall dismissed because they "promise but little to the agriculturist." The land between the hills and the river, though, was alluvial soil that Nuttall predicted would be "fertile as usual."[61] On the eastern side of the river, Nuttall noted that the Great Prairie was approximately twenty miles away and that the "the intermediate space, unbroken by hills, must necessarily afford an uninterrupted body of land little removed from the fertile character of alluvial."[62]

The settlers mentioned by Nuttall in the vicinity of Little Rock include Monsieur LaFeve, Mr. Jones, Mr. Daniels, Mr. Hogan, and Mr. Curran.[63] There were two families living near Monsieur LaFeve whom Nuttall characterized as "descendants of the ancient French settlers." As was typical when Nuttall encountered settlers of French ancestry, he remarked with aversion that Monsieur LaFeve "by his dress and manners did not appear to have had much acquaintance with the civilized world."[64] Mr. Jones did not warrant much comment from Nuttall except to say that he was "very decently entertained" at Mr. Jones's house.[65] Mr. Daniels lived alongside a second family that is not named by Nuttall. While he does not say anything about Mr. Daniels, Nuttall describes at length the geographic situation of Mr. Daniels's land. Nuttall observed that the land "appeared to be of a very superior quality, and well suited for cotton."[66] Better yet, the road to St. Louis to the northeast and the Mound Prairie Settlement and Natchitoches to the southwest ran through this area. Nuttall noted that this pathway had served people in the region for centuries.

> From all I can learn, it appears pretty evident that these extensive and convenient routes have been opened from time immemorial by the Indians; they were their war and hunting-paths, and such as in many instances have

> been tracked out instinctively by the bison in their periodical migrations. It is in these routes, conducted by the Indians, that we are to trace the adventurers De Soto and La Salle.[67]

Mr. Hogan lived in what Nuttall labeled the "settlement of the Little Rock" that was situated opposite to cliffs that Nuttall described as "declining beneath the surface at a dip or angle of not less than 45 degrees from the horizon" and "elevated from 150 to 200 feet above the level of the river."[68] There were families living on both sides of the river on "high, healthy, and fertile land." Yet, Nuttall had observed a change in the land from his earlier observations to the southeast. He commented that "this land, though fertile and healthy, cannot be compared with the alluvions of the Arkansa."[69] Despite the lesser quality of the land, Nuttall was informed by the settlers that new migrants from Tennessee and Kentucky were adding to their population. Nuttall also noted a change in the river itself. It was "no longer so tediously meandering" but presented a "stretch of six miles extent, proceeding to the west of north-west."[70]

Just beyond the Little Rock settlement lived a Mr. Curran whose house was situated opposite gentle hills.[71] A few miles beyond Mr. Curran's house, Nuttall caught his first glimpse of the Maumelle. What is now called Pinnacle Mountain was described by Nuttall as "insulated and conic like a volcano." The surrounding cliffs near the river were "decorated with the red cedar . . . and clusters of ferns." The change in scenery was inspiring to Nuttall.

> After emerging as it were from so vast a tract of alluvial lands, as that through which I had now been travelling for more than three months, it is almost impossible to describe the pleasure which these romantic prospects again afforded me. Who can be insensible to the beauty of the verdant hill and valley, to the sublimity of the clouded mountain, the fearful precipice, or the torrent of the cataract. Even bald and moss-grown rocks, without the aid of sculpture, forcibly inspire us with that veneration which we justly owe to the high antiquity of nature, and which appears to arise no less from a solemn and intuitive reflection on their vast capacity for duration, contrasted with that transient scene in which we ourselves only appear to act a momentary part.[72]

William Drope, upon whose boat Nuttall was traveling, spent March 22 and 23 visiting a Mr. Blair and a Mr. Piat.[73] The delay gave Nuttall some free time to explore the area immediately upstream from Little Rock. On the first

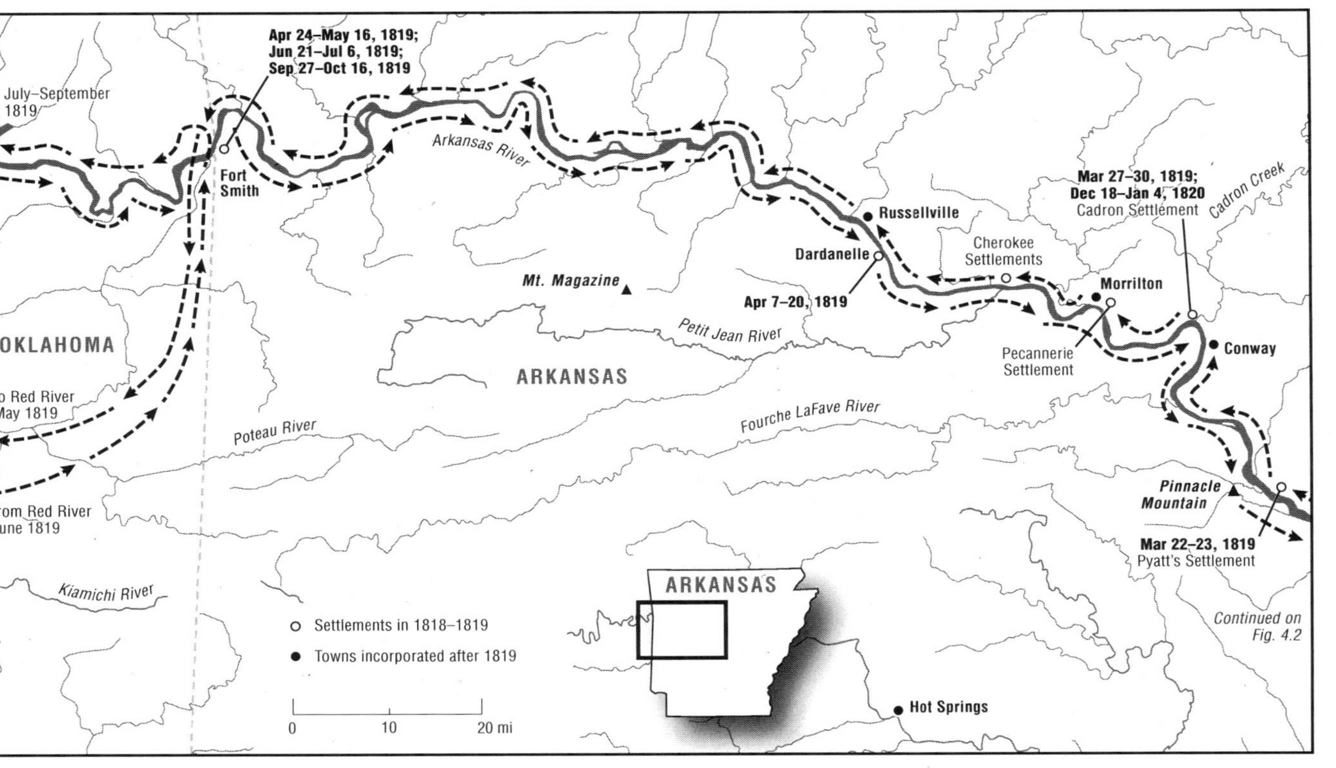

Continued on
Fig. 4.2

FIG. 4.3. Thomas Nuttall in the western Arkansas River Valley, 1819. Cartography by Erin Greb.

day, he ventured along the river to investigate a "pretended silver mine . . . about one mile below White Oak bayou."[74] Nuttall explained that the river had eroded and exposed some rocks and sediment that "present indeed an appearance somewhat remarkable." The exposed strata included layers of "fragile slate-clay" and "fine-grained siliceous sandstone" that contained mica, veins of quartz, and talc crystals.[75] Nuttall had trouble locating anything that resembled silver ore, so he investigated the slag remaining in an abandoned furnace. Here he found chunks of rock that contained pyrites, but he received conflicting accounts when he asked the locals if these specimens included what they suspected to be silver ore. After viewing the pyrites with a pocket microscope, Nuttall concluded that "like the rest of this rock, it indeed contained abundance of magnetic iron-sand, which on the disintegration of the stone, appeared scattered along the strand of the river." He also remarked, "Upon the whole, I am inclined to believe that some imposition had been practiced upon the ignorance and credulity of those who were enticed into this undertaking."[76] Nuttall was understandably skeptical of any "pretended" discoveries of precious metals in Arkansas. He noted that such claims were nothing new in the region.

> Ever since the time of Soto, reports concerning the discovery of precious metals in this territory have been cherished; we see them marked upon the maps, and although the places are easily discoverable, the gold and silver they were said to afford has entirely vanished like a fairy dream.[77]

On the following day, Nuttall sketched a distant view of the Maumelle, present-day Pinnacle Mountain, and then trekked to the summit of one of the cliffs on the opposite side of the river. From this vantage point, he described the "low mountains running in chains from the north of west to the south of east" and the "meanders of the river" that were hidden by the "pervading forests of its alluvial lands, still fertile and expansive." The Maumelle "now appeared nearly double the elevation of that on which [he] stood, probably more than 1000 feet in height" and "presented the appearance of a vast pyramid, hiding its summit in the clouds."[78]

As Nuttall joined William Drope on his boat on March 24, 1819, the scenery of "romantic cliffs" and lofty hills were a source of enjoyment for him.[79] After a day of battling a strong northwest wind and a rising river with a strong current, Nuttall and Drope arrived at the Cadron Settlement, where Cadron Creek enters the Arkansas River near present-day Conway. The settlement consisted of a group of five or six families and a "Mr. M'Ilmery

. . . is at present the only resident on the imaginary town plot."[80] The place included features that Nuttall thought boded well for the site of a settlement. There was a cove of rocks that provided a harbor that could be useful for the transfer of goods via boat and an overland route that led to the hot springs in one direction and through the great prairie in the other direction. Nuttall imagined a commercial future for this place in which a "house of public entertainment" would do a steady business serving "those southern gentlemen who pass the summer in quest of health and recreation" on their way to the hot springs.[81] Despite these geographical advantages, Nuttall doubted that a substantial city could thrive at this site. The "tiresome and lofty hills, broken into ravines, with small rills of water" left little level ground for the building of houses and other infrastructure. Nuttall concluded that "modern cities rarely thrive in such romantic situations."[82]

During the four days that Nuttall spent near the Cadron settlement, he explored the surrounding area and commented on the land, Indian mounds, the lack of education among the population, the operations of U.S. land surveyors, and the health of the country. Nuttall judged the land to be "of an inferior quality, and chiefly timbered with oaks and hickories thinly scattered," and concluded that "ages must elapse before this kind of land will be worth purchasing at any price."[83] Though the surrounding land would not be suitable for growing cotton or corn, Nuttall speculated that the place might have some commercial value as "a good range for pasturage of cattle" and the "decoctions of the wood of the sassafras and spice bush" could become "very palatable substitutes for tea." Nuttall also noted that maple trees in the area could "by a little attention afford sugar at a low rate."[84] Regarding the native landscape, Nuttall noted "a considerable collection of aboriginal tumuli." These were not the first Indian mounds that Nuttall observed in Arkansas, and he lamented, "Both they and their history are buried in impenetrable oblivion! their existence blotted out from the page of the living! . . . How dreary is this eternal night which has overtaken so many of my fellow-mortals!"[85] The dearth of schooling in the region also provoked Nuttall to observe that "the rising generation are growing up in mental darkness, like the French hunters who have preceded them, and who have almost forgot that they appertain to the civilized world."[86] Nuttall attributed the lack of education to the dispersed settlement patterns in the region and remained optimistic that future Arkansas children would be better educated as the population grew.

The likelihood of imminent population growth was evident in the work of a surveyor named Mr. Petis with whom Nuttall spoke.[87] Nuttall predicted that as the survey and sale of land proceeded there would be "ample room for the settlement of thousands of families."[88] Mr. Petis told Nuttall that he received three dollars per mile for the difficult task of surveying the lands adjacent to the river which posed the challenge of thick canebrakes, lagoons, and oxbow lakes. The hills were "not yet thought to be worth the expense of a public survey," but Nuttall concluded that such lands would still be valuable as a range for cattle.[89] The alluvial tracts of land near the river were promising for the cultivation of maize, cotton, rice, and indigo, and Nuttall noted that the military bounty lands that were awarded to soldiers of the War of 1812 had been in high demand among speculators suggesting "proof of the growing importance of this country, where lands . . . have brought a price equal to that of the best lands on the banks of the Ohio."[90] Moreover, the "general healthy appearance of the inhabitants" and the absence of doctors provided further evidence of "the prevailing salubrity of the banks of the Arkansa."[91] Yet Nuttall remarked in frustration that the existing settlers of the region were not taking full advantage of the commercial opportunities afforded them. He perceived a deficient cultural and commercial landscape because "as yet, the sum of industry calculated to afford any satisfactory experiment in agriculture or domestic economy, has not been exercised by the settlers of the Arkansa, who, with half the resolution of the German farmers of Pennsylvania, would ensure to themselves and their families comfort and affluence."[92]

On his final day near the Cadron Settlement, Nuttall observed several deer feeding while on a short hike from the river to the house of Mr. M'Ilmery. He also noted the presence of what were probably bobcats and coyotes, as well as panthers, wolves, and bears in the area. M'Ilmery, who lived "at the head of a small alluvial plain" that Nuttall believed was "well calculated for a superior farm," told Nuttall that bison could be found within "a day's ride towards the Washita."[93] Indeed, the land was already being plowed to prepare the ground for cotton. This was made easy by the "friable and loamy" soil.[94] The agricultural activity in the area would also benefit from the shorter period during which the Arkansas River inundated the surrounding land. Nuttall remarked that the spring floods were "less injurious than those of the Missouri and Mississippi" because they did not continue into the summer when the flood waters might spoil crops.[95] From this shorter flood season, he incorrectly hypothesized that the Arkansas River must be fed primarily from winter rains and not from a source in a region with snow.

As Nuttall and Drope continued their journey up the Arkansas River toward Fort Smith, the prospects for agriculture appeared to be very good.

Nuttall observed near Point Remove Creek, "Both banks of the river in this distance are one continued line of farms. Some of the cabins are well situated on agreeable rising grounds; but the nearer, I perceive, the land is to the level of inundation, the greater is its fertility."[96] There were at least fourteen families settled on the alluvial lands near the river, and several others along the banks of Point Remove. Nuttall predicted that with "slight banking" the surrounding land that was "not too deeply submerged" could be made suitable for "all kinds of produce, but more particularly maize and rice."[97] As they passed the Petit Jean Mountains, strong winds made the ascent of the river difficult. The delay gave Nuttall time to climb the "lofty ridge of broken hills" that presented "an alternation of terraces and cliffs."[98] Nuttall described the views from the summit where "a vast wilderness presented itself covered with trees, and chequered with ranges of mountains, which appeared to augment and converge toward the north-west."[99] As he peered to the southeast, Nuttall could see the peak of Pinnacle Mountain, and to the east where "a considerable plain stretches out, almost uninterrupted by elevations." To the southwest, "four distinct chains of mountains, of which the furthest, about 40 miles distant, presented in several places lofty blue peaks, much higher than any of the intermediate and less broken ridges." One portion of the plateau conjured images of home for Nuttall. He found "several enormous masses of rock so nicely balanced as almost to appear the work of art" that reminded him of "the druidical monuments of England." In addition to the vistas, Nuttall discovered a new species of anemone here and noted iron-ore nodules in the sandstone formations and "gigantic tessellated zoophytic impressions" that indicated the presence of coal.[100]

For two days after passing the confluence of the Petit Jean River and the Arkansas River, the boat crew struggled against the rising river and its strong current. Nuttall estimated that the river was nearly a mile wide and thus "little short of the Mississippi in magnitude."[101] On the first day past the Petit Jean, Nuttall and Drope hiked about five miles to a Cherokee settlement called the Galley. Nuttall described the Galley hills as "a series of low and agreeable acclivities well suited for building" where the Cherokees had "a settlement of about a dozen families." The Cherokees here appeared to Nuttall to "imitate the whites . . . in the construction and furniture of their houses and in the management of their farms," and thus "appeared to be progressing towards civilization." Yet, the Cherokee settlers also exhibited a "baneful attachment to whiskey."[102] As they made slow progress on the second day from Petit Jean, Nuttall noted that that the land on either side of the river was "elevated and fertile, and pretty thickly scattered with the cabins and farms of the Cherokees, this being the land allotted to them by congress, in exchange for others in the Mississippi Territory, where the principal part of the nation still remain." Nuttall approved of most of what he witnessed.

> Both banks of the river, as we proceeded, were lined with the houses and farms of the Cherokees, and though their dress was a mixture of indigenous and European taste, yet in their houses, which are decently furnished, and in their farms, which were well fenced and stocked with cattle, we perceive a happy approach towards civilization. Their numerous families, also, well fed and clothed, argue a propitious progress in their population. Their superior industry, either as hunters or farmers, proves the value of property among them, and they are no longer strangers to avarice, and the distinctions created by wealth; some of them are possessed of property to the amount of many thousands of dollars, have houses handsomely and conveniently furnished, and their tables spread with our dainties and luxuries.[103]

Nuttall thought that the "civilized habits, industry, and augmenting population" of the Cherokees could prove to be a "dangerous enemy to the frontiers of the Arkansa Territory" if their land claims were not settled.[104] He speculated that if the Cherokees decided to petition Spain for land across the Red River in Texas, and if they continued to embrace Anglo-American habits and industry, that they may "in time increase, and become a powerful and independent nation, subject by habit to a monarchial form of government."[105]

Dardanelle to Fort Smith, Arkansas

William Drope decided to abandon his plans to ascend the Arkansas River to Fort Smith. This disappointed Nuttall who had "entertained the hope of continuing [his] passage, without interruption or additional delay."[106] As it turned out, Nuttall would spend almost two weeks near present-day Dardanelle and Russellville. The delay gave Nuttall time to record a lengthy entry on his observations of the Cherokees. Tahlonteeskee, the chief of the Old Settlers of the Cherokee Nation West, died the year before Nuttall's arrival, and John Jolly, Tahlonteeskee's brother, had migrated to Arkansas to become chief. Nuttall described Jolly as "half Indian, and dressed as a white man" and "very plain, prudent, and unassuming in his dress and manners; a Franklin amongst his countrymen, and affectionately called the 'beloved' father." Nuttall remarked that he "should scarcely have distinguished him from an American, except by his language."[107] Drope had traded with Jolly in Mississippi Territory and vouched for his honesty and generosity. At the time of Nuttall's visit, the Cherokees were "very busily employed felling trees, and clearing their grounds preparatory to the seed-time" amid their "fine farms and comfortable cabins."[108] Nuttall was able to converse with some of the Cherokees, but "found it extremely difficult to acquire any knowledge, either of the traditions, opinions, or ancient customs of their nation." He concluded that their reluctance to discuss the past was more a matter of pride than of ignorance, noting that "the humiliating details of former poverty, ignorance, and superstition, tended to wound the feelings of those, who, besides the advantages, had also imbibed the pride and luxury of Europe."[109] In addition to the "habits of industry" that Nuttall witnessed among the Cherokees, he admired their sense of loyalty and unity.[110] He commented that their "mutual attachment" as evidenced by the "dire hatred they bore their enemies" led them to feel "for each other as members of the same family, as sons of the same father; a band of brothers mutually bound to defend and revenge the cause of each other, by a just and undeviating retaliation."[111]

The primary enemy of the Cherokees at this time were the Osages. Nuttall remarked that "the arrival of the Cherokees in this country did not fail, as might have been foreseen, to excite the jealousy of the Osages, within whose former territory they had now taken up their residence."[112] Two years prior to Nuttall's arrival, a group of Cherokees had attacked and massacred a group of Osages at Claremore mound near present-day Tulsa, Oklahoma. Nuttall was particularly incensed that a white man, John D. Chisolm, had participated in the attack. He believed that the involvement of white men in Indian wars would lead to retaliation against white settlers, merchants, and travelers and called on the Indian agent of the territory to apprehend Chisolm for trial and punishment. While Nuttall admired many of the characteristics of Cherokee society that he witnessed, he was critical of their attachment to "superstitions" and their practice of polygamy. Regarding their tendency toward superstition, Nuttall remarked:

> All the natives acknowledged the existence of a great, good, and indivisible Spirit, the author of all created being. Believing also in the immortality of the soul, and in the existence of invisible agencies, they were often subjected to superstitious fears, and the observance of omens and dreams, the workings of perturbed fancy. By these imaginary admonitions, they sometimes suffered themselves to be controlled in their most important

> undertakings, relinquishing every thing which was accidentally attended by any inauspicious presage of misfortune.[113]

Regarding Cherokee women, Nuttall observed that "the condition of the female sex bordered upon degradation" in that women were considered "objects of pleasure and necessity [rather] than as rational companions" leading to polygamous practice in which "several [women] often lived together in the house of the same husband." Yet Nuttall predicted that "polygamy among the Cherokees, without any legal restraint, will, in time, be spontaneously abandoned, as their conjugal attachment appears to be strong and sincere" and that "civilization tends to its abolition."[114] On April 15, 1819, Nuttall met with Reuben Lewis, an agent to the Cherokees and the brother of Meriwether Lewis. Lewis and Nuttall knew each other from Nuttall's 1811 travels to Fort Mandan on the Missouri River. Lewis informed Nuttall that "the progress of civilization among the Cherokees, is comparatively modern."[115]

In addition to his observations on the characteristics of the Cherokees, Nuttall explored the surrounding environmental landscape and found it to be "peculiarly agreeable."[116] On his first day in the area, Nuttall climbed to the summit of a surrounding ridge where he found a "sublime view of the surrounding country."[117] From his vantage point, he was impressed with the view of Mount Magazine and was surprised that he was still able to see Pinnacle Mountain in the distance. The following day, Nuttall amused himself by taking a leisurely stroll along another ridge and was enamored by the "gentle murmurs of a rill and pellucid water, which broke from rock to rock" and the "lugubrious vociferations of the whip-poor-will; the croaking frogs, chirping crickets, and whips and halloos of the Indians."[118] The idyllic scene was enhanced by the blooming dogwoods, violets, and Collinsia. On his third hike along the river, Nuttall came across "an enormous spider, no less than four inches from the extremity of one foot to that of the other, and two inches from head to tail, covered with long brown hair; the eyes six in number and minute, the mouth not discoverable, but in the place of jaws, as in the Monoculi, two of the six pair of feet, of a strong cartilaginous texture, very short and retracted together, each terminated by a simple hooked claw, and internally lined with a row of minute teeth for mastication." He remarked that this tarantula "entirely resembled those gigantic tropical spiders, which we see exhibited in museums."[119] Perhaps the Arkansas tarantula piqued this natural scientist's interest in locating other crawling critters, since he spent another day "chiefly in quest of insects." Nuttall did not share the details of his insect hunt other than to remark, "[I] picked off my skin and clothes more than 50 ticks, which are here more abundant and troublesome than in any other part of America in which I have yet been."[120]

On April 20, 1819, Nuttall departed Dardanelle with two French boatmen for the one-hundred-twenty-mile river journey to Fort Smith.[121] Over the next four days, Nuttall commented with approval on the environmental landscape along the river. He was impressed by the presence of fertile land, mountains, coal, wildlife, and beautiful scenery. Many of his observations are associated with the creeks they passed as the pirogue made its way upstream. Charbonnière Creek, he noted, was "so called from the occurrence of coal in its vicinity."[122] Spadra Creek, which flows through present-day Clarksville, was bordered by "considerable tracts of fertile land, well supplied with springs, and occupied by the Cherokees."[123] Coal was evident to Nuttall in the surrounding rocks, particularly what he called the Charbonnière rock that was "about 50 feet high [with] beds of a slaty sandstone . . . in which there are indications of coal."[124] In this vicinity, today an area that is submerged by Lake Dardanelle, Nuttall also saw a bear and "no less than 13 deer."[125] Present-day Short Mountain was described by Nuttall as a "lofty blue ridge" that "somewhat resembles the Magazine, being a long ridge abrupt at either end."[126] Near the present-day town of Ozark, Nuttall was impressed by the "amphitheatre of lofty cliffs, 3 to 400 feet high, having a highly romantic picturesque appearance."[127] As they neared Mulberry Creek, Nuttall recorded that "a fine stretch of about eight miles opens to view, affording an ample prospect of the river" and that "its rich alluvions were now clothed in youthful verdure, and backed in the distance by bluish and empurpled hills." The scenic view was enhanced by "the melody of innumerable birds, and the gentle humming of wild bees, feeding on the early blooming willows, which in the same manner line the picturesque banks of the Ohio." The "handsome and rising ground, flanked by a continued ridge of low hills" was home to a settlement of three or four families, presumably white.[128] The men awoke in the morning to "the sounds of thousands of birds, re-echoing through the woods, and seeking shelter from the extensive plains, which every where now border the alluvion."[129] The prairie near Vache Grasse creek, east of present-day Fort Smith, marked the "last habitation of the whites to be met with on the banks of the Arkansa, except those of the garrison."[130] In the final several miles before reaching Fort Smith, Nuttall observed a change in the environmental landscape. He noted the "first calcareous rock on ascending the Arkansa," as well as the fact that "from hence . . . the prairies or grassy plains begin to be prevalent, and the trees decrease in number and magnitude." The river close to the fort presented "long and romantic views . . . almost exclusively bordered with groves of cotton-wood, at this season extremely beautiful, resembling so many vistas clad in the softest and most vivid verdure, and crowded with innumerable birds."[131]

On April 24, 1819, Nuttall and the French boatmen arrived at Fort Smith. Major William Bradford and a company of the United States Rifle Regiment arrived to establish Fort Smith about sixteen months before Nuttall's arrival. Nuttall described the garrison as "consisting of two block-houses, and lines of cabins or barracks for the accommodation of 70 men whom it contains." The site of the new fort was "agreeably situated at the junction of the Pottoe, on a rising ground of about 50 feet elevation, and surrounded by alluvial and uplands of unusual fertility."[132] Given the other scenic views that Nuttall had enjoyed during his journey on the river, it is notable that Nuttall proclaimed that "the view [from the garrison] is more commanding and picturesque, than any other spot of equal elevation on the banks of the Arkansa."[133] Major Bradford greeted Nuttall with "politeness" but informed him that he "could not have permission to proceed any higher up the river without a special credential from the secretary of state, authorizing [him] to hold that intercourse with the natives." Nuttall was "disagreeably surprised" by this news, but after some discussion it was decided that Bradford had the authority to grant permission to travel through Indian territory.[134] The men also agreed that Nuttall would spend a few weeks at the garrison and use the fort as a jumping off point for exploring the surrounding country, as well as a place to store his collections.

For the next three weeks, Nuttall explored the surrounding territory and was quite impressed with the "whole expanse of forest, hill, and dale . . . richly enameled with a profusion of beautiful and curious flowers," the uplands that "appeared nearly as fertile as the alluvions, and affords a most productive pasture to the cattle," the soil that was "of a superior quality, and thickly covered with vegetable earth," the trees that "appear scattered as if planted by art," and the adjoining prairie that was "like an immense meadow . . . covered with a luxuriant herbage, and beautifully decorated with flowers."[135] On one of his outings, Nuttall camped overnight on the cedar prairie about ten miles southeast of the garrison. He described the "extensive and verdant meadow" as "picturesquely bounded by woody hills of different degrees of elevation and distance, and lacked nothing but human occupation to reclaim it from barren solitude, and cast over it the air of rural cheerfulness and abundance."[136] Despite the pastoral landscape, Nuttall managed little sleep overnight due to the "swarms of musquetoes," the "usual music of frogs," the "cheerless howling of a distant wolf," and the "vociferations of the . . . whip-poor-will." Dawn brought with it "the melodious chorus of many thousands of birds, agreeably dispersing the solemnity of the ambiguous twilight."[137]

A Diversion to the Red River

On May 16, 1819, Nuttall departed Fort Smith with Major Bradford, several soldiers, and an interpreter. Major Bradford was ordered to remove the white settlers who were residing in the territory of the Osages near the confluence of the Red River and the Kiamichi River in present-day southeastern Oklahoma.[138] After three weeks of exploring the surroundings of Fort Smith, Nuttall must have been pleased with the opportunity to take a trip further afield. His mood was certainly bright in his journal. He described the "delightfully clear and warm" weather that made the "whole aspect of nature . . . peculiarly charming." He also enjoyed the "picturesque mountains" and the "vast plains" that he characterized as "beautiful almost as the fancied Elysium."[139] These Elysian fields of eastern Oklahoma were decorated with a variety of blooming flowers, leading Nuttall to proclaim that the scene was "serene and charming as the blissful regions of fancy, nothing here appeared to exist but what contributes to harmony."[140] The party was on horseback and was able to cover about twenty-five miles per day despite occasionally taking paths along rocky ridges, through thickets, and over "dreary and rocky pine hills."[141] Along the way, the riflemen hunted bison and deer and the men enjoyed a breakfast of wild honey discovered in a tree.

On May 22, the soldiers and Nuttall arrived at the Red River. Nuttall noted that the "change of soil in the great Prairie of Red river now appeared obvious" in that he saw the "first calcareous rock charged with shells, &c. since my departure from the banks of the Ohio." He was also impressed by the "beauty of these plains" that were "enameled with such an uncommon variety of flowers of vivid tints, possessing all the brilliancy of tropical productions."[142] As might be expected, the white settlers in the region were not pleased to learn that they were expected to vacate their homes. Nuttall described the scene as follows:

> The people appeared but ill prepared for the unpleasant official intelligence of their ejectment. Some who had cleared considerable farms were thus unexpectedly thrust out into the inhospitable wilderness. I could not but

> sympathize with their complaints, notwithstanding the justice and propriety of the requisition. Would it had always been the liberal policy of the Europeans to act with becoming justice, and to reciprocate the law of nations with the unfortunate natives![143]

On May 26, 1819, Major Bradford and his soldiers began their return to Fort Smith. Nuttall remained behind to do some additional botanical collecting and planned to catch up with Bradford that evening. Distracted by his quest to collect "some of the new and curious plants interspersed over these enchanting prairies" and taking an incorrect route to the rendezvous point, Nuttall did not return in time to depart with Bradford and his men.[144] He attempted to catch up the following day but was unable to do so. Ever the devoted natural scientist, Nuttall remarked that his "botanical acquisitions in the prairies, proved, however, so interesting as almost to make [him] forget [his] situation," but he also recognized that he was now "cast away . . . amidst the refuse of society, without money and without acquaintance [and] unprovided with every means of subsistence."[145] Mr. Styles, one of the white settlers who was to be removed from the territory, welcomed Nuttall into his home. The Styles household had arrived recently in a "loaded wagon" with "women, and children [and] the mother of his wife, blind, and 90 years of age!" Mr. Styles and his family had settled on "the margin of the Prairie . . . a short distance from whence commences the usual bushy hills."[146]

Nuttall would spend almost three weeks with the Styles family during which he explored the surrounding land and enjoyed the songs of birds and the varieties of flora he observed. In mid-June, he arranged to travel with a group from the Red River settlement who were returning to the Fort Smith area. Nuttall was not impressed by the cultural landscape he encountered in the vicinity of the Red and Kiamichi Rivers. He described the settlers as having "the worst moral character imaginable, being many of them renegadoes from justice" who had "forfeited the esteem of civilized society" and who would head to Spanish Texas when "a further flight from justice became necessary."[147] Fortunately, the three men with whom Nuttall would travel back to Fort Smith were "men of diligence and industry" who were traveling to Fort Smith to recover horses that had been stolen from them by Cherokees.[148] Nuttall was grateful for the kind hospitality of the "poor and honest" Styles family: "they, knowing, from the first my destitute situation, separated from pecuniary resources, could scarcely be prevailed upon to accept the trifling pittance which I accidentally possessed."[149] Despite taking a circuitous and difficult route, almost losing their horses, and being tormented by prairie flies, Nuttall and his three companions eventually arrived at Fort Smith on June 21, 1819. For the next three weeks, Nuttall remained at Fort Smith, but he did not record any entries in his journal of his activities during this period.

Disease, Danger, and Disappointment in Oklahoma

In early July, Nuttall arranged to join Monsieur Bougie on his ascent of the Arkansas from Fort Smith to his trading post at the confluence of the Arkansas and Verdigris Rivers at present-day Muskogee and Fort Gibson, Oklahoma.[150] Upon their arrival on July 14, 1819, Nuttall noted that "a town will probably be founded here" due to the "irresistible tide of western emigration," the "rapids of Grand [Neosho] river [that] will afford good and convenient situations for mills," and the Osage trace that connected St. Louis to the Verdigris and "reduces the distance of those two places to about 300 miles . . . over a country scarcely obstructed by mountains."[151] The land between the Neosho and Verdigris rivers was "about two miles wide, free from inundation, and covered with larger trees than any other [he] had seen since leaving Fort Smith."[152]

A few days after arriving at the trading post, Nuttall joined two young men in a canoe to travel up the Neosho River to the salt works southeast of present-day Chouteau, Oklahoma. After ascending the river about fifty miles, Nuttall stayed with the Slover family.[153] He also visited the salt works that were at this time "lying idle, and nearly deserted in consequence of the murder of Mr. Campbell."[154] The brutal murder and scalping of Mr. Campbell by his partner and two accomplices occurred about six weeks before Nuttall arrived. Nuttall was particularly shocked to learn that one of the men who committed the crime was none other than William Childers, whom Nuttall had attempted to hire as a guide at the Cadron settlement. Despite contracting a fever while staying at the Slover household, Nuttall returned to the trading post by foot over the "Great Osage plain" through grass that was "three feet deep, often entangled with brambles" and spent one night "under the clear canopy of heaven" in the prairie where he was "alone, and without the necessary comforts of either fire, food, or water" and endured the aural assault of the "loud and shrill crepitation" of the "crickets, grasshoppers, catidids, and stocking-weavers" but fortunately was "scarcely at all molested by musquetoes."[155]

The months of August and September 1819 were the most miserable stage of Nuttall's excursion. At the end of July, Nuttall noted, "An irregular remittent fever began to show itself in our camp, with which myself and five or six others were affected."[156] The malaria he had contracted caused horrible headaches and fever for the first few days of August. To add insult to injury, Nuttall was robbed of his penknife and pocket microscope, and almost lost his horse to a thief, while he was ill. On August 11, he had recovered sufficiently to continue his journey west. Accompanied by a trapper named Lee, Nuttall set out over land toward the Cimarron River. The men planned to follow the Cimarron through the current-day Oklahoma panhandle to the present state boundaries of New Mexico and Colorado and thus avoid the northern bend of the Arkansas River that veered into Kansas before heading west. But three days into the trek Nuttall's fever returned. Although suffering from fever and diarrhea and finding it difficult to escape the "burning sun and sultry air," Nuttall was determined to continue his travels.[157] After four days of distress and a fainting spell during which Nuttall almost fell from his horse, Lee convinced the resolute traveler to return to the trading post at the Verdigris before his illness made further travel impossible or cost him his life. The situation soon turned from bad to worse. Lee's horse was weak and becoming unable to walk or carry baggage. To move forward, Lee and Nuttall had to resort to "double journeys" in which Nuttall's horse, and presumably Mr. Lee, would take half of the baggage some distance ahead, leave it, and then return for Nuttall and the remaining gear. To make matters worse, their blankets, linen, and other gear had become infested with flies and maggots.[158] Nuttall soon became "too weak to bear any exercise" and unable to eat due to the gastrointestinal distress that accompanies malaria.[159]

Lee was worried about their proximity to the Osages and their slow progress through this especially dangerous neighborhood. While Mr. Lee was away on one occasion checking beaver traps near their camp, Nuttall was attempting to rest when he spotted an Indian near their horses. Fortunately, the Indian fled when he saw Nuttall, but the brush with a potential horse thief was disturbing. Lee and Nuttall left the area immediately, fearful of the return of Indians who might rob them or worse. Nuttall noted, "As I could not possibly walk, and even required assistance to get on and off my horse . . . to have it stolen would have been to leave me to perish without hope."[160] That evening, Nuttall recorded, "[I] felt extremely unhappy, and became quite delirious; when reclined, it was with difficulty that I could rise; a kind of lethargy, almost the prelude of death, now interposed, affording an ominous relief from anxiety and pain."[161] For the next few days, the men trudged ahead as Nuttall experienced "the miseries of sickness, delirium, and despondence." In at least one instance of delirium, Nuttall's "mind became so unaccountably affected with horror and distraction, that, for a time, it was impossible to proceed to any convenient place of encampment."[162] The last shred of hope for Nuttall might have been that he was in the company of an experienced guide. That hope, too, began to wane as Nuttall noted on September 1 that "[his] companion now appeared to be ignorant of the country" and that they "saw nothing far and wide but an endless scrubby forest of dwarfish oaks."[163]

After a few days and another forty miles or so trekking through the rugged Cross Timbers region of Oklahoma, Nuttall and Lee arrived at the banks of the low, red, and muddy Cimarron River. Lee, still concerned about the nearby Osages, determined that it would be best not to travel immediately along the river, but after his horse became hopelessly mired in the mud, Lee spent a few days constructing a canoe that would carry them down the Cimarron River and back to the Arkansas River. As they neared present-day Tulsa on the Arkansas River, Nuttall and Lee could see the smoke of the Osage village. On September 11, the travelers met the Osages.

> To-day, with all our caution, it became impossible to avoid the discovery of the Indians, as two or three families were encamped along the borders of the river. They ran up to us with a confidence which was by no means reciprocal. One of the men was a blind chief, not unknown to Mr. Lee, who gave him some tobacco, with which he appeared to be satisfied. About the encampment there were a host of squaws, who were extremely impertinent. An old woman, resembling one of the imaginary witches [in] Macbeth, told me, with an air of insolence, that I must give her my horse for her daughter to ride on; I could walk;—that the Osages were numerous, and could soon take it from me. At last, the blind chief invited us to his camp to eat, but had nothing to offer us but boiled maize, sweetened with marmalade of pumpkins. When we were about to depart, they all ran to the boat, to the number of 10 or 12, showing symptoms of mischief, and could not be driven away. They held on to the canoe, and endeavored to drag it aground. Mr. Lee tried in vain to get rid of them, although armed with a rifle. At length, they got to pilfering our baggage; even the blind chief . . . also turned thief on this occasion. We had not got out of the sight of these depredators, before another fellow came after us on the run, in order to claim my horse, insisting that it was his, and I could no way satisfy his unfounded demand, but by giving him one of my blankets.[164]

Nuttall and Lee were followed by two men for the remainder of the day. Unsure of the intentions of the Osages pursuing them, Lee and Nuttall continued their canoe voyage into the night despite a thunderstorm. Nuttall noted, "[This was] the most gloomy and disagreeable situation I ever experienced in my life."[165] He struggled to get his horse to cross the river in the dark and the rain, and on one attempt both Nuttall and his horse were almost buried in quicksand. Once free, Nuttall was "drenched and shivering, almost ready to perish with cold" and convinced Lee to kindle a small fire for him to warm himself for a few hours "amidst the dreary howling of wolves."[166] By this time, the Osage pursuers were nowhere to be seen, so Lee and Nuttall enjoyed a quick meal of elk and continued the journey by moonlight. Around noon the next day, Lee and Nuttall agreed to separate. Lee continued down the Arkansas River by canoe, and Nuttall proceeded at a slower pace with his horse to complete the remaining twenty or thirty miles to the trading post. After a night in which his attempts to make a fire proved futile, Nuttall decided to leave the "hot and cheerless" sand beaches of the river and head over land. After battling through "horrible thickets," he spotted the Verdigris River across the plain and made it to the banks of the river that night where he "had to lie down alone, in the rank weeds, amidst the musquetoes, without fire, food, or water."[167]

On September 15, after more than six weeks of malaria-plagued travel, Nuttall arrived back at Mr. Bougie's trading post. His legs and feet were so swollen that his pants had to be cut off, and he was seized by terrible cramps in his hands and feet. Nuttall remained at Mr. Bougie's for another week, during which he was tormented by fever, cramps, weakness, and delirium. Though he was still weak and cramping, it was arranged by late September for Nuttall to return to Fort Smith by boat. At Fort Smith, Nuttall found that he was not alone in his suffering that season. He noted that "from July to October, the ague and bilious fever spread throughout the territory in a very unusual manner" and that "not less than 100 of the Cherokees, settled contiguous to the banks of the Arkansa, died this season of the bilious fever."[168] Both malaria and yellow fever had taken a severe toll on the population of northwest Arkansas in 1819. Nuttall was fortunate to have survived.

Descent of the Arkansas River from Fort Smith to Arkansas Post

Although Major Bradford welcomed Nuttall to stay at Fort Smith through the winter, the traveling naturalist must have been ready to return his collections and notes, along with his physically and mentally exhausted body, to Philadelphia.[169] His descent of the Arkansas and Mississippi Rivers from Fort Smith to New Orleans occurred in steps with layovers at the Pecannerie Settlement, the Cadron Settlement, and Arkansas Post. Nuttall departed Fort Smith in mid-October and arrived on November 3, 1819, at the Pecannerie settlement near present-day Morrilton and Petit Jean Mountain. Nuttall described the Pecannerie as the "most considerable settlement in the territory, except Arkansas [Post]" and explained that it "derived its name from the Pecan nut-trees, with which its forests abound."[170] There were approximately sixty families living at the settlement at the time of Nuttall's visit. He was not impressed with the cultural landscape he witnessed. Nuttall remarked that many of the settlers were "indigent" and "living in a state of ignorance and mediocrity of fortune" and determined that many "renegadoes from justice" had settled there and were "indulging themselves in indolence" and able to accomplish their "dishonest practices" and "depredations" due to "the laxity of the laws and the imperfect manner in which they are administered."[171] Compounding the troubles of the settlement were the erratic policies and misunderstandings regarding lands reserved for the Osages, Cherokees, and whites. Nuttall reported that "a number of families were now about to settle, or rather take provisionary possession of the land purchased from the Osages, situated along the banks of the Arkansa . . . a tract in which is embraced a great body of superior alluvial land. But, to their disappointment, an order recently arrived, instructing the agent of Indian affairs to put the Cherokees in possession of the Osage purchase, and to remove them from the south side of the river."[172]

On December 18, 1819, Nuttall arrived at the Cadron Settlement. The four days he spent there in March were mostly consumed with enjoyable excursions in the surrounding lands. During this visit, though, likely due to the icy weather and his continuing weakness from his bout with malaria, he was largely confined for more than two weeks to a "very ill provided" tavern that was drafty due to the "hundreds of crevices still left open" in the log walls of the rooms and "crowded with all sorts of company." Nuttall was irritated to find that "every reasonable and rational amusement appeared here to be swallowed up in dram-drinking, jockeying, and gambling" and that "our landlord, in defiance of the law, was often the ring-leader of what was his duty to suppress." While Nuttall was "perfectly steeled against games of hazard" he was nevertheless "somewhat mortified to be thus left alone, because of [his] unconquerable aversion to enter this vortex of swindling and idleness."[173]

On January 15, 1820, Nuttall arrived at Arkansas Post amidst a winter storm of snow, hail, and a heavy frost on an Arkansas River that was lower than the oldest settlers could remember it had ever been. The town had undergone important changes in the year since Nuttall had been there. When Arkansas became a U.S. territory in March 1819, Arkansas Post became the capital and Nuttall witnessed new territorial governor James Miller going to town on his "handsomely fitted" boat.[174] The new capital also had a weekly newspaper to serve a growing literate professional population. Nuttall noted with approval that the press was the "herald of public information, and the bulwark of civil liberty" and that the population was growing due to "interest, curiosity, and speculation" that had "drawn the attention of men of education and wealth toward this country, since its separation into a territory." He observed the presence of new professionals such as "lawyers, doctors, and mechanics" as well as "the retinue and friends of the governor, together with the officers of justice" that "added . . . essential importance to the territory, as well as to the growing town."[175] Nuttall did not think that the choice of "Arkansas" for the name of the town was a good one since the "name [is] by far too easily confounded with that of the river, while the name Osark, still assumed by the lower villagers of the Quapaws, and in memory of whom this place was first so called, would have been perfectly intelligible and original."[176] Nuttall's health must have improved by this time, as he spent two days exploring the prairies around Arkansas Post before departing on January 19 on the barge of Monsieur Notrebe.[177] Thus, one year after his arrival, Nuttall "bid farewell to Arkansas."[178]

Chapter Five

A Savage Sort of Country

GEORGE W. FEATHERSTONHAUGH'S ARKANSAS EXCURSION, 1834

THE EXCITEMENT WAS PALPABLE as they crossed the Mississippi River from Illinois to St. Louis. Fenston remarked that as they crossed this "noble river" he was "exceedingly gratified with the magnificent site" and that "little aid from the imagination" was needed to "make it one of the most pleasing [they had] ever met with."[1] Yet his imagination did run wild with thoughts of the early French explorers, such as Father Louis Hennepin and René-Robert Cavelier, Sieur de La Salle, who had ventured across the mighty river. He envisioned St. Louis as a French cultural landscape and imagined himself walking through streets with French names complete with shops run by the descendants of the "enterprising Canadians who first discovered and settled these shores." Deep was his disappointment when he discovered that St. Louis had become Americanized. The shops bore a "common-place appearance" and lacked French names.[2] He received "avaricious looks" from the "numerous Yankee storekeepers" and found their stores filled with "European goods from the Atlantic States." He was disappointed that "all the romance of Canadian cottages, old French physiognomies, and crowds of Indians walking about, that had been flourishing in [his] imagination, was completely dispelled." His horror soon grew when he stepped into a local tavern and found it "filled with vagabond, idle-looking fellows, drinking, smoking, and swearing in *American*." He lamented that "everything looked as if we had reached the terminus of civilisation."[3]

This was not George "Fenston" Featherstonhaugh's first encounter with an element of American society that he found revolting. Since his departure from Baltimore on August 1, 1834, he had ridden in stagecoaches and stayed in taverns in Virginia, Tennessee, and Kentucky where he repeatedly encountered and incessantly complained about gambling, swearing, smoking, tobacco-spitting, fighting, drunken American scoundrels and the wretched food and dirty lodgings that he endured. The newly appointed Geologist to the United States was on a government-sponsored expedition to conduct a geological survey between the Missouri and the Red Rivers. The Englishman, who was known as Fenston, had lived in the United States for nearly thirty years, but he had not ventured through the southern states until this journey. Fenston was eager to leave crowded stagecoaches behind and embark with a horse and wagon into the wilderness of Arkansas. It was with anticipation of better times ahead then that, after about two weeks visiting the surroundings of St. Louis, Fenston and his adult son George purchased a Dearborn wagon and an "elegant" and "good-tempered" horse that they named Missouri and set out for Arkansas.[4]

Southeastern Missouri

Fenston, his son George, and their horse Missouri would spend ten days trekking through southeastern Missouri after departing St. Louis on October 26, 1834.[5] Like Henry Rowe Schoolcraft before him, Fenston imagined as he journeyed toward Arkansas that he was departing from civilized society and into a cultural and environmental landscape that was separate physically and socially. To Fenston's mind, he was about to venture into a "savage sort of country, cut off from everything like old society."[6] The final reminder of civilization was the noisy steamboats on the Mississippi River that Fenston could hear in the distance. He described them colorfully as "monsters of the waters" that could be "heard from a distance of several miles before they are seen, and which, when they appear, come on belching and soughing out from their metallic throats as if they were huge animals in their last agony."[7] The environmental landscape on the edge of this "savage sort of country" did not fail to impress. Near the river, Fenston found quails "so numerous and tame that they would scarce get out of the way with a crack from the whiplash" and was amazed by the "whirring and croaking of tens of thousands of cranes" and the "the flocks of wild geese that rival the cranes with their harsh trumpeting."[8] He was also impressed by the amphitheater of limestone around the town of Herculaneum, and at Iron Mountain exclaimed that "everything had the appearance of being metallic matter erupted from below."[9] His geological pursuits were satiated by the strata and formations in the region.

The mining activity in what was known as the lead district of Missouri provided an opportunity for comment on both the geology and the industry of the area. At Valles Mines, Missouri, Fenston found that miners were digging shallow pits that were between six and twenty feet deep. The "wasteful" and "confused" manner of this mining, performed by "brutal" French men who were "not disposed to conversation," left the landscape so pocked that it was difficult to drive their horse and wagon through it.[10] To the south at Taplitt's and Perry's Mines, Fenston and George spent the evening with miners who were "resolute young adventurers" and "quite intelligent and obliging."[11] Fenston enjoyed the conversation and entertainment so much that he broke out a bottle of old Cognac to share. Unlike the operations at Valles Mines, Fenston observed that the "greater energy" of the Americans has resulted in "almost the whole surface of the country [being] dug up into pits of various sizes."[12] This activity seemed more like quarrying than mining to Fenston. A young miner in charge of the operation allowed Fenston to be lowered in a bucket to inspect a pit that was over one hundred feet deep. Here Fenston witnessed the thick veins of lead in the strata beneath the surface. Displaying his national bias, Fenston remarked that the English succeeded with mining better than the French because the Englishmen were more familiar with mining and more "accustomed to [following] a regular system of work." But, he noted, the Americans with their perseverance and ingenious mechanical abilities were "beginning to do very well."[13]

In some parts of southeastern Missouri, Fenston approved of the cultural landscape and the people with whom he interacted. Mrs. Gallatin, with whom they stayed in Herculaneum, was described by Fenston as "a person of great worth" for whom he felt "great respect."[14] Yet near Mine La Motte, Fenston judged the wives and mothers of the miners to be "the most ignorant human beings [he] almost ever conversed with."[15] And near Greenville, he found poor settlers from Tennessee and Kentucky who were "feeble, emaciated, and sallow" from malaria, and hunters' cabins filled with "six or seven ragged wild-looking imps, and a skinny, burnt up, dirty female."[16] Fenston found it inexplicable that people living on such fertile ground ate the "same disgusting coffee, pork, bread, and butter three times a day."[17] He also noted that a transition was taking place in the population of the region from hunters to farmers. He talked with one hunter who explained to him that the settlement of farmers drove away the wildlife they depended upon. Or, as he

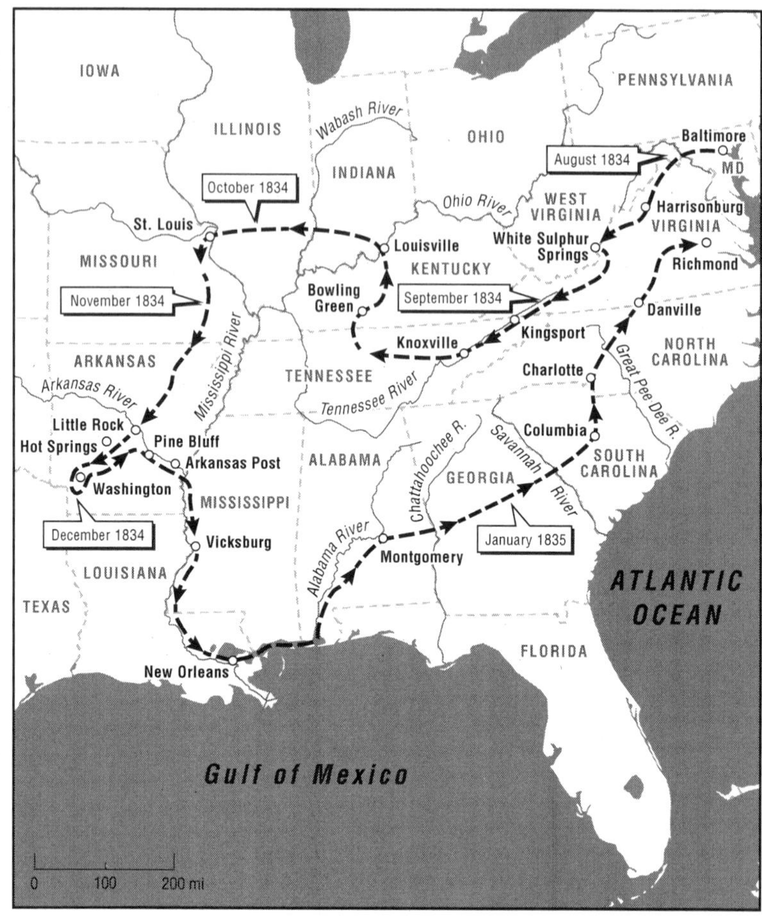

FIG. 5.1. Route of George William Featherstonhaugh, 1834–1835. Cartography by Erin Greb.

put it, "I seed the country warn't a going to be worth living in, and so I left the Gasconade Caywnty and comed here, for you'll mind that wherever the lawyers and the court-houses come, the other varmint, bars and sich like, are sure to quit."[18] Another source of tension between hunters and farmers was the hunter's practice of setting fires to drive the game out. Fenston traveled through a portion of burned and burning forest and found the hunters to be "indifferent to the devastation and inconvenience they cause" to the buildings, fences, livestock, and fields of the farmers "merely to get a few deer with greater dispatch than they would do by going a little farther into the country."[19] In present-day Ripley County, Missouri, Fenston and George experienced the fear of fires among farming families. The widow Harris and her children, "an amiable and good family," were alarmed after dark when "not a quarter of a mile from the house was a narrow edging of bright crackling fire, sometimes not more than two inches broad, but much wider when it met with large quantities of combustible matter."[20] The family rushed out to beat the edge of the fire with sticks along the line where it was advancing toward the house. With "great exertions," the family successfully fought the fire that threatened their home.

The Military Road of Northeastern Arkansas

On November 6, 1834, Fenston and George crossed the Current River on a ferryboat near the boundary of Arkansas and Missouri. Fenston described the river as a deep and "beautiful pellucid stream of from 70 to 80 yards wide" that contained salmon of twenty to thirty pounds, redhorse fish of ten to fifteen pounds, as well as buffalo fish, perch, and "large catfish of excellent quality."[21] The water was so clear that fish could rarely be caught until after dark. Fenston's first impressions of Arkansas were very positive. In addition to the beautiful river, he found the "house of entertainment" at which they stopped for a "tolerable" breakfast to be "very decent."[22] He was also pleased that a "military road" had been cut through Arkansas by the U.S. government. Of the military road, Fenston noted, "We found the trees had been razed close to the ground, and that the road was distinguished by blazes cut into some of the trees standing on the road-side, so that it could not be mistaken; a great comfort to travellers in such a wilderness."[23] Yet the road was not always easy to follow. Some of the settlers in the area had "quarreled about the direction of the Military Road" and had "taken the liberty to cut roads resembling it, and blazed the trees, to their own cabins."[24]

With their horse, Missouri, pulling their wagon, Fenston and George followed the road as best they could as it ascended from the Current River valley through a series of rocky knolls and into the forest. Fenston was impressed by the "excellent wooden bridge constructed in the best style" that spanned the Fourche River in present-day Randolph County.[25] Late in the day, after unintentionally following one of the many cutoffs that the settlers had created from the military road, Fenston and George arrived at the Russell household.[26] They were greeted by "two wild-looking urchins of boys trailing a beeve's head through the woods to bait a wolf-trap."[27] The travelers shared a room that evening with "old Mrs. Russel, a discreet matron of at least seventy" and a "sickly, unhappy-looking girl, of, perhaps, eighteen." Fenston and George were amused to the point of laughter when "without uttering a word, these amiable ladies very deliberately went through the ceremony of unrobing and getting into the other bed."[28]

Fenston praised the environmental landscape of the beautiful and clear Eleven Point River and Spring River that they crossed the following day, but the cultural landscape of people and places they encountered were judged harshly. At Eleven Point River, Fenston was annoyed by the "sorry hovel" where they had breakfast and the "awkward flat boat" that was "conducted by a girl about 16" that served as a ferry across the river.[29] The landing was so poor that Fenston was relieved to make the crossing without ruining their carriage. Approximately one mile from the Spring River, Fenston remarked that the town of Jackson was a "wretched place which passes for the county town" and was inconveniently located away from the river.[30] In present-day Lawrence County, they spent the night at the abode of widow Newland, where Fenston griped that they were "most miserably provided for, and shown to a wretched, flockbed, neither long enough nor wide enough for two to lie down upon."[31]

After an uncomfortable night with little sleep, the men were eager to move on. Perhaps too eager. They came to a "deep and dry bayou" where they successfully navigated the steep downward slope with Missouri pulling the wagon.[32] But as they attempted to ascend the opposite bank too quickly, the wagon came apart, leaving Missouri, George, and the front half of the wagon at the top of the hill while Fenston and the rear wheels tumbled back to the bottom of the bayou. Fenston and George spent the next three hours mending the wagon and were forced to walk alongside their crippled conveyance for the remainder of the day.

Amidst "flocks of parroqueets screaming," the travelers passed through the "flattish" country of southwestern Lawrence County on an early November morning.[33] Fenston heard a goose trumpeting near the Strawberry River and "took it for granted he was calling us to breakfast." His "lucky shot" at the goose "put a ball into his neck close to his head," and he proceeded to a nearby cabin where he hoped he might find some cornmeal for cooking his fresh kill. Instead of the supplies they sought, Fenston and George found people who were "steeped in poverty and broken down by fever and ague."[34]

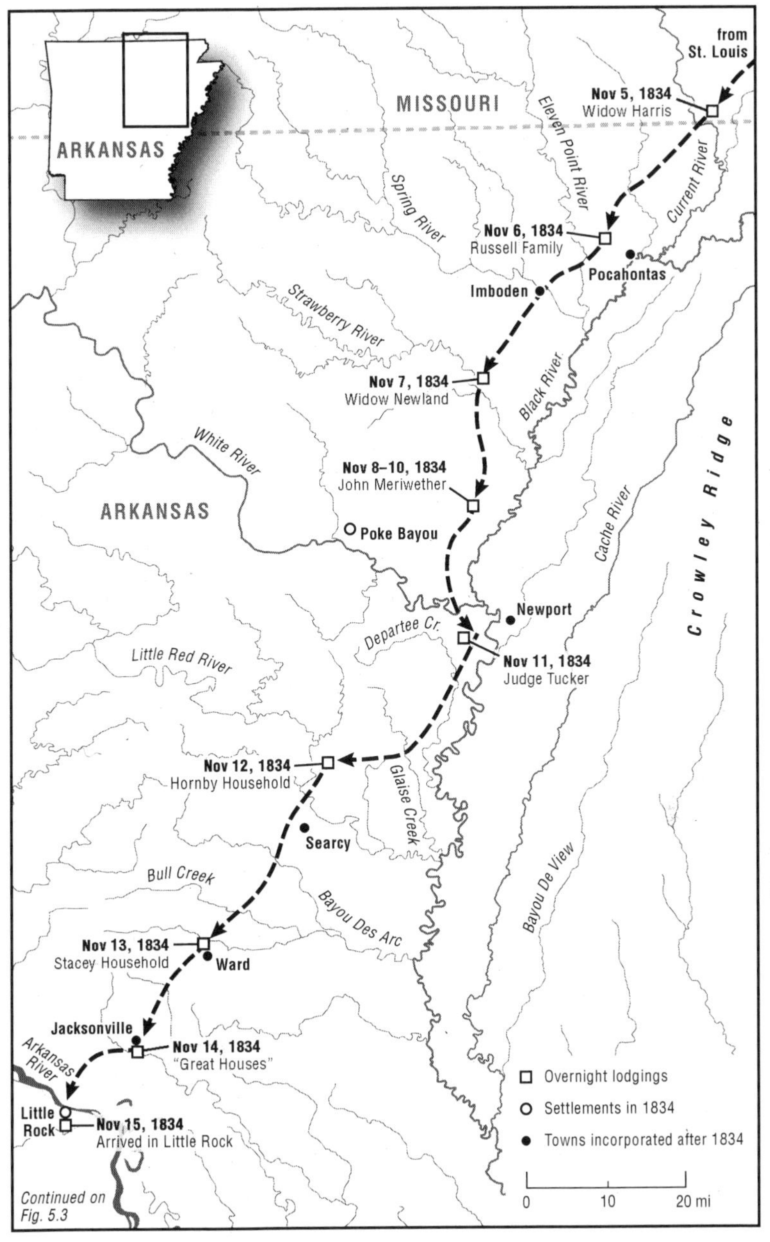

FIG. 5.2. George W. Featherstonhaugh in Northeast Arkansas, 1834. Cartography by Erin Greb.

A heavy rain soaked them during the day and their fragile wagon once again came apart. The men dragged the wagon pieces through the rain until they arrived at the log cabin of Mr. Meriwether near Curia Creek in northeastern Independence County.[35] Mr. Meriwether was a "hearty good fellow" who quickly assisted the sodden men and their horse. Mrs. Meriwether was described by Fenston unflatteringly as "six feet two inches" tall, with "an extraordinary dark, bony, hairy face" and "trimmings to match."[36] He joked that she might be mistaken for a South American soldier in women's clothing. This would not be the last time that Fenston revealed his misogynistic attitudes in his cruel characterizations and jokes about women who did not conform to his gender norms.

Fenston and George were welcomed into the Meriwether cabin where they dried themselves by a large fire, enjoyed a supper of fried pork and cornmeal, and were treated to a variety of eagerly dispensed tales. Mr. and Mrs. Meriwether were "two of the greatest talkers" that Fenston had ever heard and, having "not seen any travellers for a long time," viewed the arrival of the Featherstonhaugh men as a "fine opportunity . . . of delivering everything they had to say."[37] According to Mr. Meriwether, the route that Fenston and George had followed to the cabin was part of an "ancient Indian path" that ran from Vincennes, Indiana, to Natchitoches, Louisiana. The trail had been "adopted as the general road by white people moving in that direction," but it had also become a magnet for "desperate men" and "outlaws" who preyed on those journeying through the backwoods.[38] Fenston and George were told the tragic story of an "old bachelor" and "man of some property" named Mr. Childers, who was murdered while traveling the trail a few years earlier.[39] Fenston was shocked to learn that the man's bones still lay unburied not far from the Meriwether cabin, and, with a Meriwether son as a guide, spent part of the following day finding and burying Mr. Childers's remains.

The stories of vagabonds and villains were made more credible and urgent to Fenston with the appearance at the Meriwether door of a "tall, pale, thin young man" in a "dirty blanket coat."[40] The man told a story about his misfortunes and was given some sweet potatoes by Meriwether and a half dollar by Fenston. Mr. and Mrs. Meriwether judged the stranger's story to be "very unsatisfactory" and proclaimed the man and his companion to be "a couple of vagabonds" who were following Fenston and George with "evil intentions." Fenston and George, sufficiently warned to be "vigilant" against the "heap of villains" in the territory of Arkansas, slept with their trunks against their door to allay any suspicions they held toward their hosts and fellow travelers.[41]

The wagon was repaired once more with the assistance of Mr. Meriwether, and Fenston and George continued their journey southwesterly toward Little Rock. Accompanying the men as they departed the Meriwether household was an enormous flock of wild pigeons that was "many miles long" and so thick that it obscured the daylight. The flight of the pigeons produced a wind and rustling sound that Fenston compared to a waterfall, and that made their horse, Missouri, so nervous that he would "stand still and tremble in his harness" until they passed.[42] In addition to the disconcerting mass of pigeons, Fenston and George were uneasy about the "raw-head and bloody bones" stories they had heard from Mr. Meriwether and the shady presence of the dirty stranger who had appeared at the cabin.[43] The men adopted a defensive traveling strategy in which only one of them remained with the wagon while the other rode ahead or to the side to identify and flank potential attackers. When they encountered the suspicious strangers, Fenston decided to put on an aggressive posture and test their intentions.

> A couple of miles farther on we saw them together; and hearing our wheels, the unknown fellow turned to look at us, and spoke to the other, who did not turn round, which we construed unfavourably, perhaps putting a wrong construction upon everything they did, as I observed at the time. I now determined to get before these fellows, and putting the horse on at his best pace, with our rifles prepared, we came up to them and accosted them. Each had a gun ready cocked. The unknown fellow hung down his head; but putting a close question to him, he raised it to answer me, and I must say that a more hang-gallows-looking phiz I never saw. We now pushed on, my son driving, whilst I kept my face turned to the men, but they made no movement of an extraordinary character.[44]

The tense day of travel concluded when the sun set as they reached and crossed the White River. Fenston remarked that the river was "one of the most important and beautiful rivers of North America."[45] Despite the ferry operator's recommendation that the men would find "first-rate accommodation" with Judge Tucker, Fenston was disappointed to find that the Tuckers lived in "one of the most dirty and unprovided holes we had yet got into." The family was recovering from malaria, and Judge Tucker appeared to Fenston to be "poor and broken-spirited" though "civil and communicative." Fenston remarked on his pity for the children who were "bred up in dirt" and thus "knew not what cleanliness meant."[46] On top of the squalid setting, the sense of danger must have remained for Fenston and George. Judge Tucker regaled the Featherstonhaughs with additional details about the murder of

Mr. Childers and the brutality of backwoods justice. Moreover, the suspicious stranger who had been pacing them that day appeared momentarily at the Tucker doorstep and was deemed "a bad fellow" by Judge Tucker.[47]

Fenston and George departed the Tucker household near the banks of the White River on the morning of November 12, 1834, and traveled the remaining fifty to sixty miles to Little Rock over the next three days. Poverty and illness were common characteristics of the cultural landscape in this region of Arkansas. Fenston was alternately disgusted and dismayed by the state of society that he witnessed. One of their overnight hosts near the Little Red River, a Mr. Hornby, provoked acerbic commentary.[48]

> Hornby was a squalid, half-negro looking, piratical ruffian from Louisiana, living in a wretched, filthy cabin, with a wife to match. . . . This fellow never opened his mouth without uttering execrations of the worst kind. In this den, which had only one beastly room, we were obliged to stay, and suffer the low conversation of this horrid fellow. Some bits of filthy fried pork, and a detestable beverage they were pleased to call coffee, were set on a broken, dirty table . . . by the light of a nasty little tin lamp. . . . We passed a most disgusting night, the whole party lying down on the floor; and from the appearance of every thing around me, I should certainly, if I had been alone, have expected an attempt on my life. A place better fitted for the nefarious practices of such a set of desperate-looking human beings I never saw.[49]

After making a quick exodus from the Hornby residence the following morning, Fenston and George encountered another destitute family. Yet Fenston's judgment of the Morse family was more sympathetic.

> They had emigrated from Tennessee in the month of May last, and had been ever since so completely prostrated by the malaria, that at one time there was not, during two whole days, a single individual of them able even to draw water for the family. A more sickly, unhappy set of creatures I never beheld; livid, emaciated, helpless and all of them suffering extreme pains and nausea from an excessive use of calomel: on the floor were laid the father and five of the children, still confined to their beds; but the mother, a kind, good-hearted woman, finding that we were travellers, and were without any thing to eat, ordered one of the boys, who was still excessively weak, to show us where we could get some Indian corn, and how we could pound it so as to make a hoe cake. . . . These good people, who were

> half broken hearted, and who sighed after their dear native Tennessee, as the Jews are said to have done after Jerusalem, would not receive any compensation until I forced it upon them.[50]

Although the people in the area northeast of Little Rock were mostly "sick and miserable" and among the "poorest classes of Tennessee emigrants," Fenston found the ridges, rock formations, and wilderness landscape to be fascinating.[51] The environmental landscape of rough topography and dense vegetation, coupled with "painfully hot" temperatures, made traveling the final stretch of the road to Little Rock somewhat treacherous, but atop one rise along the way, Fenston proclaimed the view to be "one of the most striking pictures of wild American scenery" he had ever seen.[52] Another "delightful object" for the travelers to behold was the sight of the "far-famed Arkansa" river.[53] Fenston remarked that "the river was a delightful object to us; at length we saw the waters gliding along, that rise amidst the glens and valleys of the Rocky Mountains, and, to our great satisfaction, also beheld the town of Little Rock on the opposite side of the river."[54] Fenston and George were relieved to arrive at Little Rock where they hoped to enjoy better company and accommodations than they had experienced since leaving St. Louis.

Little Rock and the Maumelle Mountain

The Featherstonhaughs would spend nearly two weeks in the vicinity of Little Rock. They arrived feeling grateful, contented, and "in fine health and spirits."[55] Though the primary purpose of his excursion was to conduct a geological survey, Fenston included commentary and observations on the state of society and the cultural landscape and place features of Little Rock. According to Fenston, the town of five to six hundred inhabitants was "tolerably well laid out" with "a few brick houses, and a greater number of indifferently built wooden ones."[56] He noted that since Arkansas was on the frontier between Mexico and the United States it had become the "occasional residence of many timid and nervous persons, against whom the laws of these respective countries had a grudge."[57] Among the characters who had taken up residence in Arkansas were "*gentlemen*, who had taken the liberty to imitate the signatures of other persons; *bankrupts*, who were not disposed to be plundered by their creditors; *homicides*, *horse-stealers*, and *gamblers*." This collection of scofflaws "admired Arkansas on account of the very gentle and tolerant state of public opinion which prevailed there in regard to such fundamental points as religion, morals, and property."[58]

Despite these derogatory observations, Fenston was pleased to find an interesting assortment of people in Little Rock. At breakfast the morning after their arrival, Fenston sat across from a "dignified looking person with a well-grown set of mustachios, a round-about jacket, with other vestments made in the Spanish fashion, and a profusion of showy rings on his fingers."[59] When Fenston learned that the man was from New Spain, he became eager to talk with him in "his native tongue about his own country."[60] But the ostensible Spaniard devoured his breakfast quickly and left the room before Fenston had an opportunity to strike up a conversation. Fenston caught up with the man later and learned that he had recently arrived in Little Rock from Santa Fe and was working as a tailor due to the high wages he could earn performing that trade in Little Rock. This man seemed to Fenston to be "an odd character to begin with in Arkansas," but he was amused to find out later that, despite the man's clothing and mustache, he was "neither more nor less than a Connecticut Yankee of the name Patterson, who having occasion to leave the land of steady habits, had straggled to New Mexico."[61] A second man at the breakfast table arrived having "forgotten to wash himself and brush his hair." The unkempt man had a "tremendous red beard under his chin" and "drawled out . . . ungrammatical absurdities." Fenston asked the landlord about this man and learned that he was a "sportsman," which Fenston knew was a euphemism for a gambler who lived by "faro and rouge et noir."[62]

After two days of sharing a room with two gamblers from New Orleans, Fenston and George managed to find private accommodations with Reverend Stevenson and his family.[63] In addition to the gamblers and the sojourners, the reverend represented a third category of settlers with whom Fenston interacted in this place. Reverend Stevenson was a "somewhat dried-up looking individual, in a seedy-looking, light-coloured jacket, an old hat with a broken rim on his head, only one eye . . . and a rifle in his hand" who "turned out to be a much better man than his externals indicated."[64] At the Stevenson home, Fenston and George stayed in a "roomy bed-chamber" and found Mrs. Stevenson to be "uniformly obliging to us."[65]

One of the three other boarders at the house was a Swiss immigrant whom Fenston identifies as Mr. T. This fourth character in Little Rock society suggests how diverse the population had become by 1834. Mr. T. was a well-educated man from a "good family in Switzerland" who had been formerly "employed in one of the bureaux of the national government." Fenston was sympathetic to this educated European who was "half broken-hearted, longing to return to his native country" and laid low by his move to Arkansas. He explained that Mr. T. and a group of his countrymen "determined to abandon their country and found a colony in America" following the "revolution that overthrew the aristocratic families" in Switzerland. Mr. T. and his Swiss compatriots had decided based on a map that the "most desirable situations were to be found betwixt the 34th and 35th degrees of North latitude." Mr. T. and a companion were sent ahead to explore the situation and report back to their comrades in Switzerland. But after residing for months in the "interior of Arkansas" they ran out of money and received "no remittances nor communications of any sort from their friends at home." The Swiss men "fell into a perfect state of destitution, and led a most miserable life for a long time in the woods." After separating from his compatriot, Mr. T. arrived in Little Rock and managed to find work at the Land Office, "where his talent as a draughtsman made him very useful." Despite his employment, Mr. T. had "no prospect before him of ever getting out of Little Rock" where his income "barely sufficed to keep him alive."[66]

The Yankee poseur, the disheveled gambler, the weathered preacher, and the downhearted Swiss migrant epitomized the motley collection of Little Rock residents that Fenston observed in 1834. But Fenston also had the "good fortune to become acquainted with a few respectable and agreeable individuals" in Little Rock.[67] One of the men he met was Governor John Pope.[68] When Fenston was told where the governor lived, he proceeded to his house and knocked on the door. Mrs. Pope answered and explained that the governor was out in the woods searching for a sow and pigs that belonged to her. This activity seemed to Fenston to be appropriate for the governor of a place where "ceremony and circumlocution seem to have found no resting place amongst the inhabitants."[69] When they finally met, Fenston described Pope as "an unaffected, worthy person" who "has been of great service" and who lived "amongst the inhabitants in an unpretending and plain manner."[70] Fenston also met William Woodruff, the editor of the *Arkansas Gazette* and postmaster.[71] Woodruff was described as "always obliging" and "one of the most indefatigably industrious men of the territory."[72]

Though Fenston was impressed by Mr. Woodruff, he thought the American "passion for newspaper reading" to be troubling. He noted that in England "newspapers are too expensive for the poorer classes" and consequently their minds are not "distracted, enfeebled, and corrupted by *cheap* newspapers." Furthermore, English newspapers were "conducted by men of approved talents and fair character" and relayed to the public "all the intelligence that the inquiring spirit of a great nation requires, and assist[s] to keep down corruption rather than cherish it." Fenston was astonished and disturbed that Little Rock had "no less than three *cheap* newspapers, which are not read but devoured by everybody." Most troublesome of all to Fenston, the appetite for the "cheap poison" of newspapers made it "impossible that there should be any time or inclination for Bible reading." He concluded that this condition was the result of the "evil consequences of universal suffrage."[73]

At the Woodruff store, Fenston observed some of the "broken tradesmen, refugees from justice, travelling gamblers, and . . . young bucks and bloods, who, never having had the advantage of good examples for imitation, had set up a standard of manners consisting of everything that was extravagantly and outrageously bad."[74]

> Quarelling seemed to be their principal occupation, and these puppies, without family, education, or refinement of any kind, were continually resorting to what they called the 'Laws of Honour,' a part of the code of which, in Little Rock, is to administer justice with your own hand the first convenient opportunity. A common practice with these fellows was to fire at each other with a rifle across the street, and then dodge behind a door: every day groups were to be seen gathered round these wordy bullies, who were holding knives in their hands, and daring each other to strike, but cherishing the secret hope that the spectators would interfere.[75]

The contrast between the "respectable inhabitants" and the "desperadoes" was stark, but there was hope that the society was in a "favourable state of transition." Fenston explained,

> Disgraceful as these manners and practices must appear to Europeans, as well as to respectable Americans in the older states, it is also true that although the few individuals in Arkansas, with whom a stranger is happy to associate, sometimes express strongly their abhorrence of them, yet these things at present are so much beyond their control, and pass so constantly before their eyes, that although they do not cease to be offensive, yet you perceive that they lose with them that peculiar character of enormity in which they appear to men trained in well-ordered communities. They tell you, and not without some reason, that the rigorous criticisms that are fitted to older states of society are not strictly applicable here; that this is

> a frontier territory which, not long ago, was only inhabited by the hunter, the man who had no dependence for his existence but by killing wild animals; that the class which succeeded to this was composed of outlaws, who sought refuge here from the power of the laws they had offended; that where an absolute majority of a community consisted of criminals, gamblers, speculators, and men of broken fortunes, with no law to restrain them, no obligation to conceal their vices, no motive to induce them to appear devout or to act with sobriety, it was not surprising that such men should indulge openly in their propensities, or that public opinion—which, in fact, was constituted by themselves—should be decidedly on their side, and opposed to every thing that would seek to control them; that their consolation, however, was, that the worst of the black period had passed, that the territory was now under the government of the United States, and that a municipal magistracy was established in the town.[76]

The "respectable" class of citizens were not insulated from the violence and criminality that characterized the place during Fenston's visit. Mr. Woodruff, for example, explained to Fenston that he had tired of the outlaws who came to his store to argue and provoke one another. On one occasion, Woodruff decided to intervene. One of the young men threatened Woodruff and returned to his store in the evening. Woodruff engaged the man in a scuffle that resulted in a mortal wound to the ruffian. Woodruff showed Fenston the spot on the floor where the man "got his death by the awkward use of his own weapon." Woodruff was not charged with murder since "public opinion sided with [Woodruff], who was very popular at the period of our visit."[77] The violence was exacerbated by the widespread presence of pistols and Bowie knives. Fenston was told that most inhabitants were armed with "pistols or large hunting knives about a foot long and an inch and a half broad." These knives were "originally intended to skin and cut up animals, but . . . are now made and ornamented with great care, and kept exceedingly sharp for the purpose of slashing and sticking human beings."[78]

When the hooligans were not fighting, they were gambling and drinking and discussing their last brawl. Yet these amusements were not limited to the roughest of the inhabitants. Fenston reported, "So general is the propensity to gambling in this territory, that a very respectable person assured me he had seen the judges of their highest court playing publicly at faro" and that the "senators and members of the territorial legislature do the same thing."[79] A fellow traveler told Fenston that, when the legislature convened in town, the tavern where he was staying filled up with senators who "ordered some whiskey," "produced cards they had brought with them," and "sat up almost the whole night smoking, spitting, drinking, swearing, and gambling."[80] Again, Fenston attributed the behavior of the politicians to universal suffrage. He declared that "demagogues are already busy here" since "all the offices in the territory, except the few which are in the gift of the President of the United States, *are elective*; and candidates, if they will not wink at the vicious habits of the people, have little chance of success."[81]

Fenston anticipated that the cultural landscape of Arkansas might remain in this state for some time to come.

> Arkansas will have longer to struggle with the disadvantages which attend it than Ohio, Kentucky, and other frontier States of the Union have had, the settlers of which came from a respectable parentage, and with industrious views. These communities were never corrupted by the manners of the Gulf of Mexico, and their territories were never the refuge of outlaws. Amendment, therefore, will develop itself slowly in Arkansas, and society there will, for a long time, require a strong arm and a vigilant eye, like the wayward and spoiled child, who is compelled to conform to the hard conditions imposed upon him, until the natural love of order and justice is awakened in his heart.[82]

Fenston predicted that Little Rock could become a "respectable small town, have good seminaries of education . . . and afford agreeable society," but it could "never be very populous" and could "only have a limited share of trade" given that the town was "surrounded by extremely poor land" and was situated along a portion of the river that was "hardly navigable four months in the year."[83]

Fenston was also disappointed that the quality of the food was not any better in the capital than it had been in other parts of the territory.

> As to the manner of living here, I must confess, that although my stomach appeared to be broken in to any sort of fare before my arrival, yet I had encouraged hope that in the *capital* of the territory I should find an agreeable change. What must forcibly strike a stranger here, is the apparent total indifference of everybody to what we call personal comforts. No one seems to think that there is any thing better in the world than little square bits of pork fried in lard, bad coffee, and very indifferent bread. To this, without almost any variety, they go regularly three times a day to be fed, just as horses are fed at livery.[84]

He concluded, "We are the creatures of education and habit, and that the slovenliness and dirt, which are so revolting to those who are not accustomed to them, are not even seen by others." Fenston was also annoyed that people in Little Rock "never shut the doors" or bothered to mend broken windows, thus letting the drafty cold air blow through the shelter while they huddled by a fire. For the culture of this place to improve, Fenston expected that new settlers "from a healthier stock" who brought "examples of religion, probity, and sobriety of life" to serve as a model for "a regeneration of habits" would be needed.[85]

While visiting Little Rock, Fenston and George ventured on a three-day trip to visit the Maumelle Mountain, present-day Pinnacle Mountain. Along the way, the men encountered a group of German migrants who were recovering from malaria. Fenston noted that these people were "enfeebled and disheartened" and that their "enthusiasm for liberty and America had evaporated." It seemed to Fenston that this was "too frequently the fate of emigrants who are discontented with their native country."

> They render themselves unhappy at home by believing that everything at a distance from it is paradise; and when, after having sacrificed all their means and encountered continual privations and sickness, they have put an impassable barrier betwixt themselves and the soil they still love and the friends of their youth, they find they have accomplished nothing by expatriation, that they are in a foreign land of which they do not know the language, where everything appears barbarous to them, and that the sunshine they once inconsiderately thought belonged to the future, now, when they have paid the uttermost price for it, only beams in their sorrowful imaginations upon the past.[86]

The Germans were pleased that Fenston could converse with them and that he took interest in their adventures and predicament. Fenston gave them some money and advised them to avoid "the bottom lands where the malaria would constantly persecute them," and instead to settle on "an undulating country [with an] abundance of limestone and deciduous timber, and where the slopes of the hills would yield them grain and pasturage, and good springs."[87]

After leaving the "worthy" Germans, Fenston and George arrived at Maumelle Mountain, which they found to be a "magnificent rocky cone" that "resembles a pyramid."[88] The men rode their horses about two-thirds of the way up the mountain through a pine forest that skirted the base. The remainder of the ascent they accomplished on foot up the "naked, steep, and rugged" slope. Fenston recorded that "many acres of the western face were covered with huge blocks and fragments of the rock, without a plant or a blade of grass to relieve the rugged and desolate aspect it presented."[89] The view from the summit was "extremely characteristic of the wilds of America" and encompassed the "waving line" of the Arkansas River, the "rich bottoms" of deciduous trees that "stood in strong contrast to the pine timber growing on the ridges," the "high cones" to the northwest, and the "interminable wilderness of gray leafless forests" to the north.[90] Fenston predicted that the "great extent of these bottoms" would never be suitable for human settlement until they could be "protected by levees from the intrusion of the river."[91] As they descended into "one of those vast dark bottoms," Fenston observed that the "thick and lofty" trees were "painted a chocolate colour" up to about fifteen feet "by the red mud of the Arkansas." These "never-ending painted trees" were a constant reminder of "the wild power of the Arkansas" River.[92]

The day was nearing an end as Fenston and George left Pinnacle Mountain to find their way to a sawmill they had been told was near the river. Proceeding toward the north, the men found themselves at "a serious obstacle in a broad and deep bayou, called the Grand Maumelle."[93] The deep mud and the banks that were difficult to access presented them with a challenging ford. George led their trustworthy horse Missouri into the water first. Missouri swam "gallantly" to the opposite bank, but became mired in the bog that was "deep and plastic." The horse eventually freed himself "after many violent plunges." Fenston's horse also became "completely bogged" after crossing the river, but he lacked the "spirit" of Missouri and "seemed to give it up." Fenston recorded that the horse then "turned his eyes up to us in such a comical and reproachful way, that we simultaneously burst out a laughing." While the horse probably failed to see the humor in the situation, he eventually found his way out of the mud after "collecting his energies."[94]

Fenston soon began to worry about their circumstances. They had been told that the mill was three to four miles from the mouth of the Grand Maumelle creek. Yet, in these swampy surroundings with "an endless succession of stagnant pools" it was difficult to discern the location of the mouth. Fenston's anxiety increased as a "very cold night was coming on" and his son was "wet through" from crossing the river. Earlier in the day, Fenston and George had viewed the vast extent of this "frightful swamp" from the mountain peak and now recognized that they were lost in the dark and cold in a "horrid place" that extended for miles. If the prospect of spending the night shivering in a swamp was less than desirable, the presence of "countless gangs of savage wolves" was ample motivation to continue searching for signs of civilization. Fenston and George decided to move out of the quagmire near the river and strike a course through the forest that was "somewhat more dry and open." They were "amazingly cheered" to come across a "cowpath," and Fenston reasoned that "the cow that made that path must have some place to go to, and that something in the shape of man would probably be there." Despite losing the path multiple times, Fenston and George found a "small house on the river" where they received directions to the home of the mill operator.[95] Mr. Starbuck, who had built both a grist mill and a saw mill, was away when George and Fenston arrived, but they were greeted "in a very friendly manner" by Starbuck's in-laws, Mr. Elliot and his wife.[96] Fenston recorded that he and George spent a sleepless night at the Starbuck residence due to the frigid temperatures, the "yelling and howling of the wolves," and some "strong green tea that good Mrs. Elliot" had served them on their arrival.[97] Regardless of these discomforts, Fenston reflected on their good fortune in finding this place rather than remaining in the swamp through the night. After a day of exploring the surrounding landscape, including Crystal Hill and Mine Hill where "many persons, ignorant of minerals" believed they would find "precious metals," Fenston and George returned to Little Rock.[98]

Little Rock to the Hot Springs

Given his perceptions of Little Rock, one can imagine that it was with some sense of enthusiasm that Fenston "again put [their] little wagon in motion, and directed [their] course towards the hot springs of Washita."[99] Yet, the aggravations of Arkansas travel continued to afflict Fenston and George. The road leading to the southwest from Little Rock was "full of rocks, stumps, and deep mud holes."[100] In addition to these obstacles, the men found numerous trees that had fallen across the road. Fenston commented that these trees had "lain there many years, exhibiting an indifference on the part of the settlers unknown in the more industrious northern states." The fallen trees led to the creation of turn-outs. Fenston explained,

> When a tree falls on the narrow forest road, the first traveller that passes is obliged to make a circuitous track around it, and the rest follow him for the same reason. I have observed this peculiarity both in Missouri and

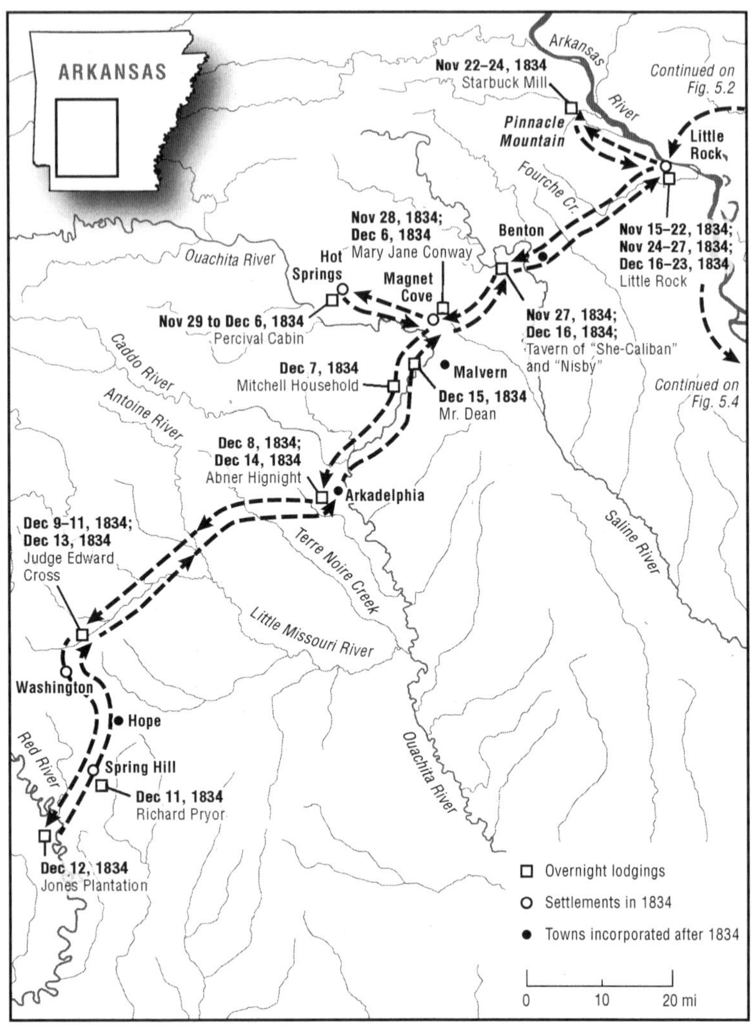

FIG. 5.3. George W. Featherstonhaugh in Southwest Arkansas, 1834. Cartography by Erin Greb.

Arkansas. If a tree is blown down near to a settler's house, and obstructs the road, he never cuts a log out of it to open a passage; it is not in *his* way, and travellers can do as they please because nobody would prevent their cutting it. But travellers feeling no inclination to do what they think is not their business, never do it. . . . But what makes this unjustifiable indolence . . .

> very absurd is that often when a track is established round the first fallen tree another obstruction shuts up this track, and so in a long period of time the established track gets removed into the woods. . . . These circuitous tracks are known by the name of *turn-outs*, and if you are inquiring towards evening how many miles it is to the next settlement, you perhaps will be told, "16 miles and a heap of *turn-outs*."[101]

That evening, Fenston and George reached a one-room tavern near present-day Benton where they spent the evening laughing and telling stories with four other travelers. The tavern was operated by two women that Fenston described as "a sort of she Caliban" who was assisted by "a stunted, big-headed negro girl, that from her size did not appear to be more than twelve, yet was not destined to see her twentieth year."[102] The woman that Fenston unkindly compared to Caliban, the beastly slave of Prospero in Shakespeare's *Tempest*, prepared a meal of "wretched coffee," "heavy cakes, one-third of which seemed to be mere dirt," and fried "little bits of fat pork." Fenston grumbled, "Everything was so dirty that my stomach revolted at what was before us" and "the old hag . . . saw well enough that we were disgusted; but as we said nothing, she made no remarks."[103]

Despite the terrible meal, Fenston and the other travelers found the African-American girl named Nisby and her interactions with the woman to be amusing. Fenston recorded, "The grotesque rags this creature was dressed in, and the broken-brimmed man's hat that was cocked on one side of her head, gave such an effect to the general attractions of Nisby . . . that she put us all into the very best possible humour, and we could not but break out into a chuckle of delight whenever she came into the room."[104] Fenston was particularly amused by Nisby's efforts to set the table and her subsequent dialogue with "the Missus." He recorded the following scene:

> "Why, how this gal has laid the table! Nisby?"
> "What's awanting, Missus?"
> "You ha-ant laid the table no hayw, you kreeter, you!"
> "I reckon I couldn't do it no better."
> "Why, whar on arth is all the forks?"
> "Why, the forks is on the table thar."
> "If you don't beat all—I mean the new forks."
> "I niver seen no new forks, you know that, Missus."
> "Whar has the kreetur put the forks, I say?"
> No answer

"Wahl! If you don't find the forks, I allow I'll give it to you!"

"I ha-ant put no forks nowhar. I niver seen no forks but them ar what's on the table; thar's five on 'em, and thar's not no more; thar's *Stump Handle*, *Crooky Prongs*, *Horny*, *Big Pewter*, and *Little Pickey*, and that's jist what thar is, and I expec they are all thar to speak for themselves."[105]

Fenston went on to explain that Stump Handle was "one prong of an old fork stuck into a stumpy piece of wood," Crooky Prongs was curled on each side, Horny was "a sort of imitation of a fork made out of a cow's horn," Big Pewter was a broken spoon, and Little Pickey was "something like a cobbler's awl fastened in a thick piece of wood."[106] Fortunately, Fenston and George carried their own knives and forks. When it came time for sleep, Fenston examined the "dingy-looking" bed and the "extraordinary bundle of rags of which [it] seemed composed." It appeared that "a score of persons" had slept on the coarse sheet, so Fenston pushed the bed rags onto the floor, "covered the pillow with a silk handkerchief," inserted himself "into a large flannel bag . . . made for the purpose," tied it closed around his neck, and wrapped himself in a "blanket-coat." He triumphantly noted that his efforts were in "defiance to the myriads of bugs that were confidently expecting their prey."[107] After a breakfast that was "more disgusting than the supper," Fenston and George left the "den of rags and nastiness" and forded the Saline River.[108]

Before they left Little Rock, James Conway, the surveyor general of the Arkansas territory and soon-to-be first governor of the state of Arkansas, provided Fenston with a letter of introduction to his wife, Polly, that requested her to host the travelers at their cottage in Magnet Cove.[109] Their experience with the "She-Caliban" and Nisby left Fenston determined to spend the next evening in more civilized company. Despite some difficulty locating the cove, the men arrived to find that Mrs. Conway was not ready for visitors. She was hosting a crew of carpenters and other workers who were constructing a cottage. Fenston was aware that he and George were "very much in the way," so they settled into a room that was "not yet enclosed, and was still open to the weather."[110] The next morning was spent collecting rock and mineral specimens along with "a great many Indian arrow heads made of a beautiful semi-transparent kind of novaculite."[111] Fenston observed that if the social conditions were more desirable in the area, then Magnet Cove would be "one of the most enviable estates in America." He was "full of admiration" for this "rare place."[112] A geologist could have spent many weeks collecting samples and studying the formations near Magnet Cove, but another rare place awaited them.

Later that day, Fenston and George arrived at "the Hot Springs of the Washita," which he remarked were "so much the object of curiosity to men of science, and so little known to the world."[113] Fenston was surprised that a place that attracted tourists seeking convalescence was a such a "ragged place" with only "four wretched-looking log cabins."[114] The men reluctantly stayed in one of the cabins that lacked furniture on its rough and uneven floor, but they made the best of the situation by constructing a table, borrowing some old chairs, and acquiring from the proprietor some skins and blankets for bedding. Following a supper of "little pieces of pork swimming in hog's grease, some very badly made bread, and much worse coffee" that was served by Mr. Percival, who had secured a monopoly as "entertainer of all visitors," Fenston and George built a fire in their primitive cabin and attempted to sleep.[115] A storm awoke them during the night, and Fenston discovered that the roof did little to prevent the rain from pouring inside and that the crawl space beneath the house served as a "good shelter to the various hogs belonging to the place, all of which had congregated immediately beneath us."[116] Despite the lodgings and food, Fenston noted, "Percival . . . was a good-natured man, could talk about things that interested us, and promised to look up some venison for another time."[117] Fenston also remarked with wry humor, "This was our first night at the Hot Springs of the Washita, but happily we were not invalids."[118]

As William Dunbar and George Hunter had done before him, Fenston occupied himself at the hot springs by observing and describing the mineral deposits, investigating the structure of the surrounding travertine, making measurements of the temperature of the water, inspecting the plant life, taking excursions to the surrounding ridges and peaks, and otherwise engaging in scientific observation. As a bonus to this scientific revel, he was also treated to a partial solar eclipse while at the hot springs. The geologist was not disappointed by his findings. On one of his jaunts, he arrived at "one of the wildest regions imaginable and singularly curious" where he found that "the mineral structure of this part of the country is as curious and rare as anything that has yet been seen."[119]

> The curious gradations of this siliceous matter, in the forms of old red sandstone, flint, hornstone, and quartzose rock, had interested me much: but my admiration was unbounded when I discovered that all the ridges and coves of the broken country I was now wandering in, were composed of a beautiful novaculite of a pearly semitransparent nature, indeed quite opalescent in places, lying in vertical lamina so brittle and so closely packed

> together, that it was very difficult to detach a piece even six inches long without the aid of proper tools; but when detached, the rock presented singularly pure glossy natural faces, and was occasionally tinged, in a very pleasing manner, with metallic solutions.[120]

In addition to his scientific endeavors, Fenston enjoyed bathing in the hot springs amidst the "picturesque effect produced upon the slope of the ridge by the volumes of vapour proceeding from so many fumeroles."[121] Fenston was also "amused" by the uses that the settlers made of the hot springs.

> The facility of obtaining hot water was fully appreciated by them, for they never seemed to boil any water for any purpose, nor to drink any cold water: a tree, smoothed off on the upper side, was laid across the stream at a narrow part, so that they could easily cross and supply themselves for the purpose of washing their clothes, and on a shelf, near the door of each cabin, was always a pail of mineral water with a gourd to drink it from.[122]

Fenston interacted with some of the hunters in the area and was entertained by dramatic stories of bear hunts past. One dedicated bear hunter explained his practices to Fenston.

> In summer, when there is no mast, Bruin is thin and hungry, and boldly intrudes upon the settlements, where there are any, to devour the hogs. If the settler catches him on his grounds he kills him, but he is too meagre and his skin is too light to tempt him far from home; he chooses another season for that, when the bears are fat, can surrender a good skin and from twenty to twenty-five gallons of oil, and have retired to the rich bottoms where the cane-brakes are. Then out he sallies, prepared for an absence of several weeks, dressed in a jacket and leggings of buckskin, for garments of any other material would soon be torn from his back by the briars. When he gets to the scene of operations he kills two or three buffaloes, if he can, for their skins, which he hangs up on poles in the form of a tent, leaving one side open in front of his fire, towards which his feet are placed when he sleeps. This is also his storehouse: his skins, his meat, his oil, are all deposited here, until their accumulation induces him either to take them home or send them by an assistant. As to what is called bear's meat, it is literally nothing but the fat of the omentum. The fleshy part is all given to the dogs. Of this fat, which the hunters call *the fleece*, they are ravenously fond, preferring it to everything else on account of its sweet taste, and because they can eat a great deal without incommoding themselves. Occasionally

> the hunter regales himself with venison when he is in a country where the deer abound, but pleasure with him is made subordinate to business, and it will take him as much time to kill and flay a deer of the value of one dollar, as it will to secure a bear worthy of twenty.[123]

On December 6, 1834, thirty years to the day after William Dunbar and his party arrived for their investigation of the hot springs, Fenston and George left the hot springs and returned to Magnet Cove to spend the evening with Mrs. Conway before continuing their journey toward Texas. Upon departing the hot springs, Fenston noted that "humble as the lodgings assigned to ourselves and the hogs had been, and rude as was our fare, yet nothing could be more obliging than the conduct of everybody to us."[124]

Southwest Arkansas to the Red River

From Hot Springs, Fenston had hoped to continue in a westward direction through the Ouachita Mountains and to Fort Towson near the Red River in present-day Oklahoma, but he would need a guide to do so since "all roads of every kind terminate at the Hot Springs; beyond them there is nothing but the unbroken wilderness, the trails and fords of which are only known to a few hunters."[125] The potential guides were all busy with the bear hunting season though and none could be persuaded to give up the hunt to lead the two gentlemen through the wilderness. Fenston and George decided that going alone would be a bad idea given the cold weather and the difficulty they would have finding their way and acquiring food. Instead, they agreed to follow "a more frequented and practicable route."[126] The route they would follow cut across the Arkansas counties of Clark, Hempstead, Pike, and Miller in a southwest direction toward the Red River boundary with Mexican Texas.

Their first evening on the trail was spent at the Mitchell home near Prairie Bayou.[127] Fenston's commentary on the lodgings and food at this household repeated a familiar theme. Given all of the places that Fenston had encountered thus far that he found to be "wretched," it is notable that Fenston described this as "one of the most wretched places we had yet met with in our journey."[128] He grumbled that the "supper consisted of some pieces of dirty-looking fried pork, corn-bread eight days old, mixed up with lumps of dirt, and coffee made of burnt acorns and maize."[129] James Conway, soon to become the first governor of the state, happened to stop in at the Mitchell home as Fenston and George were attempting to swallow the repulsive meal. Conway "laughed at [their] fastidiousness" and showed them how to drink the corn-coffee by "nipping his nose with his fingers and swallowing it exactly as if it had been castor-oil."[130]

Fenston and George realized that their wagon was in desperate need of repair and would probably not survive the remainder of the journey to the Red River. Consequently, they left the wagon and their trunks behind with Mr. Mitchell and acquired a second horse and saddle. Although the accommodations and other cultural attributes of the place had been dreadful to Fenston's eyes, he found the surrounding environmental landscape of southwest Arkansas to be very attractive. He described the views as "very beautiful" along the "fine wild romantic ride" through "broken hills" and "numerous streams" that "flowed through limited bottoms of great fertility."[131] The ride was also enhanced by the abundant candleberry myrtle on the surrounding knolls and the presence of "numerous flocks of well-grown wild turkeys" that "often came strutting across the road showing their beautiful glossy plumage to the greatest advantage" and then took flight "with as strong a wing as the wild-goose, wheeling around and then alighting upon the tallest pine trees."[132]

Near present-day Arkadelphia, Arkansas, the Featherstonhaughs arrived at the brick house of Jacob Barkman and his wife, Rebecca.[133] Fenston was amused by the mannish characteristics he witnessed in Rebecca Davis Barkman.

> I have never seen any one, as far as manners and exterior went, with less pretensions to be classed with the feminine gender. All her accomplishments seemed to me to have a decided learning the other way. She chewed tobacco, she smoked a pipe, she drank whiskey, and cursed and swore as heartily as any backwoodsman, all at the same time; doing quite as much vulgarity as four male blackguards could do, and with as much ease as if she had been an automaton set to do it with clockwork machinery. She must have been a person of surprising powers in her youth, for I was informed that she was now comparatively refined to what she had been before her marriage; at that period, so full of interest to a lover, she was commonly known by the name of old Davis's "She Bar."[134]

Notwithstanding her coarse appearance and habits, Fenston was pleased with Mrs. Barkman's "good nature to [them]" as well as the "excellent" dinner of "fat boiled ribs . . . with good bread" that she prepared.[135]

Fenston and George departed the Barkman residence on December 8, 1834, and continued their journey through Clark County on a southwesterly course. The men visited an ancient Caddo mound and speculated that the location must have been "a sweet sequestered situation" for the Indians due to the "good fish" in the river, the abundant game, and "a loose soil of the greatest fertility."[136] Fenston noted that he and George were "exceedingly pleased with the scene around us" due to the sun that was "shining brilliantly," the "flocks of parroquets" that were "wheeling and screaming around," and the "trumpet tone of the ivory-billed woodpecker" that they could hear frequently.[137] After crossing Terre Noire Creek and several other large creeks during the afternoon, the men arrived at the cabin of Abner Hignight, an early settler of Clark County.[138] Fenston described Hignight as a "famous" hunter who "lived in a solitary log cabin that had once been the court-house for the county of Clark" and was an "honest" and "soberly-disposed person."[139]

At the Hignight residence, Fenston and George encountered a group of "sportsmen," or gamblers, whom Fenston labeled "knights of the faro and rouge et noir tables."[140] The leader of the gang was a Mr. Tunstall. During his stay with John Meriwether in Independence County, Fenston had been warned about Mr. Tunstall. According to Mr. Meriwether and others, Tunstall was "said to be a very enterprising man, to possess some property, but to indulge excessively in horse-racing and cards."[141] Apparently, Tunstall was known to travel with others who "passed for travellers like himself, but who, in fact, were in his pay, for the purpose of inciting others to play and to procure him bets."[142] Tunstall told Fenston that he was returning from horse races near the Red River where government lands were being sold. He lamented though that it was "dull times" since "people seemed to be thinking of nothing but going to Texas."[143] As they talked while supper was being prepared, the other men with Tunstall pretended not to know him. Fenston found Tunstall's conversation with him to be "sensible and entertaining" and deduced that Tunstall was attempting to "inspire [him] with a favourable opinion of himself."[144] After supper, one of Tunstall's confederates took out a deck of cards and two others joined him as one of them drawled "I reckon I'll take a hand." Tunstall continued to chat with Fenston by the fire for a while before turning to him and "in a very winning manner" saying, "Well, I don't care if I take a hand, if you do." Fenston replied that he and George were fatigued and were going to go to bed soon. One of the men at the table then turned to Fenston and said, "Mister, if you *prefar* roulette, I'll take one out of the box what I've got here."[145] Tunstall joined the men at the table and waited about fifteen minutes before pulling out some brandy, pouring it, and politely offering it to Fenston and George. When Fenston replied that they did not drink liquor but preferred milk instead, Tunstall poured the brandy back into the cask and the men packed up their cards. Fenston was pleased with himself for resisting "such a coarse trap . . . set in such a coarse manner" by these "low gamblers."[146]

The following morning, after a miserable night "stretched on some wretched boards," Fenston and George listened to the "contemptible wretches" boast about "all sorts of frauds and villainies" in which they had been engaged. The band dropped the pretense that they were strangers, and Mr. Tunstall "could not avoid seeing that [Fenston] was aware he was the head of a travelling gang of sharpers."[147] Before Tunstall and his associates departed, they managed to cheat a "foolish Irishman" out of his pony by filling him with brandy and then convincing him to swap the pony for a "huge raw-boned animal." Mr. Hignight encouraged the Irishman to hold on to his pony, but "brandy and ambition got the better of him."[148] Tunstall and his men quickly exchanged saddles and rode away laughing.

Abner Hignight was preparing for a bear hunt on the morning that Fenston and George continued their trek through southwestern Arkansas. Fenston was impressed by Hignight's preparation for the hunt.

> We . . . saw with admiration how perfectly he was prepared to supply all his wants during his absence, without assistance from any one. His dress consisted of a hunting jacket and leggings, made of skins tanned by himself, and secured by strings formed either of the same materials or the integuments of animals. He had a close cap on made of skin, a girdle round his waist, in which were stuck his hatchet and his butcher's knife, and a heavy rifle weighing sixteen pounds on his shoulder. He had two pack-horses to carry Indian corn for their subsistence, some necessary articles for himself, and to bring back the returns of his hunting. The most important part of his retinue consisted of eight dogs, which he valued very highly, especially the old ones, on account of their great sagacity and prudence.[149]

Fenston regretted that he and George did not have time to join Mr. Hignight on the hunt, but they were pleased to hear the stories of such hunts from Mr. Hignight as he joined them on the first part of their journey the following day.

The environmental landscape of present-day Clark and Pike counties was described by Fenston as "good bottom land" that included a "great abundance of holly and laurel growing in every direction" along with "hills of moderate elevation of sandstone, with pine trees" and streams that were "transparent" with "gravelly bottoms."[150] The men crossed the Little Missouri River on a ferry boat and entered present-day Hempstead County on December 9, 1834. Fenston depicted the northern edge of Hempstead County as "a close low bottom, densely covered with cane, laurel, holly, and swamp timber of every kind" leading to a rise where "a new kind of soil appeared of a singularly waxy nature, and a dark black carbonaceous colour."[151]

Over the numerous streams that crossed the land, nine bridges had been built along the military road. Unfortunately, Fenston found that the bridges were useless, since the floor planks had not been secured by nails and had therefore drifted away with the first flood following construction. Fenston speculated that "this had been purposely neglected by the contractors who built the bridges that they might make a second job out of it."[152] The travelers who preceded the Featherstonhaughs on this road had ingeniously taken the remaining bridge planks and laid them across the river at shallow locations to enable them to cross. The military road did not impress Fenston.

> Thus have the provident cares of the United States government been frustrated, travellers placed in great danger, and a state of things produced which in a short time will render this route impracticable; for although this military road, opened at so great an expense by the government, has been made the county road in the counties it passes through, the overseers of the road pay no attention to it, and far from repairing the floors of the bridges, will not even cut a tree out when one falls across the road.[153]

As they crossed through Hempstead County, Fenston and George "made the unpleasant discovery" that the horse they had obtained from Mr. Mitchell was becoming lame.[154] Since they had left their wagon and supplies with Mr. Mitchell as collateral for the horse, and it seemed unlikely that the horse would make it to the Red River and back, George proposed that he return to Mitchell's with the horse to allow Fenston to continue the journey. Fenston agreed that this was the best course of action, so he and his son "after sharing each other's privations and being most faithful and inseparable companions to each other for four months . . . shook hands" and parted ways for the time being.[155]

After sunset on December 9, 1834, Fenston arrived at the home of Judge Edward Cross.[156] The Cross home was a "neat-looking wooden house, built upon the double cabin plan" sitting on a knoll about one half mile from the road.[157] When Fenston arrived, he observed "a cheerful light in the room to the right" and, after knocking on the door, he "modestly entered a neat parlour, and saw a lady and two gentlemen sitting near a blazing fire."[158] What amazed and impressed Fenston most about the Cross home was "a real carpet" on the floor that led him to feel "doubly full of respect for everybody and everything." Fenston presented a letter of introduction to the judge and was received with "the most unaffected kind reception."[159]

Judge Cross was described by Fenston as a "gentlemanly-looking person, about thirty-five years old" who was "well acquainted with everything that was going on around him," and a "man of candour" who "entertained, in common with his countrymen, the opinion that the United States were always in the right, and that all countries that differed with them were necessarily in the wrong."[160] Fenston found Mrs. Laura Elliott Cross to be a "lady-like and agreeable woman, full of the most amiable attentions" who prepared an "excellent" supper.[161] The evening was spent in conversation about the "geography of the country, its mineral resources, and the movements . . . in relation to the Mexican province of Texas."[162] Fenston learned that the judge considered his jurisdiction to extend nearly two hundred miles to the west.

> Although by a treaty between Mexico and the United States the boundary betwixt the two countries was settled to be by a north line to Red River, from where the 32nd degree of N. lat. intersects the Sabine River, yet, to the astonishment of the Mexicans, a pretension was set up by the American speculators that the river—which from time immemorial had been known as the Sabine, there never having been any other stream which bore that name—was not the Sabine, but that in fact another stream lying farther to the west, and which was known by the name of *Neches*, was the true Sabine. Unfortunately for this pretension, the 32nd degree did not intersect this Neches; but as the claim had been asserted, this was deemed of no consequence by the speculators, so the territory involved in the dispute fell under the jurisdiction of Judge Cross until the dispute was adjusted; for the land being valuable, American settlers had flocked into it, and there he was obliged to go to administer justice, traversing the wilderness alone, swimming the rivers upon his horse, and picking up his jurymen here and there, as he went along, to try his causes.[163]

After an excellent supper and an informative conversation, the evening ended with a particularly welcome sight for Fenston. He was shown to a bedroom with "a good fire, nicely plastered walls, and not a space in any part of them through which you could put your head to see what it was the hogs were making such a noise about." The bed was "nice and clean" with "two fine white linen sheets" and led Fenston to exclaim that "never did a man feel more delighted at drawing the highest prize in the lottery."[164]

The joy continued the following morning when Fenston "walked out to look at one of the most lovely countries [he] had ever seen." He admired the prairie land that was a "fine, gentle, undulating country" and the soil that was a "dark waxy substance" that was "as black as charred wood" with "a much more inky colour that the rich vegetable mould usually found in low ground."[165] Over breakfast, Judge Cross explained that his cornfields were part of a vast, natural prairie that stretched to the west. His curiosity piqued, Fenston accompanied Judge Cross on an "agreeable excursion in the neighbourhood" during which they stopped in the "little insignificant village of Washington, where the government land-sales were holding."[166] The men found Sam Houston staying at Washington and "leading a mysterious sort of life, shut up in a small tavern, seeing nobody by day and sitting up all night." Fenston did not wish to remain in Washington for very long.

> I had been in communication with too many persons of late, and had seen too much passing before my eyes, to be ignorant that this little place was the rendezvous where a much deeper game than faro or rouge-et-noir was playing. There were many persons at this time in the village from the States lying adjacent to the Mississippi, under the pretence of purchasing government lands, but whose real object was to encourage the settlers in Texas to throw off their allegiance to the Mexican government. Many of these individuals were personally acquainted with me; they knew I was not with them, and would naturally conclude I was against them.[167]

As Judge Cross and Fenston returned to the Cross home, Fenston was impressed by the environmental landscape that he described as "very lovely and desirable country" with "picturesque prairies, charming woods, and lively streams."[168] He found it disturbing that "one of the most salubrious parts of Arkansas" was being overlooked by emigrants on their way to Texas.

> Hundreds of thousands of acres of the very first quality, and which they could obtain at the insignificant price established by law of a dollar and a quarter an acre, are passed by as if they did not deserve their attention. Put in motion by the insidious arts of the unprincipled adventurers who have for a long period contemplated this great robbery of the Mexican government, and their cupidity awakened by the vision of magnificent farms *to be*

> *obtained for nothing*, they hasten on to a country possessing fewer advantages, little suspecting that they are but tools employed by their tempters to defend the plunder these have in contemplation. I never meet with wagons filled with these Texas emigrants, without looking upon the men as victims and the women and children as widows and orphans.[169]

On the morning of December 11, 1834, Fenston departed the Cross home and headed on horseback toward the Red River. Fenston made his way to Washington again and serendipitously crossed paths with a Mr. Pryor whom he had met on his visit the day before. Mr. Pryor was a "Virginian, who had moved into the neighborhood of Red River about three years before and had established a cotton plantation in Texas."[170] The two men were heading in the same direction, so they agreed to travel together, and Mr. Pryor offered to provide Fenston with lodging for the night at his cabin. The ride through Hempstead County was made even more pleasant by the fact that Fenston found Mr. Pryor to be a "gentlemanly and intelligent person" who was "*wide awake* to everything that was passing around him."[171] One of the topics about which Mr. Pryor was wide awake was the prevalence of land speculation and fraud. Fenston was told of settlers who were cheated out of their land by speculators who would outbid them when it came up for sale. In some cases, a speculator would approach a settler and tell them ahead of the sale that he intended to outbid him. Fenston learned that the settler then had "to choose . . . between abandoning the land where he has expended so much labour, and to which he and his family have become attached, or to make a ruinous compromise."[172] Thus, a settler might consent to allowing the speculator to purchase the land and then mortgage it from him. Fenston seethed that "in many cases the poor settlers have agreed to pay ten dollars an acre to these rapacious and unfeeling wretches, delivering to them the ready money they had prepared to pay to the government, and executing a mortgage to them for the remainder." The settler was then saddled with debt and "converted into the slave of a set of unprincipled harpies who make enormous profits by their nefarious transactions."[173] Fenston also learned that the agents at the land office engaged in deception to allow the speculators who purchased the land out from under a settler to do so at the government rate of a $1.25 per acre. This state of affairs seemed to Fenston to be the result of the American quest for the "almighty dollar." He remarked that among Americans, "wealth . . . must be had at any cost; and good faith and fair dealing, both public and private, are not to be permitted to stand too inconveniently in the way of its acquisition."[174]

While Mr. Pryor shocked Fenston with stories of the evils of land speculation in Arkansas, the men rode through a series of landscapes, including "sandy pine land," "a dead level of fine black land," and on to a ridge covered with oaks and pines that "assumed an astonishing height and diameter, such as [he] had never before seen out of Canada."[175] Fenston was impressed with Mr. Pryor's home. It was situated in the midst of a forest of large pine trees where Mr. Pryor had cleared a few acres, erected "an admirable fence," divided the plot into "regular compartments," and built "several detached buildings made of hewn logs, but finished in a very neat manner." Fenston was exuberant.

> On entering this precinct, at a distance of perhaps a hundred yards from the buildings, I hardly knew how to repress my admiration. I had been forming to myself an idea of a humble cabin hastily got together in the woods, when a villa of very neat proportions appeared before me, with a quadrangle bordered with plants here and there, regularly laid out into broad walks; whilst the squares between the walks, so far from having been ploughed or dug up, were still filled with the huge stumps of the pines that had grown there only eighteen months before. . . . Another compartment had been turned into an excellent vegetable garden, where all sorts of good things were growing.[176]

The surprises continued when Fenston approached the house and heard a piano—"a piano in the wilderness, within ten miles of a Mexican province!"

Once again, Fenston found himself in a household where he received a good supper, a good bed, and "hospitable attentions" from the lady of the house.[177] The only scene that appeared to cause Fenston some distress was the enormous pile of hundreds of large pine logs "without a single knot in them" that Mr. Pryor was in the process of drying and burning. Fenston understood that, without a saw mill in the area, Mr. Pryor had to resort to this action that Fenston noted would have "broken the heart of a regular timber merchant."[178] Fenston was pleased to learn that there was "talk . . . of building a church" and that the settlers near Mr. Pryor thus had a "cheerful prospect before them of establishing a social and moral colony of educated people in this part of Arkansas."[179] The example of the industrious Mr. Pryor led Fenston to pontificate about the contrasts between the landscape of educated versus uneducated settlers.

> The [uneducated], notwithstanding the "sovereign" privileges with which they are dignified, seem, wherever I have had an opportunity of observing

> them, to have but one object in view, which is the immediate gratification of animal wants. Order, cleanliness, propriety, seem never to be thought of; they build a rude cabin, they remain in it till it rots, they patch it up as long as they can, and only when it has begun to tumble down, build another as rude as the first. They live twenty or thirty years in the same place without discovering that they have a single moral want. Religion is never spoken of, and the Sabbath day to them is nothing but a day when it is a custom for the husband to shave himself, and the wife to go out a visiting. If an individual comes amongst them with higher views, they do not aspire to his standard but seek to drag him down to their level, as being exactly the situation they would choose if they were in his place, for nothing seems to appear more natural to democracy than dirt.[180]

Mr. Pryor and others of the educated class were to be commended, according to Fenston, for their attempts to "establish a rational mode of existence" since "the degraded state of things which prevails amongst the lower classes cannot improve of itself, but must grow worse from generation to generation, without the aid of living moral examples."[181]

On the morning of December 11, 1834, Fenston departed with a Mr. Williams, a native of Connecticut who was visiting Judge Cross and then returning to his cabin near the Red River. The men traveled about ten miles along the edge of the pine hills and the fertile plain of the Red River which Fenston noted was "considered to be of the very first class of cotton lands in this part of North America."[182] As the men rode through southwestern Hempstead county, Mr. Williams told Fenston about his adventures in Texas and Mexico. According to his story, Williams had joined James Long on one of his filibustering expeditions to conquer Texas between 1819 and 1821. After Long was killed by a Mexican prison guard in 1822, Williams joined forces with Benjamin Rush "Ben" Milam. For the past few years, Williams had been living alone in a cabin on Milam's Red River land grant. Although Fenston found Williams "a short thin man, looking much older than he was, from the effects of exposure and various hardships," to be "an interesting person," he was not sympathetic to the cause of the Anglo-American settlers in Texas, such as Long, Milam, and ostensibly Mr. Williams.[183] He remarked that the Mexican government understandably kept a "jealous eye" on the movements of men like Ben Milam since it was well known that "persons occupying land on the frontier consider themselves in the United States or in Texas, just as it suits their interests."

> They are Mexicans until they get a title from the Mexican Government, but as the Americans are the only settlers who give an intrinsic value to the land by their labour, it becomes the interest of every proprietor to encourage the annexation of the country to the United States, a measure, any serious attempt to consummate which, will be a severe trial to the Federal Union. Nor can the Mexicans be blind to the movement that is now going on in relation to the province of Texas, or fail to have their doubts about the fidelity of individuals situated as Colonel Milam is. Indeed all the persons who have possessions on the disputed line, being native-born citizens of the United States, may be considered as pioneers of the advancing Anglo-American population, and to be only waiting for favourable opportunities to indulge in their irresistible propensity to spread themselves over conterminous territories, with or without any title to them.[184]

Fenston predicted that "Mexico will find that it would have been easier to have kept them out, than it will be to turn them out."[185] Just ten months after Fenston and Williams rode through southwestern Arkansas, the Battle of Gonzales and the Siege of Bexar would serve as the beginning of the conflict that resulted in Texas's independence.

Fenston and his trusty steed Missouri crossed the Red River at Dooley's Ferry on December 12, 1834.[186] He was glad to have "successfully penetrated to this extreme frontier," but he was not impressed by the environmental landscape. He lamented that "nothing could be less beautiful or picturesque than the river and its shores."[187] The ferryman who ushered Fenston across the two-hundred-yard-wide river told him to move quickly once they reached the opposite bank, since the ground would "scarcely bear the weight of a horse, and might *suck* him in."[188] The situation improved soon as Fenston and Missouri traveled into present-day Miller County, Arkansas, to the cotton plantation of a Dr. Jones.[189]

The Lost Prairie, as it was known, was described by Fenston as "a tract of about 2000 acres of incredible beauty and fertility, bearing extraordinary crops of cotton, and gracefully surrounded by picturesque woods."[190] The cotton plants were particularly impressive. While the cotton districts through which Fenston had traveled so far contained "a low dwarfed bush not exceeding two feet high," the Red River cotton country was "filled with stately and umbrageous bushes five feet high, covered with innumerable pods resembling large white roses." The high-yield cotton, that he was told was called "Mexican white-seeded cotton," was "so dazzling white to look upon as to create rather a painful sensation in the eyes."[191] Fenston observed the layers of rich earth visible in a thirty-foot well and proclaimed that "it would seem impossible to exhaust a soil of this kind."[192]

The fertility of the soil and the productivity of the cotton crops encouraged a slave-based plantation economy that Fenston found reprehensible. When he arrived at the Jones plantation he was welcomed by the Jones family but found that Dr. Jones was away from home purchasing slaves. Fenston seethed that "the occupation of Texas by the Americans, where there are so many millions of acres of the most fertile cotton lands, will convert the old slave-holding part of the United States into a disgusting nursery for young slaves, because the *black crop* will produce more money to the proprietors than any other crop they can cultivate."[193] The hypocrisy of the slave owners in Texas was particularly galling to Fenston.

> To believe them, they have no motive but to establish "free institutions, civil and religious." Yet, in defiance of human freedom, just laws, and true religion, they proceed to consummate their real purpose, which is to people the country with slaves in order to cover it with cotton crops. The poor slaves I saw here did not appear to me to stand any higher in the scale of animal existence than the horse; the horse does his daily task, eats his changeless provender, and at night is driven to his stable to be shut in, until he is again drawn forth at the earliest dawn to go through the same unpitied routine until he dies. This is the history of the slave in Texas, differing in nothing from that of the horse, except that instead of maize and straw he is supplied with a little salt pork to his maize, day after day, without any change, until death relieves him from his wearisome existence.[194]

Fenston lamented the inability of the Mexican government to control the territory, and thus avert the spread of American slavery. The apparently inevitable independence of Texas and subsequent accelerated extension of slavery seemed to Fenston to be "one of the greatest misfortunes that could have happened to the human family in our times."[195] The settlers that Fenston encountered during his one-day excursion in the neighborhood of Lost Prairie appeared to have been "spoiled by the possession of land that merely wants fencing and ploughing." He noted that "any land that requires to be cleared and drained, whatever its quality may be, they consider a 'hard bargain.'"[196]

Fenston had decided before arriving at the Red River that he would not linger in the area or proceed further into Texas since, according to his sources, conflict between the Anglo-American settlers and the Mexican government seemed imminent. He also decided that it would be prudent to keep his thoughts on this subject to himself. Consequently, after reaching the westernmost point of his long excursion, Fenston "turned [his] back upon the fair and sunny fields of Texas, now doomed to the curse of slave-labour" and returned to Judge Cross's house on a "serene, beautiful, and soft . . . December morning."[197]

Over the next five days, Fenston retraced his path across southwestern Arkansas and returned to Little Rock on December 17, 1834. Along the way, he spent evenings with Edward Cross, Abner Hignight, and at the tavern of the "She-Caliban" and Nisby. At a stop at the Barkman house to feed his horse, Fenston heard the final word on Texas from Rebecca Barkman.

> The old lady, who was standing at the door, with her pipe in her left hand, and a comfortable chew of tobacco in her cheek, shook hands heartily with me, and asked me how I liked Texas, adding before I could give her an answer that she "could not see what folks was such [damned] fools as to go there for."[198]

Fenston and George reunited at the Mitchell household, where they collected their wagon, hitched up Missouri, and continued the return trek without delay. The men would spend the next week in Little Rock packing up specimens, updating journals, and otherwise preparing for the return to Virginia. Fenston noted that there was no need to spend any more time than necessary in Little Rock since they "found the same people and the same unvarying occurrences" and had "seen everything in the neighbourhood."[199]

A Steamboat from Little Rock to the Mississippi River

Their plan was to return to Virginia via Alabama, Georgia, and the Carolinas, since Fenston and George were "desirous of seeing other portions of the southern country."[200] They were faced with a dilemma, though. The rainy season was about to wreak havoc on the roads and make fording rivers difficult, if not impossible. A return trip via wagon thus seemed unwise. The choice to leave the wagon behind was an easy one, but parting ways with their horse, Missouri, was a much more difficult prospect. As Fenston explained, Missouri was "a beautiful animal, was docile, had served us faithfully, and we were unwilling to part with him." Fenston and George decided that George would "make Missouri the partner of his fortunes, and . . . follow an entirely new line of country," while Fenston would follow the Arkansas River to its mouth, proceed down the Mississippi River to New Orleans, sail to Mobile, and then journey through Alabama, Georgia, and the Carolinas via steamboat and stagecoach.[201] Fenston justified the difficult choice to part with his son by imagining the amount of territory the two men would cover.

> By taking these two distinct lines of country we should have an opportunity of examining 4000 miles more of the surface and strata south of the Potomac, an amount of observation which, added to the 2000 miles at least which we had already made, would furnish a great many data for forming an approximate view of the geology of the southern portions of the United States.[202]

Fenston also decided to invite the dejected Swiss immigrant, Mr. T., to join him for the remainder of the journey.

> [Mr. T.] was a person of considerable talent, and appeared to feel as if he were shipwrecked for life, and thrown upon a barren coast without any rational hope of ever being restored to society again, or of meeting a brother he had in the United States, but whom he was without the means of joining. I could not bear to see a gentlemanly person of so much merit left in such a painful and hopeless condition: if I had left Little Rock without him, I should have felt as much remorse as if I had abandoned one whom I was bound to protect; and having got into that sort of kind feeling, I thought it right to let in a ray of sunshine upon his existence, and proposed to him to accompany me. I imagine Mr. T. packed up his portmanteau with as much pleasure as I had done my own, and from that moment he became my companion for the rest of my journey.[203]

Timing was of the essence if one was to leave Little Rock by steamboat in late December. The Arkansas River was low and, as Fenston explained, "steamers, especially if they are bound down the river, sometimes only touch at Little Rock for an hour or two, and if a boat is missed at this time of the year a traveller, who has no other means of getting away, may be detained all the winter."[204] Fenston planned to remain in Little Rock, if possible, until after Christmas so that he could witness a ball at one of the taverns. In Fenston's judgment, most American Protestants "seem to prefer to desecrate than to celebrate the great Christian festivals," so he was eager to experience a Christmas Eve ball in Little Rock, where he mused sarcastically that "it was probable that all the devotional piety of the territory of Arkansas would

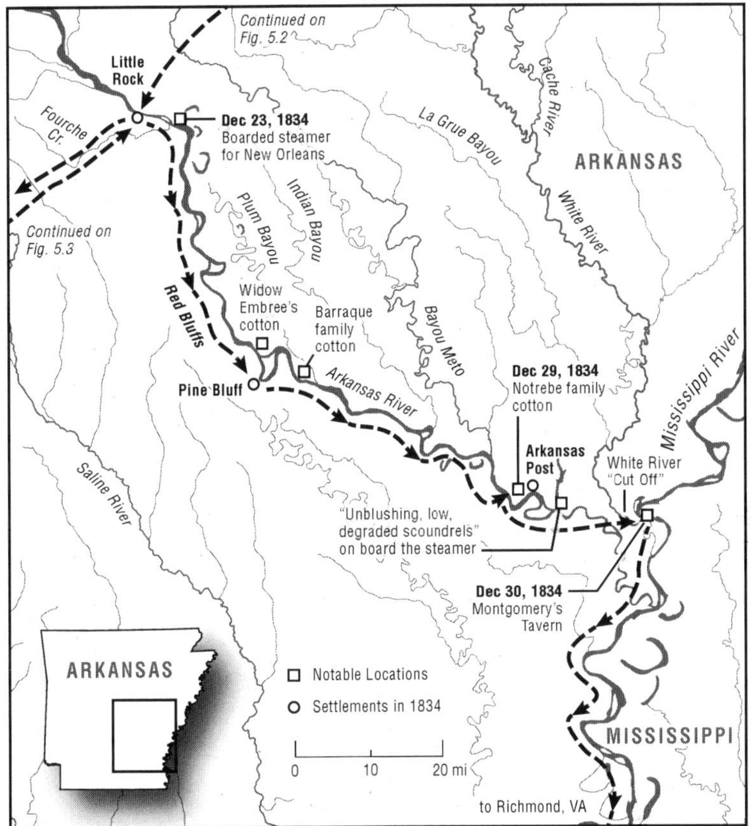

FIG. 5.4. George W. Featherstonhaugh in Southeast Arkansas, 1834. Cartography by Erin Greb.

break out upon the occasion."[205] The ball of the previous year was described in colorful detail to Fenston by a participant.

> There were about 100 men and 3 women. The men had their hats on, and danced armed with pistols and bowie knives, whilst the landlord, assisted by two of his people, with his hat cocked on one side, took pitchers of strong whiskey-punch round the room, and clapping the gentlemen on the back, gave them to drink. As this was the principal business of the evening, and the pitchers unceasingly went round, the whole party soon got amazingly

drunk, but were very good-natured, 'for there were only a few shots fired in fun.'[206]

Fenston's opportunity to witness the Arkansas Christmas bacchanal was lost, though, when he learned on December 22 that a steamer had arrived twenty miles downstream and would depart the following day. Fenston rushed ahead to catch the steamboat while George and Mr. T. followed with their baggage in the wagon. Following a breathless dash to the steamer through flooded lagoons and soaking rain, Fenston managed to secure passage. The captain agreed to leave a small boat behind with one of his men so that George and Mr. T. could catch up. After traversing the distance from Little Rock to the steamboat landing through boggy mud and swollen streams in a derelict wagon, the men got their baggage on the steamboat and Mr. T. and Fenston settled into their berths by dusk.

Despite their success at catching the departing vessel, the moment was bittersweet since, for Fenston, parting with his son was "the most painful part of the business." His fatherly emotions were a combination of worry about leaving his son behind "in a wilderness, without anyone to assist him" and pride in the ability of the young man and confidence that "he would do very well." Nevertheless, the "moment of parting was painful to both of us" and as Fenston "beheld [George] standing on the desolate bank of the Arkansas," he was "very much affected, and thought it would have been better to have spared [them] both such a moment."[207]

The steamer was underway early on the morning of December 24, 1834. Fenston was impressed with neither the environmental landscape nor the cultural attributes of his fellow passengers as he steamed down the Arkansas River from Little Rock to the Mississippi River. The course of the Arkansas River was "extremely serpentine," filled with snags and sawyers, and, in general, Fenston proclaimed, "nothing can be more monotonous than the country through which this muddy stream holds its course."[208] The river was also very shallow, so the steamboat ran aground frequently. Fortunately, the captain was experienced with navigation of the low river, and when the steamboat became stuck he "always succeeded in backing the steamer or forcing it through the mud."[209] Though the scenery was not particularly stimulating, the passengers on the boat provoked Fenston's characteristic acerbic commentary. He remarked that these "low persons" and "animals" who were traveling from the Red River to New Orleans "gave themselves unrestrainedly up to such beastly vulgar habits, even when at the table, that it became impossible to remain a spectator of their stercorarious proceedings."[210] Fenston and

Mr. T. attempted to "put matters upon a better footing," but their fellow travelers did not have the "slightest idea of there being such a thing as indecency."[211] One fellow passenger, or "young reprobate" as Fenston called him, named Mr. Powers was a twenty-one-year-old New Englander who was in "a constant state of intoxication" and "behaved in the most ungovernable and ruffian-like manner." Fenston had "cautiously abstained from having anything to do with him," but the "drunken puppy" became upset when Fenston failed to offer him some of his wine one evening.[212] Powers came at Fenston with a knife and threatened to cut his throat. Fenston recorded that he "never was more tempted to knock a fellow's brains out," but he calmed himself and told Powers that if the young man made one step towards him he would "put him to death on the spot."[213] Later that evening the "young brute became so beastly drunk that he lay down in a berth belonging to one of the other passengers and vomited upon his clothes."[214]

Down the river at Arkansas Post, the boat was boarded by another crew of "notorious swindlers and gamblers" who "lived by the most desperate cheating and bullying, and who skulked about alternately betwixt Little Rock, Natchez, and New Orleans, in search of any plunder that violent and base means could bring into their hands."[215] These "scoundrels of the worst class" included two American army officers who engaged with the others in "unrestrained indulgence of every vicious extravagance, night and day." Fenston described the scene when the men boarded as that of a "peaceful vessel forcibly boarded by pirates of the most desperate character."

> Putting on a determined bullying air of doing what they pleased because they were the majority, and armed with pistols and knives, expressly made for cutting and stabbing, eight inches long and an inch and a half broad; noise, confusion, spitting, smoking, cursing and swearing, drawn from the most remorseless pages of blasphemy, commenced and prevailed from the moment of this invasion.[216]

Fenston was concerned that confronting these men might result in a murder, so he appealed to the captain to enforce the printed rules for his vessel that called for passengers to be put ashore if their conduct was offensive to others. But the captain knew his customers. He told Fenston that he "did not pretend to execute" the rules because what Fenston complained about were "the customs and manners of the country" and that if the captain removed the men from the boat "he should never get another passenger" or any of the freight from the planters.[217] The captain explained one occasion in which he "put a disorderly fellow belonging to Vicksburg on shore" and "when he stopped there on his return [was] boarded by fifteen persons, armed with knives and pistols, who proceeded to spit in his face, kick him, and treat him in the most savage manner."[218] Fenston and Mr. T. were thus forced to endure and witness the antics of this "collection of unblushing, low, degraded scoundrels."[219]

The one positive aspect of the voyage down the Arkansas River were the settlers with whom Fenston interacted when the boat stopped to collect their cotton. Indeed, the primary purpose of the steamer appeared not to be collecting passengers but stopping to collect cotton bales to be hauled to market in New Orleans and beyond.

> These stoppages gave me frequent opportunities of looking at the country, and calling to see the different families, all of whom, by their affability showed how happy they were to offer civilities to a stranger who visited their country for the first time. The French families were delighted, too, that I could converse with them in their native language, and were in raptures when they heard that I had even been in Paris.[220]

Near Pine Bluff, Fenston recorded that the boat stopped to collect the cotton crop of widow Embree, who "appeared to be an active and respectable person and lived with some order and comfort in her double cabin."[221] About twenty miles down the river, the boat arrived at the planation of Monsieur Antoine Barraque, whose "family were all French, and occupied a house containing two large and very comfortable rooms, neatly and sufficiently furnished."[222] Fenston proclaimed the plantation to be "one of the best cotton plantations on the river, to judge from the size and luxuriance of the plants." Fenston engaged "Madame Barraque, four young ladies, and some of their friends" in "an interesting chat" and noted the Madame Barraque appeared to have "no small portion of the Quapaw blood in her" but was nevertheless "a very good-looking woman notwithstanding her Indian blood, has *French* manners, and has produced a fine young family."[223] Fenston was pleased to learn that Monsieur Barraque would be joining them on the boat. Barraque was "full of conversation, his adventures and opinions were amusing" and he was "a very intelligent and agreeable fellow-passenger."[224]

When the boat arrived at Arkansas Post, Fenston became acquainted with Barraque's partner, friend, and compatriot Frederick Notrebe. Fenston explained that Notrebe was the "great man of the place" and had "accumulated a considerable fortune."

> His house appears to be a comfortable one, and has a store attached to it, where the principal business of this part of the country is transacted. Notrebe preceded M. Barraque in Arkansas, and also married a Creole with Indian blood in her veins. Cultivating cotton himself, advancing money to other planters to carry on their business with, upon condition of taking their crops when gathered at a given price, and taking skins and peltry of every kind in payment of goods obtained at his store—of which whiskey forms no small item—he has contrived to secure a monopoly of almost all the business of the country, and after a vigorous struggle has compelled all his competitors to withdraw from the trade.[225]

Fenston described Arkansas Post as "situated on the edge of an extensive prairie" with "a few straggling houses, principally occupied by some descendants of the ancient French settlers, who live in [a] comfortless way."[226] As for the environmental landscape, Fenston was "pleased" that "nature assumes a somewhat different appearance at this place." Instead of "endless forests and cane-brakes" that caused a "sense of weariness" that "oppresses the mind," Fenston found that "the Arkansas forms a beautiful sweep for two or three miles" with banks that were "about eighty feet high."[227] Fenston explored the surrounding landscape and noted the violence of the water in this delta region.

> I examined the neighbourhood for several miles, and found the country a dead flat, with a few stunted trees growing here and there, and the land so cut up by broad channels or gullies made by the rain, that even within 300 yards of the settlement they had been obliged to construct bridges over some of them. There is a track on the bank of the river which I followed some distance, until it stopped at a precipice of near 100 feet high, with a wide chasm, on my left, the solid contents of the whole having, as I was informed, fallen into the water within the last twelve months. All this might have been avoided if they had, in the first instance, constructed proper passages for the atmospheric waters to pass off.[228]

The boat, so overloaded with Notrebe's cotton shipment that "she looked from the shore like an immense collection of bales of cotton amongst which some pieces of machinery had been stuck," departed Arkansas Post on December 30, 1834.[229] The boat followed a "cut-off" channel that led to the White River and then on to the Mississippi River. Fenston explained that it was "more convenient to take this Cut-off to reach the Mississippi, as it is a clear canal-like navigation about 250 feet broad, without any snags or sawyers."[230]

Along the way, Fenston noted that they saw "two miserable cabins" and "lofty canes about 25 feet high."[231] When they arrived at the confluence of the White River and the Mississippi River, Fenston and Mr. T. reflected on their location on the "great fluviatile highway" that was "about three-quarters of a mile wide" and a "fine open stream without sandbars and snags."[232] Thus, as 1834 came to a close, Fenston departed Arkansas, and he and Mr. T. "rejoiced at [their] escape from the contracted banks and endless forests of the Arkansas, the very air of which seemed to breathe of corruption."[233]

Chapter Six

Deep Mapping Travelers' Perceptions of the Arkansas Past

One hundred fifty-eight years after Fenston's tour ended, a young Arkansas governor was elected president of the United States. During the final months of the 1992 presidential campaign, Governor Bill Clinton was challenged by his opponents, President George H. W. Bush and billionaire H. Ross Perot, to explain the relevance of Arkansas.

> Jim Lehrer: Mr. Perot, if you were sitting at home now and just heard this exchange about Arkansas, who would you believe?
>
> H. Ross Perot: I grew up five blocks from Arkansas. [Laughter] Let's put it in perspective. It's a beautiful state. It's a fairly rural state. It has a population less than Chicago or Los Angeles, about the size of Dallas and Fort Worth combined. So, I think probably we're making a mistake night after night after night to cast the nation's future on a unit that small.
>
> Lehrer: Why is that a mistake?
>
> Perot: It's irrelevant. [Laughter]
>
> Lehrer: What he did as Governor of Arkansas—
>
> Perot: No, no, no. But you can't—I could say that I ran a small grocery store on the corner, therefore, I extrapolate that into the fact that I could run Wal-Mart. That's not true. I carefully picked an Arkansas company, you notice there, Governor.
>
> Lehrer: Governor?
>
> Bill Clinton: Mr. Perot, with all respect, I think it is highly relevant, and I think that a four-billion-dollar budget in state and federal funds is not all that small. I think the fact that I took a state that was one of the poorest states in the country and had been for one hundred and fifty-three years and tried my best to modernize its economy and to make the kind

of changes that have generated support from people like the presidents of Apple Computer and Hewlett-Packard and some of the biggest companies in this country, twenty-four retired generals and admirals, and hundreds of business executives are highly relevant. And you know, I'm frankly amazed that since you grew up five blocks from there you would think that what goes on in that State is irrelevant. I think it's been pretty impressive.

Perot: It's not.[1]

Although Perot tossed out a few geographical facts about the state that might have made him sound like an objective, outside observer, he used those basic characterizations to make a more consequential judgment about the significance of Arkansas places and landscapes. Though made within the sordid context of presidential politics during a televised debate, the depiction of Arkansas as an irrelevant and impoverished backwater resonated with the audience. It is doubtful that the giggling spectators in the Michigan State University auditorium, or those watching on television at home, had read the travel narratives of Dunbar, Schoolcraft, Nuttall, or Featherstonhaugh. Furthermore, it is unlikely that many of the audience members had ever been to Arkansas. Yet, like William Foote Pope one hundred years before him, Bill Clinton was obligated to defend the honor of his state against the entrenched place and landscape perceptions that many Americans held about Arkansas. The laughter that Ross Perot provoked with his clever jibes at the expense of Arkansas suggests that such perceptions were alive and well in the late twentieth century.

Perceptions of Place and Landscape

How are place and landscape perceptions created and why do they persist? News stories, literature, art, comedy, photographs, cartoons, film, television, maps, boosterism, and other visual and written media are some of the obvious sources of social and geographic perceptions. Of course, the personal experience of travel and interaction with people and environments also shapes perceptions. But, any attempt to give credit or lay blame for the perceptions of any particular place on any particular source would be foolish. It is impossible, for example, to know with any certainty how the writings of George W. Featherstonhaugh contributed to his readers' perceptions of Arkansas. Each reader over time brought his or her own experience and social perspectives to the interpretation of Featherstonhaugh's narrative. What went on in the mind of a thirty-five-year-old reader in Philadelphia in 1854 or a sixty-eight-year-old reader in Paris in 1972 is impossible to know.

Instead of asking how Featherstonhaugh, Schoolcraft, Nuttall, or Dunbar contributed to any generalized social perceptions of Arkansas over time, I aim to map the perceptions that these travelers communicated through their writings. What did Featherstonhaugh make people think about Arkansas? This is a question that simply cannot be answered. How does Featherstonhaugh's narrative reveal *his* perceptions of the people and environments that he encountered in Arkansas? I believe this question can be explored through an analysis of Featherstonhaugh's language and a mapping of this language. Each of the travelers discussed in this book described the cultural and environmental landscapes that he encountered and offered his opinions about the value of these peoples and places. Since each traveler was in motion, these descriptive and subjective observations are made in different spaces. By mapping these observations, it is possible to represent the perceptions of these travelers visually in a way that aids in comprehending the spatial patterns evident in their writings. In this chapter, I present and discuss the perception maps that I created to explore the spatial patterns evident in these travelers' perceptions of Arkansas places and landscapes.[2]

William Dunbar and George Hunter

The observations and perceptions of William Dunbar and George Hunter on their 1804 to 1805 expedition on the Ouachita River are illustrated in figures 6.1 through 6.4. The maps reveal that, in both the Louisiana portion of the journey and the Arkansas portion of the journey, the men recorded environmental observations and perceptions at a much greater rate than cultural observations and perceptions. This pattern is to be expected, given the sparse population in the area they traversed. The cultural perceptions of Dunbar and Hunter in Louisiana, shown in figure 6.1, are clustered at two locations—near present-day Jonesville and present-day Monroe. In the first instance, the men described a French man who operated a ferry at the site and had built a house on an Indian mound. At Fort Miró, the men discussed the American military men and their perceptions of the quality of the fort and its surroundings. In both cases the men confine most of their commentary to descriptive observations but offer a few positive perceptions and a couple of negative judgments as well. Both men are at their most negative about the cultural features of Louisiana when they encounter what they perceive as "indolence" and poverty among settlers near present-day Sterlington, Louisiana. While in Arkansas, the men described relics of cultural features on the landscape. In most cases, these objects were not paired with the people who created or left them behind. The few people the expedition encountered in Arkansas were transitory rather than settled. Thus, the map of the cultural perceptions of Dunbar and Hunter in Arkansas, as seen in figure 6.2, reveals a space through which people were in motion rather than rooted in place. From the Indian mounds to the hunters' caches to the pathways that crossed the river to the empty cabins at the hot springs, the party encountered objects of culture rather than actual human beings. In one exception, the expedition encountered the camp of a man near the Little Missouri River who Dunbar identified as "M. Le Fevre" and described as "intelligent" and a "gentleman." This is the solitary positive cultural perception that appears on the Arkansas landscape of William Dunbar.

The environmental observations and perceptions recorded by Dunbar and Hunter in their journals are much more numerous and frequent than their observations and perceptions of the cultural landscape. Consistent with the purpose of their expedition, the journals are devoted mostly to descriptions of the flora, fauna, soils, minerals, and waterways that they encountered along their route. Through Louisiana, shown in figure 6.3, Dunbar and Hunter recorded several positive perceptions that often intersect with possible human uses for these landscapes. Where they found the soils to be fertile, the game to be plentiful, the timber to be hardy, the shrubs to be thriving, the minerals to be valuable, and the river to be navigable, Dunbar and Hunter were approving. Where the river was broken by gravel and sandy shoals, or lands were inundated, or rocky, or pine-covered, the men were rarely impressed. Thus, environmental perceptions were colored more by commercial and human settlement considerations than by aesthetic sensibilities. The exception to this pattern of human-use standards is evident in the environmental perceptions revealed in figure 6.4. While in Arkansas, the men allowed their aesthetic sentiments to surface as they marveled at the beauty of rocky outcrops along the Ouachita River between present-day Arkadelphia and Hot Springs. Yet the travelers continued their negative judgments of Arkansas environments when they recorded their disappointment in the commercial potential for coal, precious metals, or valuable minerals in their short excursions away from the river and the springs.

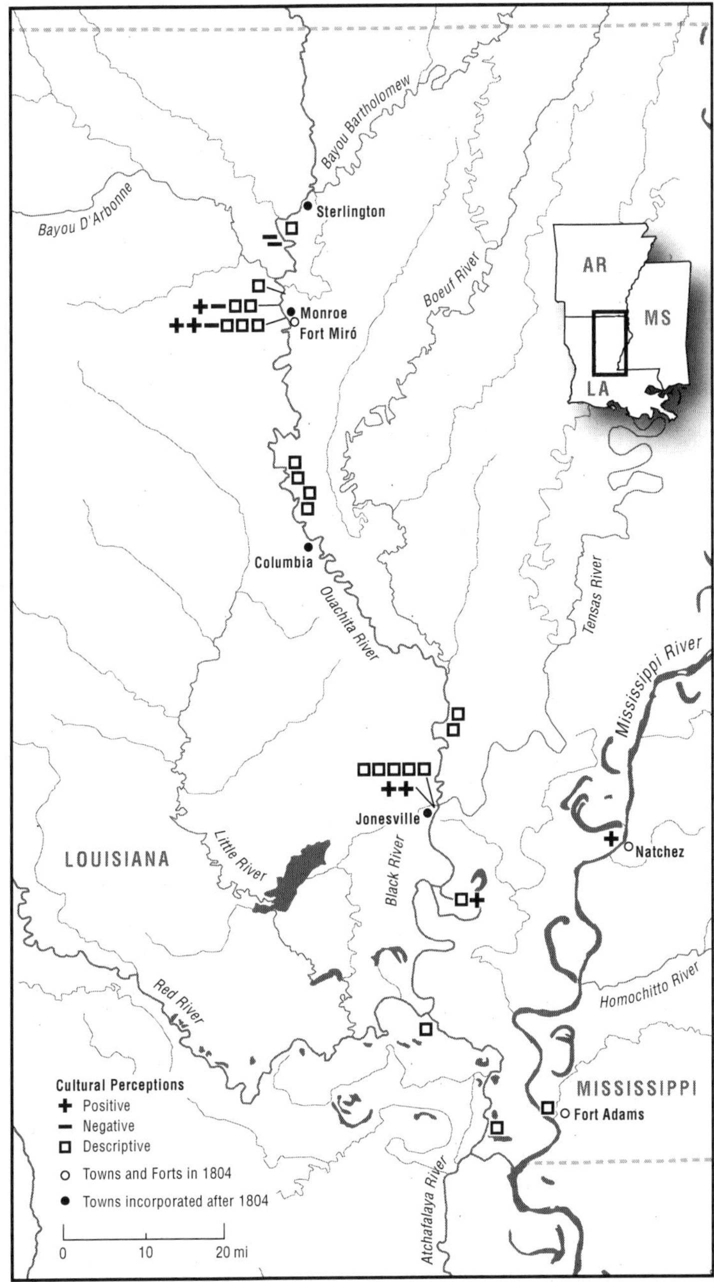

FIG. 6.1. William Dunbar's and George Hunter's Perceptions of the Cultural Landscape of Louisiana, 1804–1805. Cartography by Erin Greb.

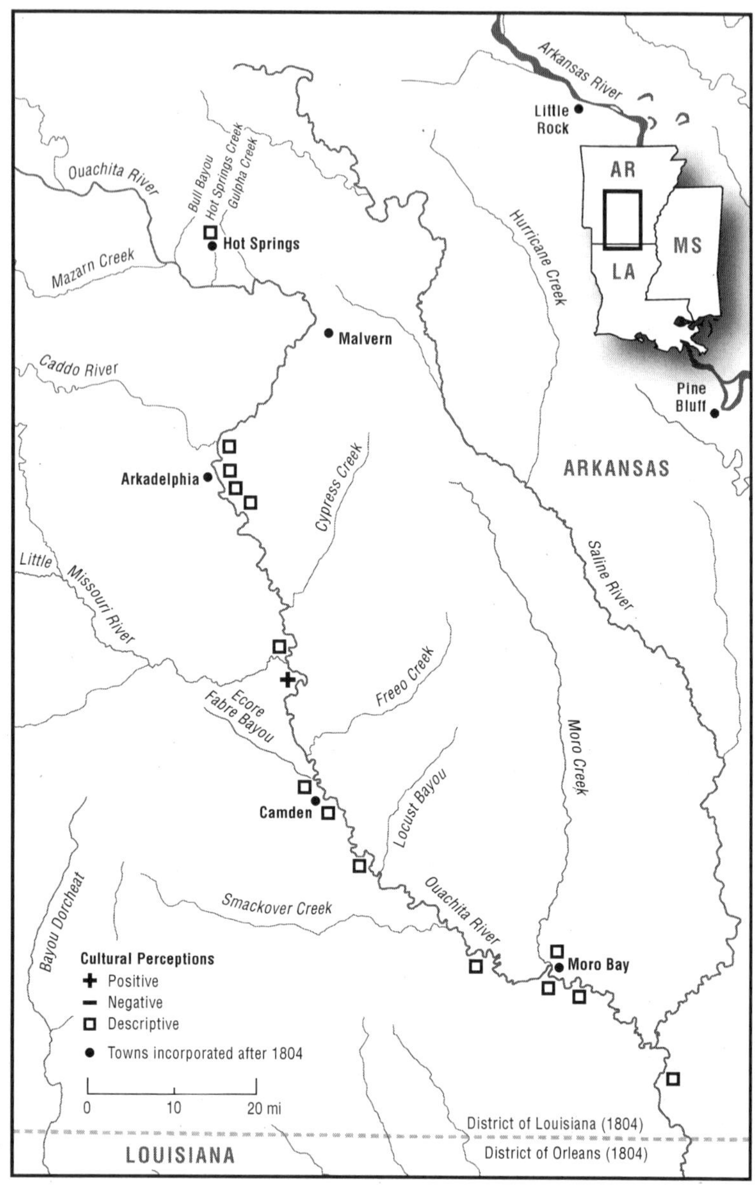

FIG. 6.2. William Dunbar's and George Hunter's Perceptions of the Cultural Landscape of Arkansas, 1804–1805. Cartography by Erin Greb.

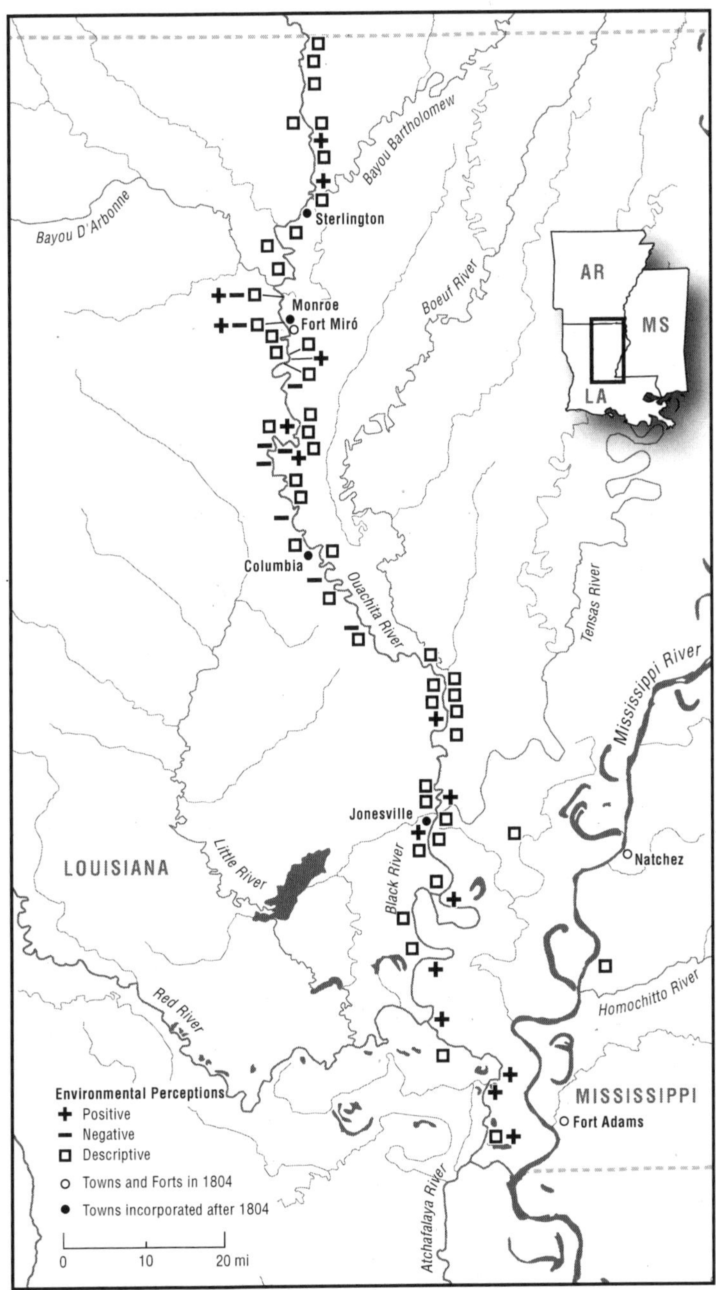

FIG. 6.3. William Dunbar's and George Hunter's Perceptions of the Environmental Landscape of Louisiana, 1804–1805. Cartography by Erin Greb.

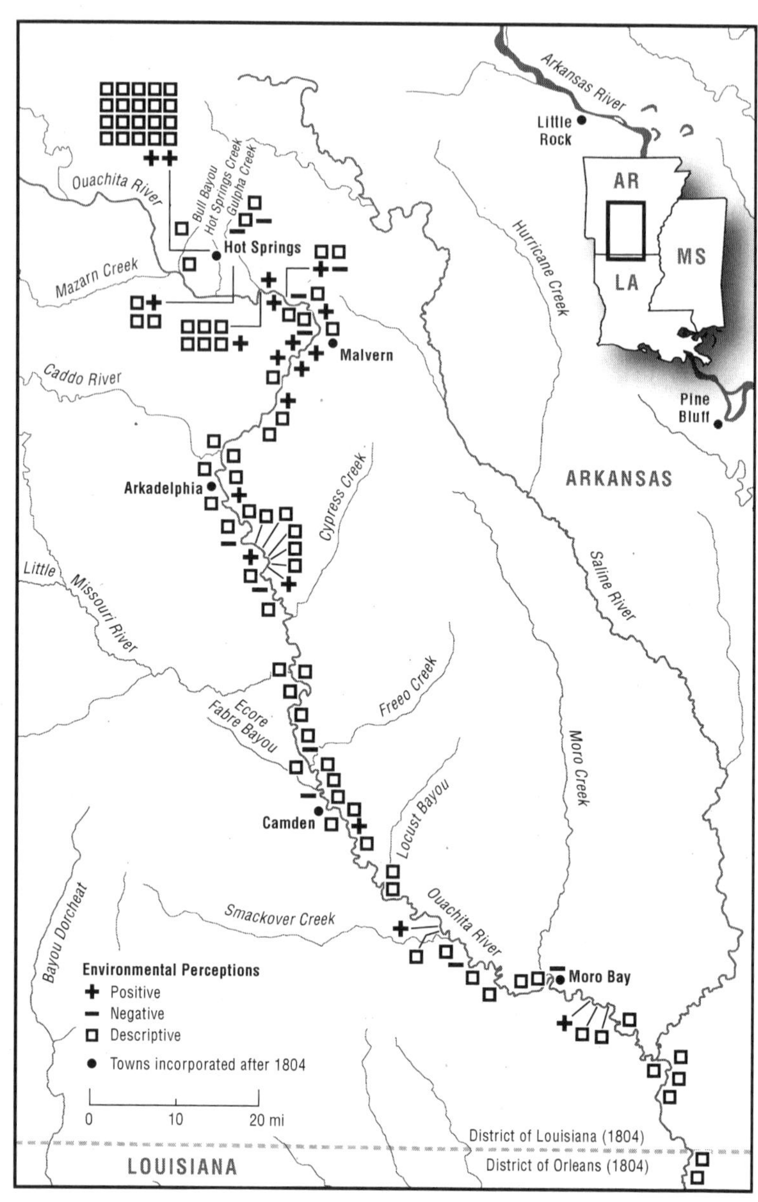

FIG. 6.4. William Dunbar's and George Hunter's Perceptions of the Environmental Landscape of Arkansas, 1804–1805. Cartography by Erin Greb.

Henry Rowe Schoolcraft

Henry Rowe Schoolcraft commented frequently on both the environmental and the cultural characteristics that he observed in the Ozarks in late 1818 and early 1819. Schoolcraft was not reticent about offering his opinion on the settlers and other cultural features that he recorded in his journal during his tour. In two instances, as shown in figure 6.5, Schoolcraft was quite negative about the cultural attributes he encountered during the first part of his trek. His experiences with Mr. Wells near Bennetts Bayou in Arkansas and with the Holt and Fisher families near Beaver Creek in Missouri are the two locations where he recorded his most derogatory statements. It was in these two places where Schoolcraft found families that he considered dirty, disheveled, uneducated, irreligious, bad-mannered, and otherwise uncivilized. It might be coincidence, but it is interesting to note that both encounters took place when Schoolcraft was on his way to his intended destination on the James River. Perhaps stress, exhaustion, fear, and impatience colored his experiences with these people. On his return journey, Schoolcraft engaged in much less cultural criticism.

At the beginning of his journey, Schoolcraft was critical of the land he traversed. As shown in figure 6.6, Schoolcraft recorded several negative environmental perceptions as he trekked through the present-day Missouri counties of Crawford, Dent, Texas, Douglas, and Ozark. He repeatedly described the land as "sterile," "rough," and "barren." His less-frequent positive environmental perceptions in this portion of Missouri occurred where he encountered pure water, beautiful vistas, and awe-inspiring caves. Schoolcraft became almost exclusively positive when he described the environments he witnessed further west in the present-day Missouri counties of Taney, Christian, and Greene. Here he found "enchanting" rivers, "delightful" scenery, "transparent" waters, "sublime" views, "vigorous" forests, "beautiful" prairies, and "rich" alluvial soils. Similarly, Schoolcraft was impressed by the "diversified" and "picturesque" scenery that he encountered along the White River near Norfork and Calico Rock, Arkansas. Like his cultural commentary, there is a spatial pattern to Schoolcraft's environmental commentary. Schoolcraft was much more sharp-tongued during the first half of his journey than he was on his return. Along with his bias toward cultivable land and environmental features with high human-use potential, perhaps his inexperience with the rigors of backcountry travel and his fears of hunger and injury negatively affected his perceptions of the environmental landscape early in his trek.

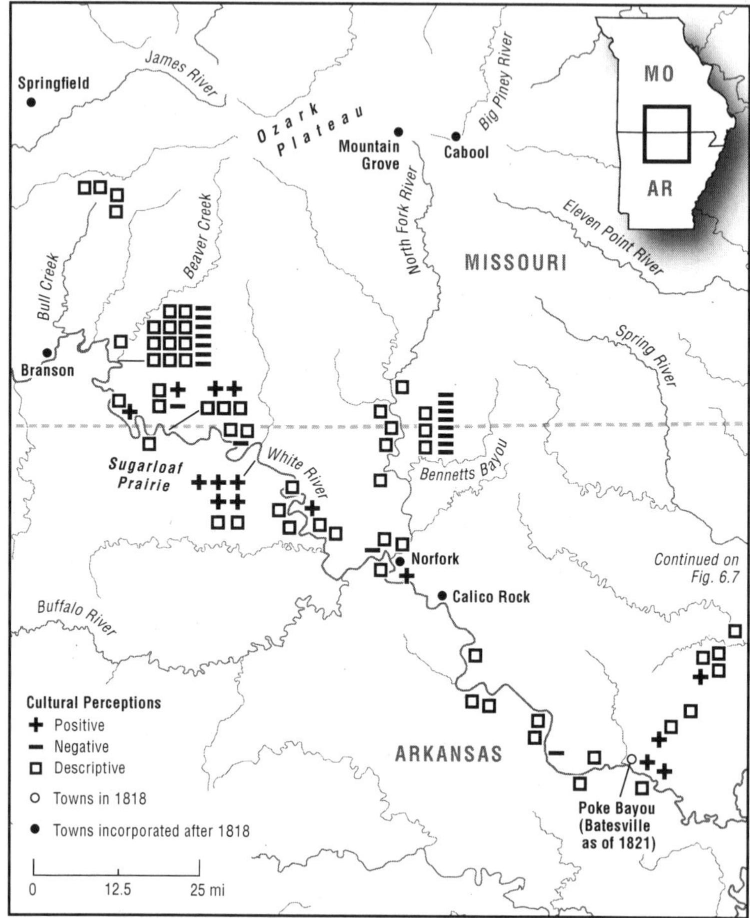

FIG. 6.5. Henry Rowe Schoolcraft's Perceptions of the Cultural Landscape of the Central Ozarks, 1818–1819. Cartography by Erin Greb.

During the final leg of his journey, displayed in figures 6.7 and 6.8, Schoolcraft's observations are mostly descriptive or positive.[3] In contrast to his cultural perceptions during the first half of his trip, Schoolcraft did not record any negative perceptions of the settlers in the eastern portion of the Ozarks. Instead, Schoolcraft approved of the "agricultural industry," "increasing population," and other "improvements" that he observed among the recent settlers of the present-day counties of Independence and Randolph

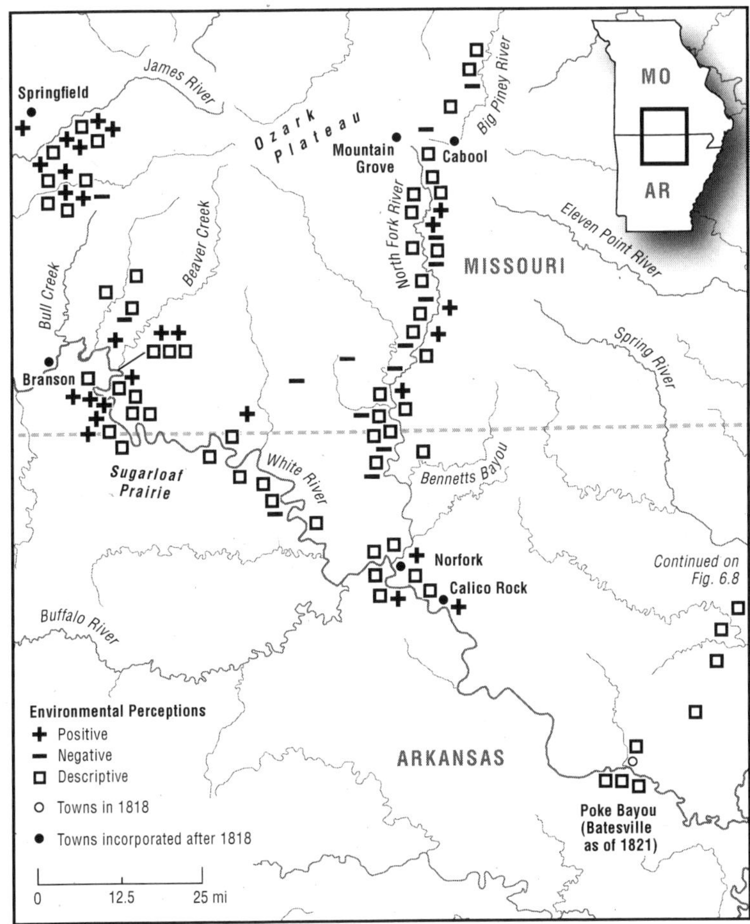

FIG. 6.6. Henry Rowe Schoolcraft's Perceptions of the Environmental Landscape of the Central Ozarks, 1818–1819. Cartography by Erin Greb.

in Arkansas and Ripley and St. Francois in Missouri. Similarly, Schoolcraft was either descriptive or positive about the environmental landscapes of this eastern section of the Ozarks. The alluvial soil, limestone outcrops, granite deposits, and wide streams are all perceived as desirable and worthy of the attention of the American settlers flowing in from Kentucky, Tennessee, the Carolinas, and Pennsylvania. The spatial patterns evident in Schoolcraft's commentary further support the long-recognized biases of American men of

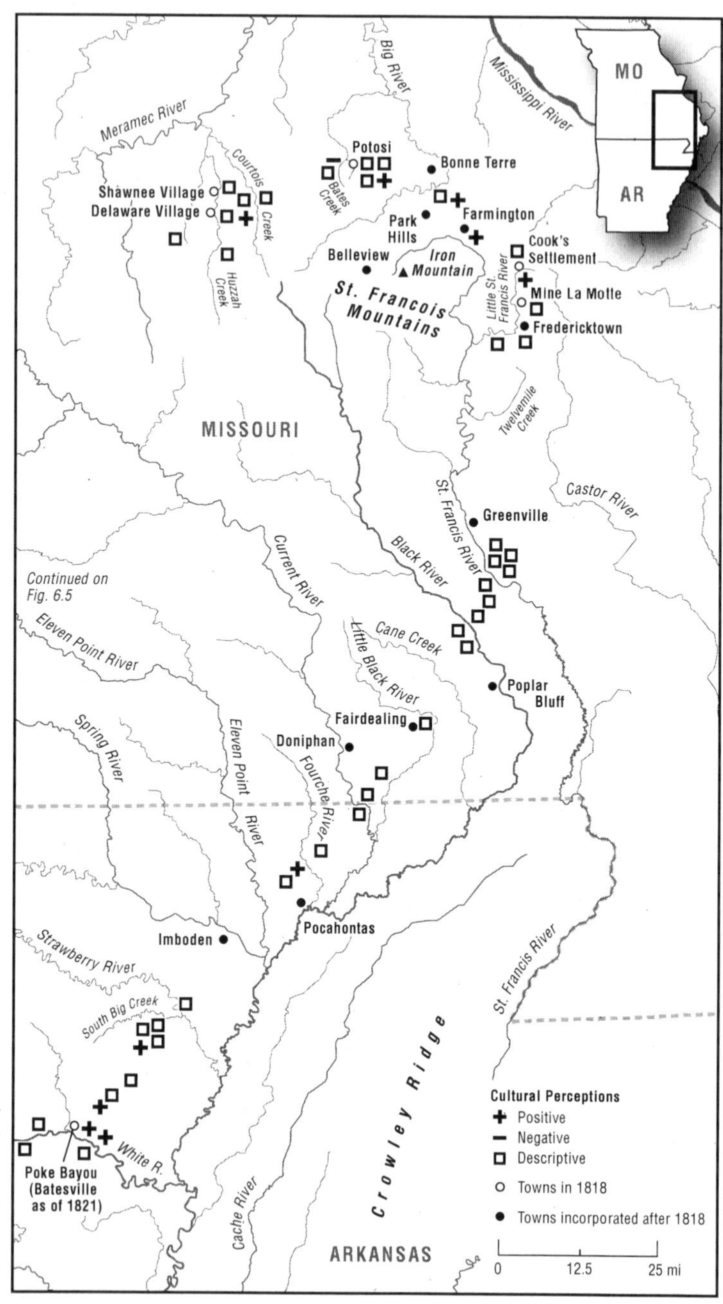

FIG. 6.7. Henry Rowe Schoolcraft's Perceptions of the Cultural Landscape of the Eastern Ozarks, 1818–1819. Cartography by Erin Greb.

Schoolcraft's class and regional background in favor of cultural ecologies and cultural landscapes that are settled, commercial, and agricultural.

Thomas Nuttall

Thomas Nuttall insisted in the preface to his narrative that his purpose was to publish his journal for the good of science rather than to entertain the readers of travel tales. Although much of his journal is indeed descriptive in nature, Nuttall frequently offered his opinions about the cultural and environmental landscapes he witnessed. The cultural perceptions evident in Nuttall's narrative, as illustrated in figure 6.9, reveal a few spatial clusters of cultural commentary that is mostly descriptive yet also rather negative. The few people with whom Nuttall mingled along the Mississippi River were viewed with scorn. There was nothing positive to say about the culture of boatmen, Indian traders, drunkenness, and poverty that he witnessed along the shores of the river. The month that Nuttall spent near Arkansas Post allowed him time to interact with the diverse peoples who had settled the area. Here Nuttall tended to reveal his class and national biases when evaluating cultural landscapes. Where he witnessed his version of civilization, his commentary was full of praise. The industriousness and manners of the merchants of Arkansas Post, such as William Drope and Joseph Bogy Sr., impressed Nuttall. Also evident were positive and sympathetic perceptions of some of the cultural attributes of the Quapaw. Despite his praise for some individuals though, Nuttall disparaged those of French and métis heritage whom he found to be ignorant, idle, extravagant, and otherwise too similar to the "savages" in their cultural practices and attitudes. Like Schoolcraft, Nuttall preferred those who embraced agriculture and commerce.

The map of Nuttall's environmental perceptions of southeast Arkansas, shown in figure 6.10, also illustrates Nuttall's preference for description over judgment. Nuttall was diligent in his recording of the flora, fauna, soils, and minerals that he encountered. Like his perceptions of the cultural landscapes along the Mississippi River, Nuttall was quite negative in his perceptions of the environmental landscape of the violent river and its forsaken surroundings. Yet, once Nuttall arrived on the Arkansas River, his perceptions of the environment became much more positive. Like Dunbar and Schoolcraft, Nuttall applauded environments where he saw potential for agricultural and commercial development. This was particularly true of the area around present-day Pine Bluff, Arkansas, where Nuttall saw the combination of fertile

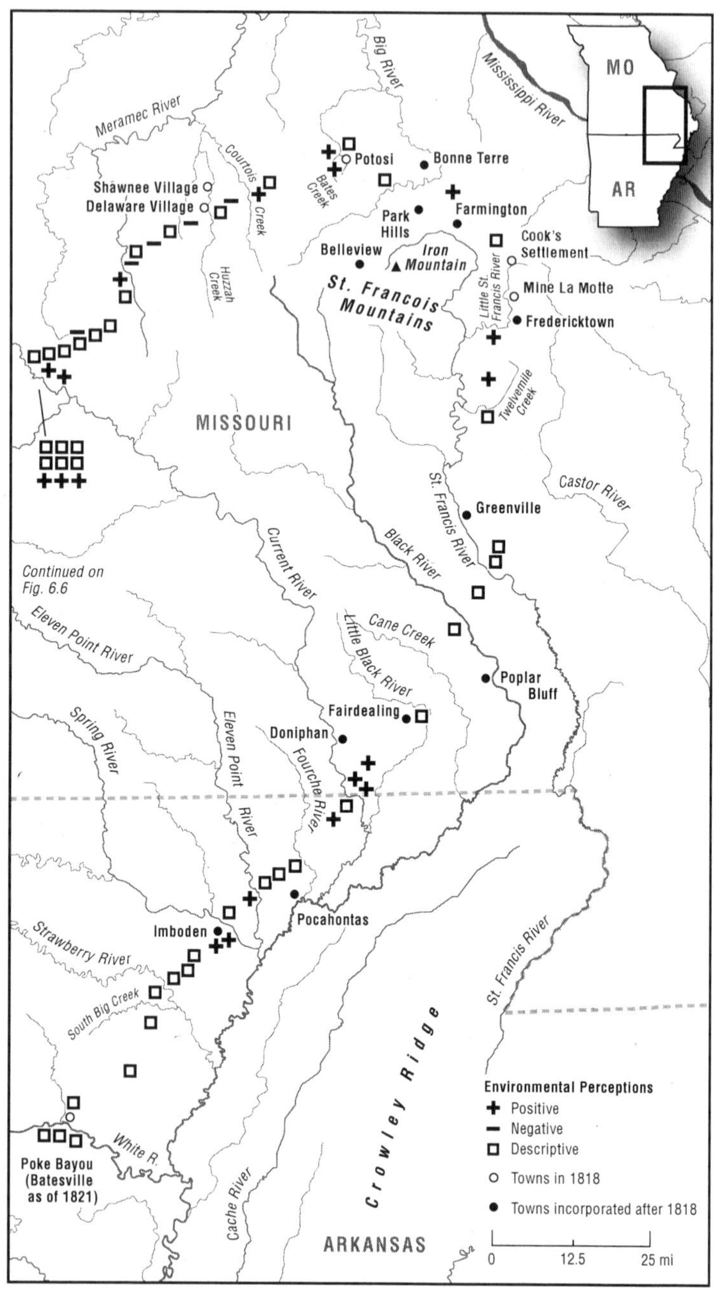

FIG. 6.8. Henry Rowe Schoolcraft's Perceptions of the Environmental Landscape of the Eastern Ozarks, 1818–1819. Cartography by Erin Greb.

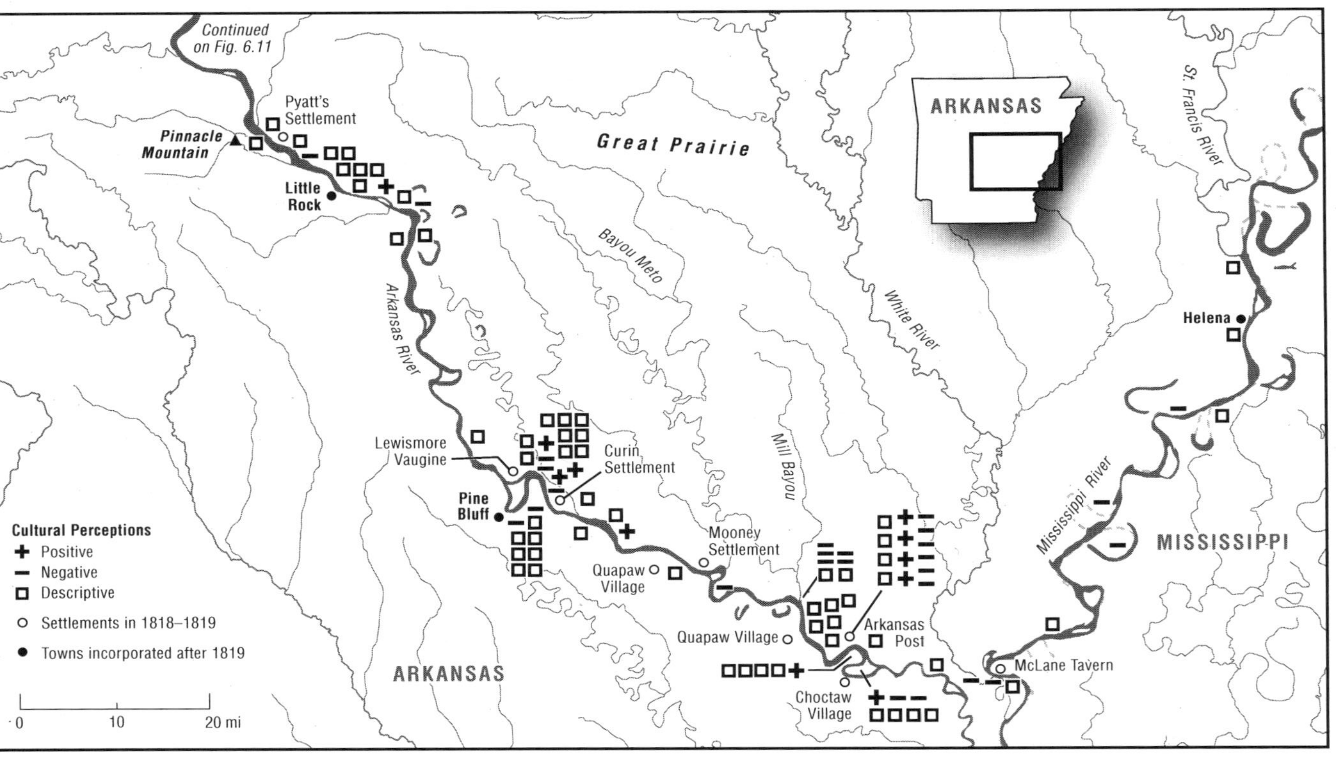

FIG. 6.9. Thomas Nuttall's Perceptions of the Cultural Landscape of Southeast Arkansas, 1819–1820. Cartography by Erin Greb.

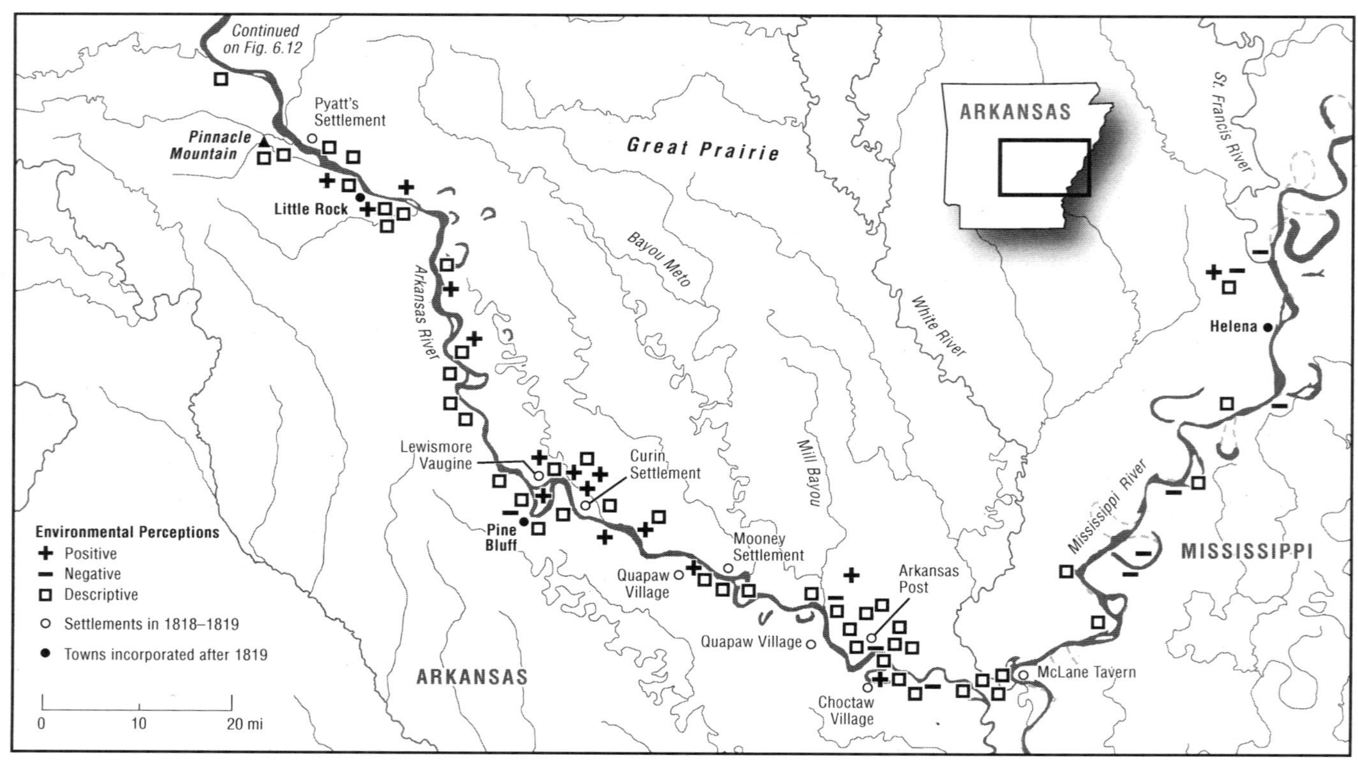

FIG. 6.10. Thomas Nuttall's Perceptions of the Environmental Landscape of Southeast Arkansas, 1819–1820. Cartography by Erin Greb.

land, a healthy climate, and proximity to river transportation and markets as a positive sign for human settlement and industry. In fact, Nuttall projected a positive future for environmental landscapes like these if future settlers used these lands for farming and ranching and established mills for processing the bounty. Like Dunbar and Schoolcraft, Nuttall approved of people doing what he thought should be done with the land, while he criticized those who seemed incapable of capitalizing on the environmental blessings at their feet.

Nuttall's narrative of his travels from Little Rock through the Arkansas River valley to Fort Smith also includes more attention to environmental than cultural landscapes. As the maps of his perceptions, shown in figures 6.11 and 6.12, display, Nuttall was almost universally positive about the environments he encountered in this portion of Arkansas. He was enamored with the scenic beauty of the rugged river valley and its contrast to the river environments of southeast Arkansas. In fact, Nuttall's only negative statement about the environment of the river valley appeared when he judged the land near the Cadron Settlement to be "inferior." Otherwise, he was effusive in his admiration for the "romantic," "sublime," and "picturesque" scenes of "lofty" cliffs and "verdure." In addition to the aesthetic beauty of the landscape, Nuttall frequently commented on the fertility of the elevated land adjacent to the river. Likewise, Nuttall was usually positive in those cases when he offered his opinion on the cultural attributes of the people who had settled this beautiful and rich environment. Despite his concern near the Cadron Settlement that the "rising generation are growing up in mental darkness," Nuttall anticipated that future settlement and industry would resolve this temporary state-of-affairs. After all, the possibility of cultural transformation was evident among the Cherokees in the region. The Cherokees with whom Nuttall interacted were admired for the construction of their houses and the management of their farms. What Nuttall perceived as a "happy advance toward civilization." As with Dunbar and Schoolcraft, the perception maps of Nuttall's journey reveal spatial patterns in his reactions to cultural and environmental landscapes along the Arkansas River. These patterns, and the prejudices they expose, are vital to understanding the narrative of a man who claimed no other purpose than the advancement of science.

George William Featherstonhaugh

By the time of Featherstonhaugh's tour in 1834, cultural and environmental transformation was accelerating in Arkansas beyond the preliminary

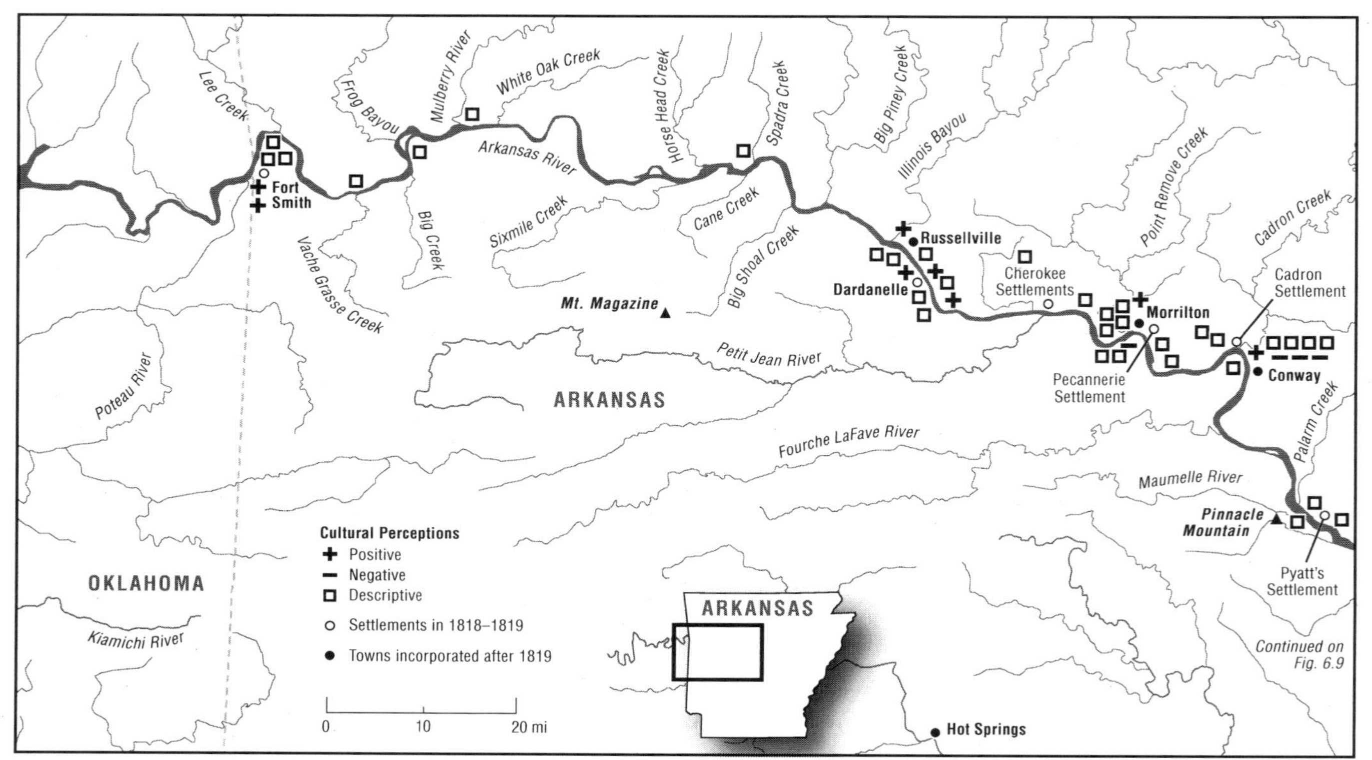

FIG. 6.11. Thomas Nuttall's Perceptions of the Cultural Landscape of the Western Arkansas River Valley, 1819. Cartography by Erin Greb.

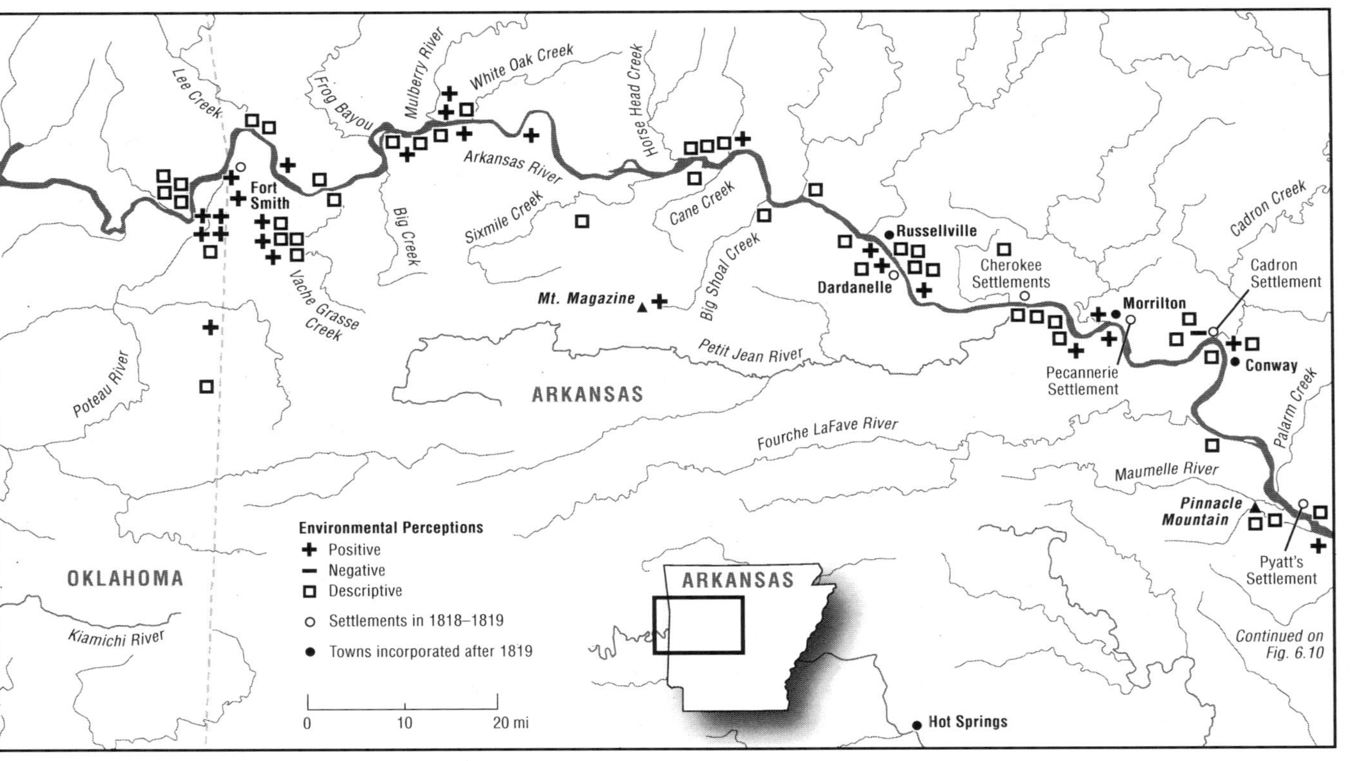

FIG. 6.12. Thomas Nuttall's Perceptions of the Environmental Landscape of the Western Arkansas River Valley, 1819. Cartography by Erin Greb.

changes that Nuttall and Schoolcraft had witnessed fifteen years earlier. White migration, Indian removal, territorial status, and impending statehood had reshaped the human geography of the region. Unlike Dunbar, Schoolcraft, and Nuttall before him, Fenston chose to publish a narrative that would appeal to the penchants of the readers of travel literature published by John Murray in London. Yet Fenston carried most of the same prejudices toward the poor, the non-white, and the non-agriculturally or -commercially engaged that were evident in the language of the other travelers. Like Schoolcraft, Fenston was unreserved in using his pen to criticize, even ridicule, the cultural attributes that he found lacking. Although the primary purpose of his U.S. government-sponsored expedition was to conduct a geological survey, Fenston recorded substantial information about the people and places he encountered. Unlike the other travelers depicted in this book, the language of Fenston's travel narrative relied less on descriptive observations and more on a lively telling of his perceptions of cultural and environmental landscapes.

As Fenston journeyed through northeastern Arkansas in early November 1834, he was impressed by the beautiful and "pellucid" rivers he crossed. As shown in figure 6.14, his first perceptions of the environmental landscape of Arkansas, particularly its clear rivers, were positive. His perceptions of the cultural landscape, however, as shown in figure 6.13, were a mixture of respect for "worthy" people, such as Mr. and Mrs. Meriwether, and disgust at the "wretched" food, cabins, and beds along the way. He also evoked a sense of danger in his narrative when describing the suspicious-looking men who seemed to be following them and the settlers' tales of murder and robbery. Finally, Fenston recorded how sickly and poor many of the households in this region were at the time of his trip. The contrast between beautiful land and miserable people was stark in northeast Arkansas.

Fenston arrived in Little Rock on November 15, 1834, and found a town of five to six hundred inhabitants. This was the first urbanized area Fenston had encountered since he departed St. Louis in late October. As shown in figure 6.15, his commentary on the cultural landscape was deeply reproachful. Despite the presence of a few gentlemen, such as Reverend Stevenson, William Woodruff, and Governor John Pope, Fenston described a population of scofflaws, bullies, gamblers, renegades, murderers, and thieves. The theme of beautiful land and impoverished people continued as Fenston headed southwest toward the Red River. As shown in figure 6.16, he was almost universally positive about the environment of broken hills, rich soil, beautiful

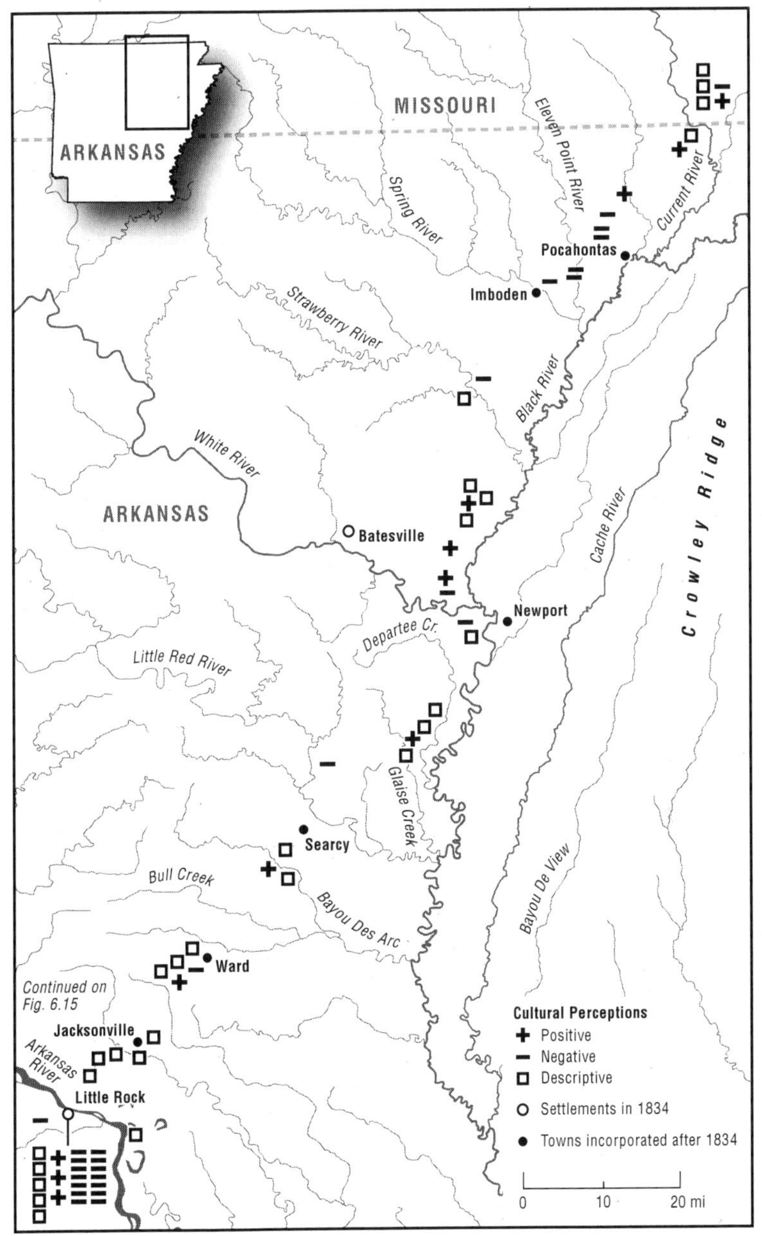

FIG. 6.13. George W. Featherstonhaugh's Perceptions of the Cultural Landscape of Northeast Arkansas, 1834. Cartography by Erin Greb.

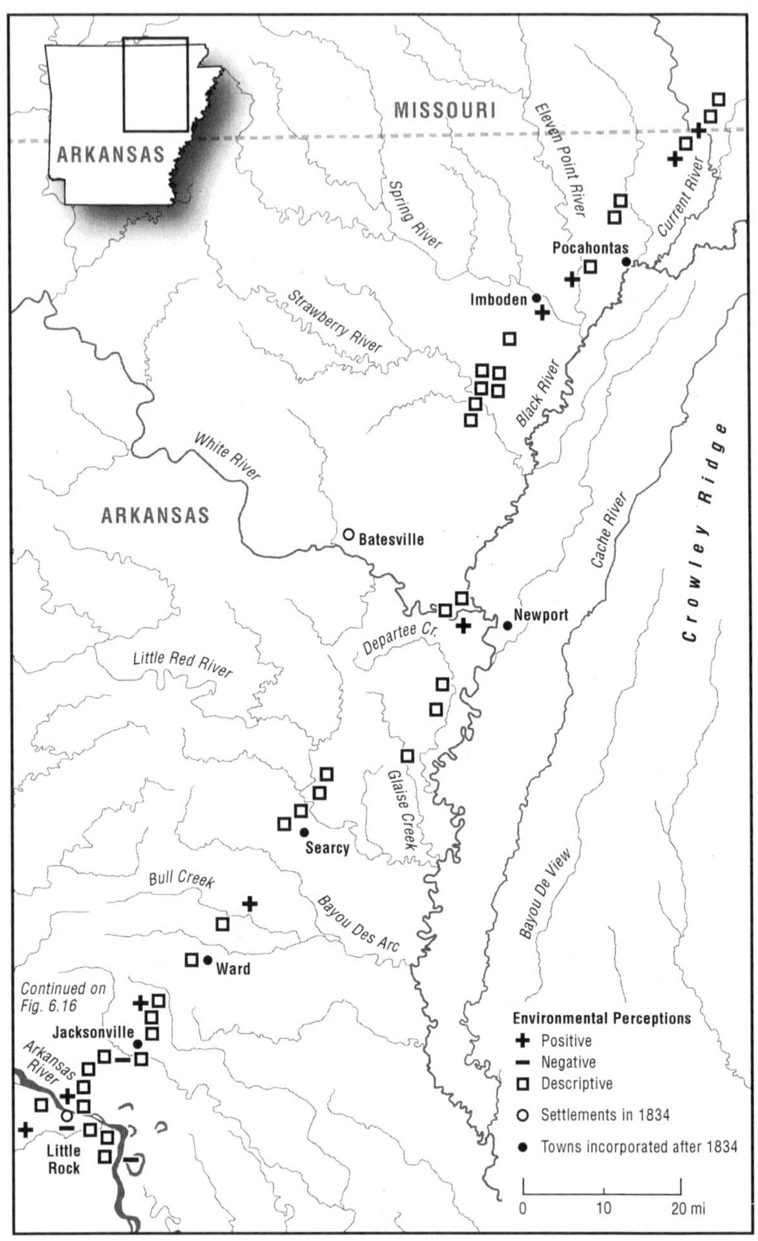

FIG. 6.14. George W. Featherstonhaugh's Perceptions of the Environmental Landscape of Northeast Arkansas, 1834. Cartography by Erin Greb.

minerals, clear streams, and picturesque prairies, but his complaints about the wretched food, miserable lodgings, and deceitful characters of the cultural landscape continued. Here, Fenston's perceptions of cultural merit tended along class lines. Where he found poor settlers, he mocked them and complained about the circumstances of their poverty. Where he found the wealthier and educated class of Judge Edward Cross, Richard Pryor, and James and Polly Conway, he approved of their civilized habits and admired what they had accomplished on the distant frontier. Fenston also equated wealth with morality when he imagined the wealthy Virginians of Spring Hill in Hempstead County as the beacon of education, religion, and civilization on the frontier. In addition to class bias, Fenston's language reveals his gender biases. Where he found women who did not meet his standards of femininity—Mrs. Meriwether, the "she-Caliban," and Rebecca Barkman—he ridiculed them for their ugliness and failure to adopt the ladylike manners he expected. Where he encountered married women who conformed to his gender norms—Mrs. Conway and Mrs. Cross—he praised them for being "agreeable" and for demonstrating their skills in cooking and keeping a clean and comfortable house. Fenston also exposed his political opinions through his assessment of the cultural landscape of southwest Arkansas. He is unrestrained in his disdain for the "mysterious" Sam Houston, the Texans plotting to overthrow Mexican rule, the plantation slavery along the Red River, and the dangers of universal suffrage. Unlike Dunbar, Schoolcraft, and Nuttall, Fenston published his thoughts at a time in his career when he did not need to be concerned with the political implications of criticizing Americans and their government. It is also likely that his later experience with the boundary dispute along the Maine and New Brunswick border between the United States and Canada may have hardened his attitudes further toward American expansionism.

The third region of Arkansas through which Fenston traveled was the southeastern path of the Arkansas River. Once again, Fenston found little to admire in the cultural landscape he encountered. The map shown in figure 6.17 reveals that Fenston had only one positive comment to make about the people along the Arkansas River. The wealthy plantation owner and founder of New Gascony, Antoine Barraque, drew Fenston's praise. Fenston seemed not to share fellow Englishman Thomas Nuttall's dislike of French cultural attributes. Unlike his penchant for offering his judgments of the settlers in the other regions he traversed, Fenston tended toward descriptive statements of the cultural landscape in this region, such as the quantity of cotton brought

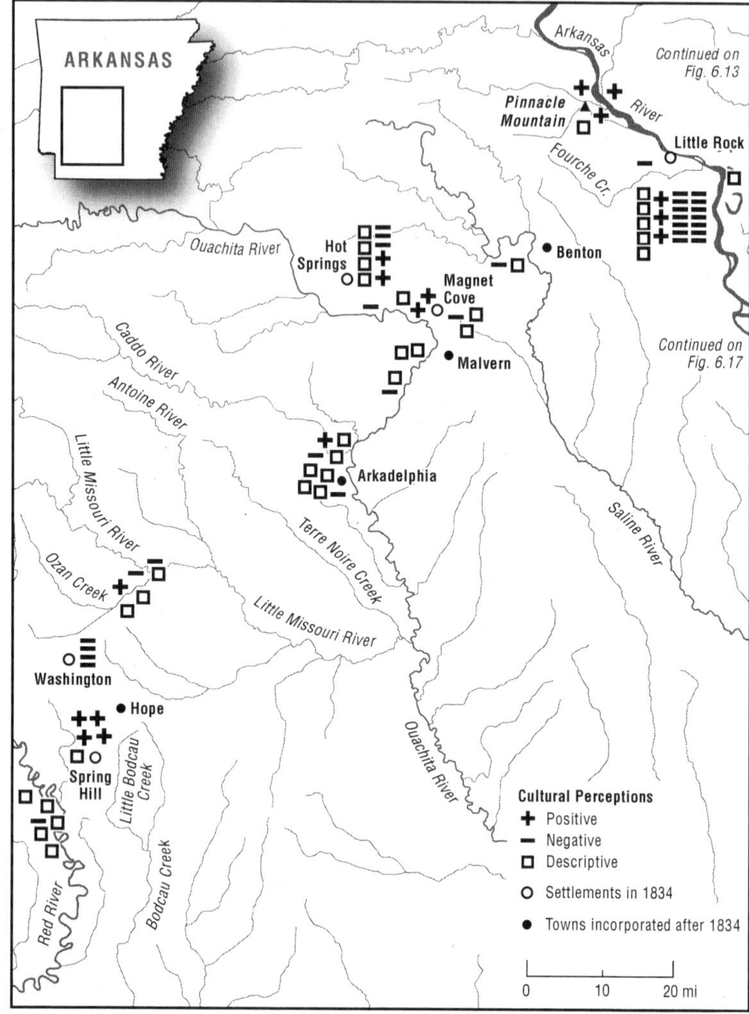

FIG. 6.15. George W. Featherstonhaugh's Perceptions of the Cultural Landscape of Southwest Arkansas, 1834. Cartography by Erin Greb.

aboard at the plantations of Widow Embree and Frederick Notrebe. Only in Arkansas Post did Fenston continue his pattern of denigrating the "straggling houses" and "miserable taverns" of the settlers. Fenston is also mostly descriptive, rather than judgmental, about the environmental landscape he encountered along the Arkansas River. As shown in figure 6.18, Fenston's

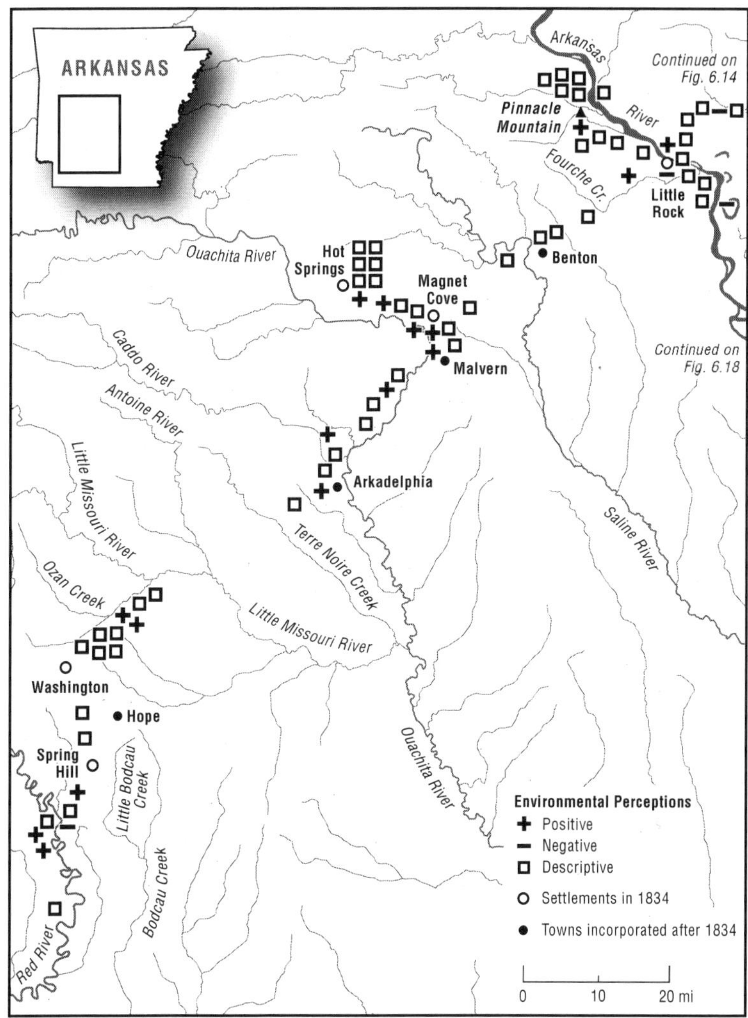

FIG. 6.16. George W. Featherstonhaugh's Perceptions of the Environmental Landscape of Southwest Arkansas, 1834. Cartography by Erin Greb.

perceptions of the "beautiful sweep" of the river near Arkansas Post were positive, while his judgments of the "monotonous country" and the snags, sawyers, and sandbars of much of the serpentine river's course from Little Rock to the Mississippi River were negative. One important difference in Fenston's travel through this region is that, unlike his sojourn from St. Louis

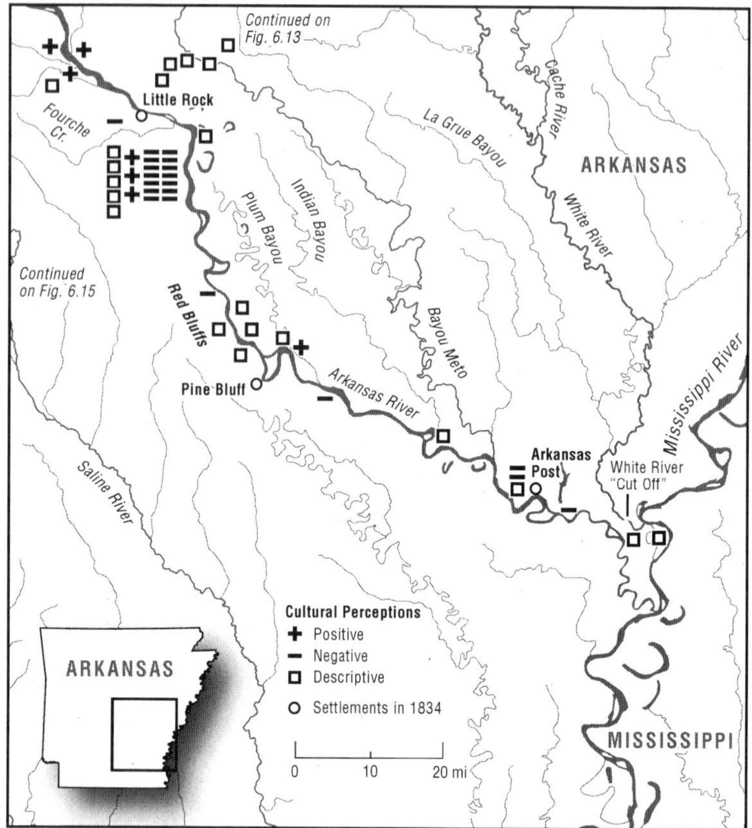

FIG. 6.17. George W. Featherstonhaugh's Perceptions of the Cultural Landscape of Southeast Arkansas, 1834. Cartography by Erin Greb.

to the Red River, he was in the company of others in the confines of a steamboat. In other portions of Fenston's narrative as he traveled through Virginia, Tennessee, and Kentucky, he complained incessantly about the crude manners of his fellow stagecoach passengers. Once again, Fenston found himself in the company of others. And, once again, he was incensed by the drunken, gambling, swindling, violent, scoundrels with whom he was forced to share close quarters. Thus, his commentary about "low, degraded scoundrels" was not directed toward Arkansas residents of this region, but rather toward the transient steamboat passengers who appeared to live lives of gambling, drinking, fighting, and cheating.

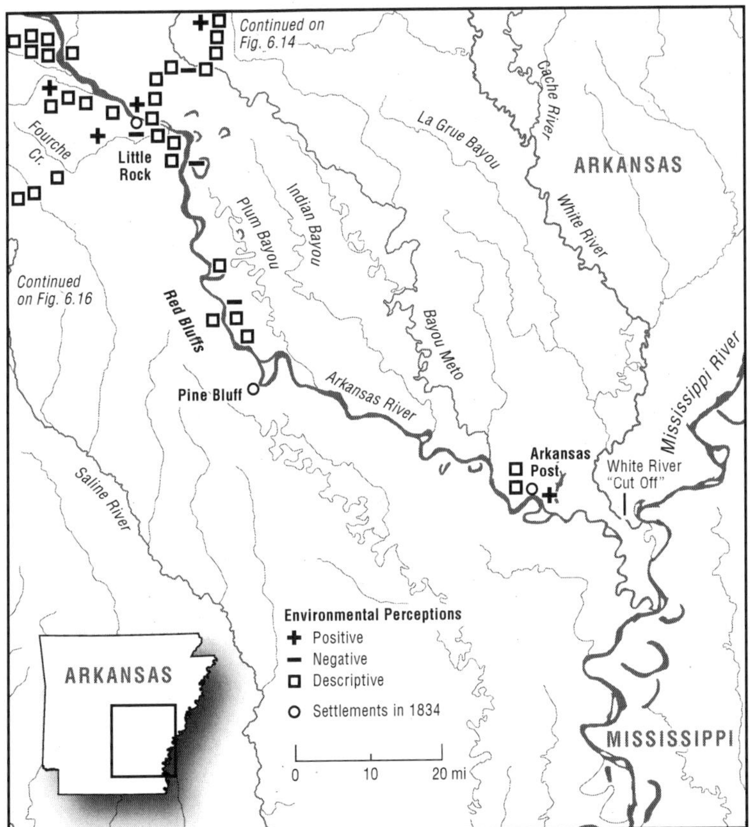

FIG. 6.18. George W. Featherstonhaugh's Perceptions of the Environmental Landscape of Southeast Arkansas, 1834. Cartography by Erin Greb.

Spaces Traversed, Places Experienced, and Landscapes Perceived

Arkansas experienced a momentous transformation of cultural and environmental landscapes in the early nineteenth century. The travelers depicted in this book were eyewitnesses to these transforming places and landscapes during a critical period from the Louisiana Purchase of 1803 to the admission of Arkansas as the twenty-fifth state of the United States in 1836. Each of these travelers left behind a record of the spaces he traversed. These routes can be mapped, with varying degrees of precision, to illustrate that, together, these men explored a variety of Arkansas spaces from the south-central coastal plains to the southeastern delta to the southwestern blackland prairie to the western Arkansas River valley to the northern Ozarks. While these compass point directions, physiographic regions, and mapped route lines provide an important layer to understanding the spaces crossed by these travelers, a more complete understanding of these travelers is found in an analysis of their perceptions of the places and landscapes they explored. Each traveler traversed Arkansas spaces, but each traveler also perceived Arkansas places. These travelers' perceptions of place and landscape have been the focus of this book and the mapping presented in this chapter. When mapped, traveler perceptions reveal not just *what* the traveler said, but *where* he said it. Furthermore, the language used by these travelers to describe the places and landscapes they encountered reveals more about the traveler himself than the people and places he portrayed. Each traveler inevitably carried his own biases and priorities as he interpreted the landscapes he explored and analyzing this language brings into better focus the lenses through which these men viewed their world. Mapping the perceptions of the travelers has illustrated the places experienced and perceived by these men rather than simply the spaces they traversed. This geographical focus on the history of these spaces yields a deeper understanding—a deeper map—of the Arkansas past.

Notes

Introduction

1. Mercer, "On the Track of 'The Arkansas Traveler.'"
2. Pope and Pope, *Early Days in Arkansas*, 230–31.
3. Blevins, *Arkansas/Arkansaw*, 6.
4. Masterson, *Arkansas Folklore*; Blevins, *Arkansas/Arkansaw*.
5. Keighren, Withers, and Bell, *Travels into Print*.
6. The sensationalistic aspects of travel literature have received significant attention from scholars who have critiqued the literature through multiple theoretical lenses. See Pratt, *Imperial Eyes*; Thompson, *Travel Writing*.
7. It is common for Arkansas historians to discuss the negative commentary of these early travelers and to associate that commentary with the negative reputation and stereotypes of Arkansas. In particular, see Cochran, "'Low, Degrading Scoundrels'"; Williams, "Bear State Image"; Blevins, *Arkansas/Arkansaw*; Bolton, *Arkansas, 1800–1860*.
8. Geographers John Wylie, Tim Cresswell, and Denis Cosgrove have written respected works on the topics of place and landscape. Wylie, *Landscape*; Cresswell, *Place: A Short Introduction*; Cosgrove, *Geography and Vision*.
9. DuVal, "Debating Identity, Sovereignty, and Civilization"; DuVal, "'A Good Relationship, & Commerce'"; Arnold, "Indians and Immigrants in the Arkansas Colonial Era"; Arnold, *Colonial Arkansas, 1686–1804*; Whayne, "Turbulent Path to Statehood"; Bolton, *Arkansas, 1800–1860*.
10. The travel writer William Least Heat Moon used the concept of deep mapping to describe his approach. See Heat Moon, *PrairyErth*. This work builds on the field of spatial humanities, HGIS, and the concept of deep mapping. See Bodenhamer, Corrigan, and Harris, *Spatial Humanities*; Maher, *Deep Map Country*; Sturges, "Deep Map of the South"; Dunn, Kadish, and Pasquier, "Religious Centre with a Civic Circumference"; Ridge, Lafreniere, and Nesbit, "Creating Deep Maps"; Bodenhamer, Harris, and Corrigan, "Deep Mapping and the Spatial Humanities"; Fishkin, "'Deep Maps'"; Oxx, Brimicombe, and Rush, "Envisioning Deep Maps."

1. Eyewitnesses to Geographical Transformation

1. DeRosier, *William Dunbar*, 14.
2. DeRosier, *William Dunbar*.
3. Dunbar and Rowland, *Life, Letters, and Papers of William Dunbar*, 23.
4. Dunbar and Rowland, 30.
5. Dunbar and Rowland, 27.
6. Dunbar and Rowland, 60–61.
7. Dunbar and Rowland, 62.
8. See DeRosier, *William Dunbar*. Diana Clark was fifteen years old at the time of the marriage and was originally from England. She was a relative of the Ross family with whom Dunbar had done business since his arrival in Pennsylvania.
9. DeRosier, *William Dunbar*.
10. Jefferson, Thomas Jefferson to William Dunbar, June 24, 1799.
11. Clark, Daniel Clark, Jr to Thomas Jefferson, February 12, 1799; DeRosier, *William Dunbar*; Dunbar and Rowland, *Life, Letters, and Papers of William Dunbar*; Jefferson, Thomas Jefferson to William Dunbar, January 12, 1801.
12. Jackson, *Thomas Jefferson and the Rocky Mountains*; Ronda, "Exploring the West in the Age of Jefferson"; Harris and Buckley, *Zebulon Pike, Thomas Jefferson, and the Opening of the American West*; Koelsch, "Thomas Jefferson, American Geographers"; Allen, "Thomas Jefferson and the Mountain of Salt."
13. Dunbar, William Dunbar to Thomas Jefferson, May 13, 1804; Holmes, "Casa Calvo, Marques de"; Jefferson, Thomas Jefferson to William Dunbar, July 17, 1804; Dunbar, William Dunbar to Thomas Jefferson, June 1, 1804; Dunbar, William Dunbar to Thomas Jefferson, August 18, 1804.
14. Dunbar, William Dunbar to Thomas Jefferson, February 2, 1805.
15. Jefferson, Thomas Jefferson to William Dunbar, March 14, 1805.
16. Dunbar and Rowland, *Life, Letters, and Papers of William Dunbar*.
17. Cited in Freeman and Custis, *Southern Counterpart to Lewis and Clark*, 204–5.
18. DeRosier, *William Dunbar*, 203.
19. Schoolcraft, *Personal Memoirs of a Residence*, xxx.
20. Bremer, *Indian Agent and Wilderness Scholar*, 11.
21. Schoolcraft describes his travel to Missouri in Schoolcraft, *Scenes and Adventures*.
22. Moses Austin (1761–1821) established himself in the lead-mining business in Virginia in the 1780s in partnership with his brother Stephen. In 1798 he established a settlement and lead mining operation at Mine a Breton, present-day Potosi, Missouri. Through expansions of his holdings and innovations in mining techniques, he became wealthy and influential. In 1820 he traveled to San Antonio where he secured permission to establish a colony in Spanish Texas with the help of Baron de Bastrop. He contracted pneumonia during his journey in Texas and died June 10, 1821. One of his sons, Stephen Fuller Austin (1793–1836) carried out his father's wish to establish a colony in Texas. It

is possible that Moses Austin funded Schoolcraft's tour of the Ozarks.

23. Bremer, *Indian Agent and Wilderness Scholar.* According to his headstone in West Farmington Cemetery, Farmington Hills, Michigan, Levi Pettibone was born January 23, 1792, in Manchester, Bennington County, Vermont, and died April 27, 1868, in Farmington, Michigan. He was the son of Deborah Purdy and Seth Pettibone. He was a resident of Vermont at the time of the 1820, 1830, and 1840 U.S. federal censuses. The 1850 census indicates that he was a farmer in Farmington, Michigan, with his wife Huldah, fifty-six, and their son John, eighteen, and owned $4,000 in real estate. Huldah Strait Pettibone died in 1874.
24. Stephen Harriman Long (1784–1864) was a U.S. Army topographical engineer who was selected, along with General Henry W. Atkinson, to lead an expedition to build a fort near the confluence of the Yellowstone River and the Missouri River in present-day North Dakota. The expedition included the zoologist Thomas Say (1787–1834), who recorded descriptions of previously unknown species of reptiles, amphibians, birds, mammals, and invertebrates.
25. Schoolcraft, *Personal Memoirs*, 40.
26. Schoolcraft, *View of the Lead Mines of Missouri*, 21–22.
27. Schoolcraft, 22.
28. Schoolcraft, *Narrative Journal of Travels*, 131–32.
29. Mumford, "Mixed-Race Identity in a Nineteenth-Century Family," 20.
30. Bremer, *Indian Agent and Wilderness Scholar*, 214.
31. Through Professor Barton, Nuttall was introduced to the famous botanist and traveler William Bartram. William Bartram (1739–1823) was the son of John Bartram (1699–1777) an early American botanist and explorer.
32. Nuttall read William Dunbar's journal of the Ouachita River expedition and he hoped to accomplish the goal of ascending the Arkansas River to the Rocky Mountains.
33. Graustein, *Thomas Nuttall.*
34. Nuttall, *Journal of Travels*, 7.
35. Bigelow, "Review of Thomas Nuttall's *A Journal of Travels.*"
36. Nathaniel Jarvis Wyeth (1802–56) amassed wealth through his innovations in the ice industry in Boston. In the 1830s, he sought to extend his business endeavors to the Oregon Country by pursuing prospects in fur, farming, and fishing, but was unable to compete with the powerful Hudson's Bay Company. Milton Sublette (1801–37) and the Rocky Mountain Fur Company were rivals of the American Fur Company and the Hudson's Bay Company for dominance in the western fur trade. John Kirk Townsend (1809–51) had recently joined the American Philosophical Society and the Academy of Natural Sciences of Philadelphia when he was invited to by Nuttall to join the Wyeth expedition.
37. Townsend, *Narrative of a Journey*, 141.
38. Townsend, 179; emphasis in original.
39. Townsend, 225; emphasis in original.

40. Townsend, 289; emphasis in original.
41. Townsend, 296. McLoughlin was a French-Canadian who was about the same age as Nuttall and was serving as the chief factor for the Columbia district of the Hudson's Bay Company. He later supported the American cause in Oregon and became an American citizen.
42. Graustein, *Thomas Nuttall.*
43. The surname *Featherstonhaugh* was most likely pronounced *FAN-shaw.* His biographers, Berkeley and Berkeley, spelled his nickname as "Featherston." I've chosen to spell his nickname as "Fenston" to match the likely pronunciation. I appreciate the assistance of Charles W. J. Withers of the University of Edinburgh with the probable pronunciation of the surname and nickname.
44. Berkeley and Berkeley, *George William Featherstonhaugh.*
45. Featherstonhaugh, *Geological Report,* 51.
46. Featherstonhaugh, 57.
47. Featherstonhaugh, 92.
48. Berkeley and Berkeley, *George William Featherstonhaugh.*
49. Berkeley and Berkeley.
50. Featherstonhaugh, George W. Featherstonhaugh to John Murray, February 3, 1844; underlining in original.

2. A Very Great Natural Curiosity

1. Dunbar and Hunter, *Forgotten Expedition,* 10, 12.
2. Dunbar and Hunter, 22.
3. Dunbar and Hunter, 14.
4. George Hunter (1755–1832) was selected as co-commander of the expedition based on his experience and reputation as a chemist and druggist in Philadelphia. Hunter also had prior experience with wilderness travel, having made journeys to St. Louis in 1796 and Lexington, Kentucky, in 1802. Following the War of 1812, Hunter moved from Philadelphia to New Orleans, where he continued his work as a pharmacist.
5. Dunbar and Hunter, *Forgotten Expedition,* 9.
6. Dunbar and Hunter, 13.
7. Dunbar and Hunter, 32.
8. Dunbar and Hunter, 15. It is difficult to know what to make of Dunbar's reference to European peasants here. He did not appear to have any qualms about the inhumanity of slavery and seemed to blame any poverty he saw on the supposed laziness of the poor. Any concern for the oppressed in society is doubtful. But Dunbar had demonstrated a canny ability to gauge the direction of the political winds through changing regimes in west Florida, so it is conceivable that Dunbar was paying homage to the Jeffersonian ideal of agrarian virtue in a republican society in contrast to the feudal hierarchies of monarchical Europe.
9. Dunbar and Hunter, *Forgotten Expedition,* 15.
10. Dunbar and Hunter, 15.
11. Dunbar and Hunter, 15.

12. Meinig, *Continental America.*
13. The location is notable not only because it is the beginning of the journey on the Ouachita, but because Jonesville, Louisiana, is almost due west of Natchez, Mississippi. The expedition spent one week traveling a circuitous river route to advance a distance that today would require a mere thirty-minute drive west on Highway 84.
14. Dunbar and Hunter, *Forgotten Expedition*, 20.
15. Dunbar and Hunter, 22.
16. Dunbar and Hunter, 18.
17. The ancient mounds at this location date to approximately 100 BCE to 700 CE. It is believed to be one of the tallest pre-Columbian mounds in North America.
18. Dunbar and Hunter, *Forgotten Expedition*, 24–25.
19. Dunbar and Hunter, 9.
20. Dunbar and Hunter, 22.
21. Dunbar and Hunter, 26–27.
22. Dunbar and Hunter, 36.
23. Dunbar and Hunter, 36.
24. Dunbar and Hunter, 40.
25. Dunbar and Hunter, 46.
26. Dunbar and Hunter, 45.
27. Dunbar and Hunter, 47.
28. Dunbar and Hunter, 44.
29. Dunbar and Hunter, 45.
30. Dunbar and Hunter, 49.
31. Dunbar and Hunter, 52.
32. Dunbar and Hunter, 45–49, 52. For more on the class and national biases revealed in Dunbar's and Hunter's perceptions of poverty, see Owsley, *Plain Folk of the Old South*; McWhiney, *Cracker Culture*; Winders, "Imperfectly Imperial"; Pratt, *Imperial Eyes.*
33. Dunbar, William Dunbar to Thomas Jefferson, November 9, 1804.
34. Dunbar and Hunter, *Forgotten Expedition*, 53. According to the 1810 U.S. federal census, Samuel Blazier was a resident of Ouachita Parish, Louisiana, and the head of a household that included one male under 10, one male 26–44, one female 10–15, two females 16–25, and one female over 45. According to records on Ancestry.com, Blazier was born about 1765 and died about 1835. He married Francoise Avignon in about 1792 and their children were Elizabeth Blazier (1797–1856), Maria Lucia Blazier (1799–unknown), Lenora Maria Blazier (1802–unknown), John Blazier (1804–50), and Samuel Alexander Blazier (1807–60).
35. Dunbar and Hunter, *Forgotten Expedition*, 55.
36. Dunbar and Hunter, 62.
37. Dunbar and Hunter, 82.
38. Dunbar and Hunter, 93.
39. Dunbar and Hunter, 91.
40. Dunbar and Hunter, 60.
41. Dunbar and Hunter, 63.
42. Dunbar and Hunter, 67.
43. Dunbar and Hunter, 70.
44. Dunbar and Hunter, 84.
45. Dunbar and Hunter, 70.
46. Dunbar and Hunter, 77. It is notable that Dunbar records what he considers to be information "with truth" as well as that which might have been reported "falsely." Hunter relates at one point that they have doubts about the "judgment and

veracity" of Blazier. The acquisition of geographical knowledge was thus taken with a healthy grain of salt.

47. Dunbar and Hunter, *Forgotten Expedition*, 173.
48. For more on the Osages, see Rollings, *Osage*; Burns, *History of the Osage People*. The Osages resisted the encroachment of Americans and other Indian groups in their territory. They held important commercial and political power in the region due to their eighteenth-century alliances with the French and their partnerships with fur traders such as René Auguste Chouteau.
49. Dunbar and Hunter, *Forgotten Expedition*, 84–85.
50. Dunbar and Hunter, 172.
51. Dunbar and Hunter, 85.
52. Dunbar and Hunter, 192.
53. Dunbar and Hunter, 188.
54. Dunbar and Hunter, 62.
55. Dunbar and Hunter, 95.
56. Dunbar and Hunter, 93.
57. Dunbar and Hunter, 97.
58. Dunbar and Hunter, 98.
59. Dunbar and Hunter, 99.
60. Dunbar and Hunter, 99.
61. Dunbar and Hunter, 102.
62. Dunbar and Hunter, 95.
63. Dunbar and Hunter, 98.
64. Dunbar and Hunter, 106.
65. Dunbar and Hunter, 106.
66. Dunbar and Hunter, 105.
67. Dunbar and Hunter, 107.
68. Dunbar and Hunter, 107–8.
69. Dunbar and Hunter, 108.
70. Dunbar and Hunter, 108.
71. Dunbar and Hunter, 108.
72. Dunbar and Hunter, 109.
73. Dunbar and Hunter, 110.
74. Dunbar and Hunter, 111.
75. Dunbar and Hunter, 123.
76. Dunbar and Hunter, 131.
77. Dunbar and Hunter, 131.
78. Dunbar and Hunter, 141.
79. Dunbar and Hunter, 110, 123.
80. Dunbar and Hunter, 123.
81. Dunbar and Hunter, 124.
82. Dunbar and Hunter, 139.
83. Dunbar and Hunter, 140.
84. Dunbar and Hunter, 149.
85. Dunbar and Hunter, 127.
86. Dunbar and Hunter, 127.
87. Dunbar and Hunter, 128.
88. Dunbar and Hunter, 154.
89. Dunbar and Hunter, 139.
90. Dunbar and Hunter, 135.
91. Dunbar and Hunter, 144.
92. Dunbar and Hunter, 135.
93. Dunbar and Hunter, 138.
94. Dunbar and Hunter, 120.
95. Dunbar and Hunter, 120.
96. Dunbar and Hunter, 120.
97. Dunbar and Hunter, 132.
98. Dunbar and Hunter, 142.
99. Dunbar and Hunter, 143.
100. Dunbar and Hunter, 142.
101. Dunbar and Hunter, 159.
102. Dunbar and Hunter, 162.
103. Dunbar and Hunter, 164.
104. According to his headstone in Mount Holly Cemetery in Little Rock, Pierre LeFevre was born in 1750, came to Arkansas from Canada in 1770, and died in 1820. When Dunbar and Hunter met him, he was a wealthy landowner and Indian trader settled near Arkansas Post. He went bankrupt in 1810. See Arnold, *Rumble of a Distant Drum*.

105. Dunbar and Hunter, *Forgotten Expedition*, 167.
106. Dunbar and Hunter, 168.
107. Dunbar and Hunter, 171.
108. Dunbar and Hunter, 170.
109. Dunbar and Hunter, 167. The course of the rivers through the plains was based on the mistaken idea that the western rivers all flowed from some single high point in the mountainous west. This imagined geography placed the sources of the rivers close to one another.
110. Dunbar and Hunter, *Forgotten Expedition*, 172.
111. Dunbar and Hunter, 167.
112. Dunbar and Hunter, 188.
113. Dunbar and Hunter, 194.
114. Dunbar and Hunter, 183.
115. Dunbar and Hunter, 184.
116. Don Juan "Caddy" Hebrard de Baillion was an early settler of Catahoula Parish who operated a ferry across the Black River. Dunbar refers to the man as Hebrard, while Hunter calls him Cadits. See Kilpatrick, "Historical and Statistical Collections of Louisiana."
117. Dunbar and Hunter, *Forgotten Expedition*, 196–97.
118. Dunbar and Hunter, 191.
119. Dunbar and Hunter, 191–92.
120. Dunbar and Hunter, 192.
121. Dunbar and Hunter, 188.
122. Dunbar and Hunter, 197.
123. Dunbar and Hunter, 197.
124. Dunbar and Hunter, 198.

3. A Greenhorn in the Ozarks

1. Schoolcraft, *Rude Pursuits and Rugged Peaks*, 19.
2. Schoolcraft, *Rude Pursuits and Rugged Peaks*, 22. Levi Pettibone was about the same age as Henry Schoolcraft and also from New England. Thus, both men were in their mid-twenties and inexperienced with overland and backcountry travel in a region like the Ozarks.
3. Schoolcraft, *Rude Pursuits and Rugged Peaks*, 20.
4. Schoolcraft, 22.
5. Schoolcraft, 19.
6. Schoolcraft, 19.
7. Schoolcraft, 19–20.
8. Schoolcraft, 20.
9. Schoolcraft, 21.
10. Schoolcraft, 23.
11. The Roberts name is a common one. According to census records, John, Thomas, and William Roberts were residents of southeastern Missouri during this period. Leandre Leon Polite-Raubert "Lonzo" Robert is an interesting possibility for the Mr. Roberts that Henry and Levi encountered. He was born in Sainte Genevieve, Missouri, in 1792—thus about the same age as Schoolcraft and Pettibone—and died in 1859 in Old Mines, Washington County, Missouri. He is buried at Saint Joachim Cemetery in Washington County, Missouri. If this is the correct Roberts family, then Mrs. Roberts was Mary Anne Sylvain Roberts (1799–1840).

12. Schoolcraft, *Rude Pursuits and Rugged Peaks*, 23.
13. These villages and the Roberts cabin were in today's Mark Twain National Forest. Schoolcraft explains in his journal that they crossed the creek at the site of a Delaware village in which most of the men were out hunting, while women, children, and older men remained. The second Delaware village was three miles upstream, and the Shawnee village was four miles downstream.
14. Schoolcraft, *Rude Pursuits and Rugged Peaks*, 24.
15. Schoolcraft, 26.
16. Schoolcraft, 24, 25, 26.
17. The men were in in present-day Montauk State Park.
18. Schoolcraft, *Rude Pursuits and Rugged Peaks*, 26, 27, 28.
19. Schoolcraft, 29.
20. Schoolcraft, 29.
21. After ceasing mining operations in 1818, Ashley was active in the fur trade and made journeys to the Rocky Mountains in the 1820s. He became a U.S. congressman from Missouri in the 1830s. For more on the caves of Missouri, see Weaver, *Missouri Caves in History and Legend.*
22. Schoolcraft, *Rude Pursuits and Rugged Peaks*, 31.
23. Schoolcraft, 31.
24. Schoolcraft, 31.
25. Schoolcraft, 33.
26. Schoolcraft, 35.
27. Schoolcraft, 35–36.
28. Schoolcraft, 36.
29. Schoolcraft, 36.
30. Schoolcraft, 38.
31. Schoolcraft, 38.
32. Schoolcraft, 38.
33. The Gasconade River, and its major tributary, the Big Piney River, flow to the north-northeast and drain into the Missouri River. To the west of the Gasconade watershed is the Osage River system, which includes several rivers and streams that also flow into the Missouri.
34. Schoolcraft, *Rude Pursuits and Rugged Peaks*, 38.
35. Schoolcraft, 39.
36. Schoolcraft, 39.
37. Schoolcraft, 40.
38. Schoolcraft, 40–41.
39. Schoolcraft, 41. In his journal, Schoolcraft referred to the present-day North Fork of the White River as the "Limestone River."
40. Schoolcraft, *Rude Pursuits and Rugged Peaks*, 42. Milton Rafferty identified Elkhorn Spring as current-day Topaz Spring.
41. Schoolcraft, 43.
42. Schoolcraft, 42.
43. Schoolcraft, 40.
44. Schoolcraft, 42.
45. Schoolcraft, 42.
46. Schoolcraft, 42.
47. Schoolcraft, 44.
48. Schoolcraft, 44.
49. Schoolcraft, 44.
50. Schoolcraft, 47.
51. Schoolcraft, 47.
52. Schoolcraft, 47.
53. Schoolcraft, 47.
54. Schoolcraft, 48.
55. Schoolcraft, 50.
56. Schoolcraft, 49.
57. Schoolcraft, 51.

58. The men were in present-day Baxter County, Arkansas, near present-day Norfork Lake and Mountain Home.
59. Schoolcraft, *Rude Pursuits and Rugged Peaks*, 52.
60. No document that verifies the precise identity of the Wells family could be found, but one possibility is the family of Charles Wells Sr., who was born in Pennsylvania in 1773 and died in 1836 in Missouri. His wife was Sarah "Sally" Lewis Wells (1775–1857). By 1819, Charles and Sally had approximately ten children, including seven sons—three of whom would have been over the age of twenty—and three daughters. Although Charles Wells Sr. appears to have made his home in St. Charles County and Montgomery County, Missouri, near St. Louis, two of his sons—Jacob Wells and Charles Wells Jr.—had a presence in Arkansas. In 1822 Charles Wells (presumably Junior) married Jenny Newcomb and Jacob Wells married Rosanna Newcomb in Lawrence County, Arkansas. The 1830 U.S. federal census enumerates a Charles Wells, of the right age to be Charles Jr., in Wayne County, Missouri. Charles Wells appears again in the 1840 U.S. federal census in Gasconade County, Missouri.
61. Schoolcraft, *Rude Pursuits and Rugged Peaks*, 52.
62. Schoolcraft, 53.
63. Schoolcraft, 52–53.
64. Schoolcraft, 54.
65. Schoolcraft, 55.
66. Schoolcraft, 55.
67. Schoolcraft, 55.
68. Schoolcraft, 56.
69. Schoolcraft, 56–57.
70. Schoolcraft, 57.
71. Schoolcraft, 58.
72. The men were near the section of the White River that flows into Bull Shoals Lake today and runs along the state line of Arkansas and Missouri.
73. George James McGarrah was born in 1760 in South Carolina, where he and Mary Rowell married in 1797. The ages of their children fit Schoolcraft's description of "a numerous family of sons and daughters, all grown up." James McGarrah died in Washington County, Arkansas, in 1840.
74. Schoolcraft, *Rude Pursuits and Rugged Peaks*, 60.
75. Schoolcraft, 60.
76. Schoolcraft, 61.
77. Schoolcraft, 61.
78. Schoolcraft, 61.
79. Schoolcraft, 61.
80. In his journal, Schoolcraft spells the surname "M'Gary." The man was probably James McGarrah of Marion County, Arkansas.
81. Schoolcraft, *Rude Pursuits and Rugged Peaks*, 62.
82. Schoolcraft, 62.
83. According to Turnbo's *White River Chronicles*, Joe Coker (1787–1862) and his father, William "Buck" Coker (1769–1855), reached the Sugar Loaf country in 1814 and 1815, respectively. Numerous members of the Coker family lived in this vicinity. See Turnbo, *White River Chronicles*.
84. Schoolcraft, *Rude Pursuits and Rugged Peaks*, 64. The present-day

towns in the vicinity of the Sugar Loaf Prairie Settlement are Leadhill and Diamond City, Arkansas. The settlement was named for a bald knob along the White River that is now forested at the top.

85. Schoolcraft, *Rude Pursuits and Rugged Peaks*, 63.
86. Schoolcraft, 64.
87. Schoolcraft, 63.
88. Schoolcraft, 63.
89. Schoolcraft, 63.
90. Schoolcraft, 64.
91. Schoolcraft, 64.
92. Schoolcraft, 65.
93. Schoolcraft, 66.
94. Schoolcraft, 66.
95. The families with whom Schoolcraft and Pettibone stayed were probably those of William Holt (ca. 1790–1853) and his wife Sophia Warwick Maloney Holt (ca. 1791–1838), and James Fisher (ca. 1798–1842).
96. Schoolcraft, *Rude Pursuits and Rugged Peaks*, 67.
97. Schoolcraft, 67.
98. Beaver Creek flows into the White River just east of present-day Branson, Missouri.
99. Schoolcraft, *Rude Pursuits and Rugged Peaks*, 69.
100. Schoolcraft, 69.
101. Schoolcraft, 71.
102. Schoolcraft, 73.
103. Schoolcraft, 73.
104. Schoolcraft, 75.
105. Schoolcraft, 74.
106. Schoolcraft, 74.
107. Schoolcraft, 74.
108. Schoolcraft, 74.
109. Schoolcraft, 74.
110. Schoolcraft, 74.
111. Schoolcraft, 72.
112. Schoolcraft, 73.
113. Schoolcraft, 78.
114. Schoolcraft, 78–79.
115. Schoolcraft, 79–80. According to Milton Rafferty, the cave they explored was Smallin Cave near present-day Ozark, Missouri.
116. Schoolcraft, *Rude Pursuits and Rugged Peaks*, 80–81.
117. Schoolcraft does not make it clear whether these lead mines were abandoned or simply closed for the winter.
118. Schoolcraft, *Rude Pursuits and Rugged Peaks*, 83.
119. Schoolcraft, 82.
120. Schoolcraft, 82.
121. Schoolcraft, 82.
122. Schoolcraft, 83.
123. Schoolcraft, 84. One can only speculate about the reasons that Schoolcraft did not attempt to move to this area and establish the operations that he envisioned. The simplest explanation is that he lacked funding, entrepreneurial skill, or both.
124. Schoolcraft, *Rude Pursuits and Rugged Peaks*, 84.
125. Schoolcraft, 86.
126. Schoolcraft, 88.
127. Schoolcraft, 90.
128. Schoolcraft, 89.
129. Schoolcraft, 89.
130. Schoolcraft, 92–93.
131. Schoolcraft, 92.
132. Schoolcraft, 94.
133. Schoolcraft, 95.
134. Schoolcraft, 95–96. Bull Shoals Lake above Bull Shoals Dam covers most

of this portion of the White River today.

135. Schoolcraft spelled the surname as "Yochem." Henry and Levi visited two Yocums on White River. These men were most likely Solomon Yocum (ca. 1773–1850) and Jacob Yocum (ca. 1791–1850). According to Turnbo, the Yocum brothers Jess, Mike, Jacob, and Solomon immigrated to the United States (Pennsylvania) from Germany as children. See Turnbo, *White River Chronicles.*

136. Schoolcraft, Rude Pursuits and Rugged Peaks, 97.

137. Schoolcraft, 99.

138. Schoolcraft, 98.

139. Schoolcraft, 98.

140. Schoolcraft, 99.

141. This man was probably Augustine John Friend (ca. 1770–1840).

142. Schoolcraft, *Rude Pursuits and Rugged Peaks*, 100.

143. This man was probably Jacob Yocum (ca. 1791–1850).

144. Schoolcraft, *Rude Pursuits and Rugged Peaks*, 103.

145. This man was probably William Matney (ca. 1783–1854). Matney married Sarah Yocum, one of the daughters of Solomon Yocum. See Clouston-Becker, *Lives and Legends of the Ozark Yoakums*; Goodspeed, *Biographical and Historical Memoirs.*

146. Schoolcraft, *Rude Pursuits and Rugged Peaks*, 103.

147. Schoolcraft, 108–9.

148. Poke Bayou is present-day Batesville, Arkansas.

149. Schoolcraft, *Rude Pursuits and Rugged Peaks*, 109.

150. Schoolcraft, 111.

151. Mrs. Lafferty was most likely Sarah Lindsey Lafferty, the widow of John Lafferty. John Lafferty was wounded in the Battle of New Orleans in 1815 and died sometime between 1816 and 1817. Thus, Sarah Lafferty was a recent widow when Schoolcraft and Pettibone arrived in early 1819. See Miller and Elrod, "John Lafferty (1759–1816)."

152. Schoolcraft, *Rude Pursuits and Rugged Peaks*, 110.

153. Schoolcraft, 111–12.

154. Schoolcraft, 111–12.

155. According to Goodspeed, "Col. Robert Bean ran the first keel-boat up White River and established himself at the mouth of Poke Bayou in 1814." See Goodspeed, *Biographical and Historical Memoirs.*

156. Schoolcraft, *Rude Pursuits and Rugged Peaks*, 113.

157. The published version of Schoolcraft's journal does not include most of the names of the settlers that Schoolcraft encountered in northeast Arkansas and southeast Missouri. Schoolcraft's original journal, available in the Henry Rowe Schoolcraft Papers at the Library of Congress (Henry Rowe Schoolcraft papers, 1788–1941 [bulk 1820–1856], https://lccn.loc.gov/mm 73039115), includes the names Mr. Hudson, Maj. Hynes, Widow Black, Harn, Reeves, Matthews, Solomon Bollinger, Col. Esty, Dr. Bettis, Smith, Swain, Tucker, Burdett, Cook, and Hale. I appreciate the assistance of Blake Perkins in locating the original journal.

158. Schoolcraft, *Rude Pursuits and Rugged Peaks*, 118.
159. Schoolcraft, 119.
160. Schoolcraft, 119.
161. Schoolcraft, 119–20.
162. Schoolcraft, 124.
163. Schoolcraft, 124.
164. Schoolcraft, 124–25.
165. Schoolcraft, *Personal Memoirs*, 38.

4. A View from the Banks of the Arkansas River

1. Nuttall, *Travels into the Arkansas Territory*, 58–59.
2. Nuttall, 59–60.
3. Nuttall, 57–58.
4. Nuttall, *Travels into the Arkansas Territory*, 49.
5. Nuttall, 49–50.
6. Nuttall, 54.
7. Nuttall, 54–55. For more on the New Madrid earthquakes, see Valenčius, *Lost History of the New Madrid Earthquakes*.
8. Nuttall, *Travels into the Arkansas Territory*, 60.
9. Nuttall, 64.
10. Nuttall, 65.
11. Nuttall, 65.
12. Nuttall, 66.
13. Nuttall, 69.
14. According to Josiah Shinn, there was a resident in this area named J. McLean. The tavern owner is sometimes identified as Neil McLane, but McLane was a lawyer and circuit judge from New Hampshire who died in Little Rock in 1821 at the age of twenty-nine. According to Shinn, Neil McLane had "only been in the state a short time." See Shinn, *Pioneers and Makers of Arkansas*.
15. Nuttall, *Travels into the Arkansas Territory*, 72.
16. Nuttall, 76.
17. Edwin Godfrey and his father, who had accompanied Nuttall since they departed from Louisville in early December left Nuttall here and continued their journey down the Mississippi River to New Orleans on another flatboat.
18. Nuttall, *Travels into the Arkansas Territory*, 77.
19. Nuttall, 78.
20. Nuttall, 77.
21. Nuttall, 78. For more on the Arkansas Delta, see Whayne and Gatewood, *Arkansas Delta*.
22. Nuttall, *Travels into the Arkansas Territory*, 78.
23. Nuttall, 87.
24. Nuttall, 85.
25. Nuttall, 89.
26. Joseph Bogy (alternately Baugis, Baugy, Bougie) was born circa 1752 in Quebec. He married Della Marie Louise DuGuay Duplassy (ca. 1761–1847) at Kaskaskia and established himself as a trader at Arkansas Post around 1786. He extended his trading operations to the Three Forks area in present-day Oklahoma where the Verdigris, Grand, and Arkansas Rivers converge near present-day Muskogee, Oklahoma. According to his headstone at Saint Peters

Cemetery in New Gascony, Jefferson County, Arkansas, Bogy died in November 1831. Kuhlman, "Bogy, Joseph (ca. 1749–?)."

27. Nuttall, *Travels into the Arkansas Territory*, 83.
28. The identity of "Braham" is unknown, but Nuttall might have meant to spell the name "Barham." If so, he may have been referring to Jacob Barkman (1784–1852). According to Josiah Shinn, in Arkansas Post in 1819 "the principal cotton factor was William Drope of New Orleans, and Frederick Notrebe acted as his agent at the post. Drope ran this business in conjunction with a store which carried everything from sugar to sawmills . . . Eli J. Lewis was postmaster, clerk of the Circuit Court, tanner and storekeeper, and the boomer of the town." Eli Lewis committed suicide in 1822. See Sesser, "Jacob Barkman (1784–1852)"; Shinn, *Pioneers and Makers of Arkansas*.
29. Nuttall, *Travels into the Arkansas Territory*, 83.
30. Nuttall, 86.
31. Nuttall, 88.
32. Nuttall, 93–94.
33. Nuttall, 80.
34. Nuttall, 100.
35. Nuttall, 100.
36. Nuttall, 101.
37. Nuttall, 100.
38. Nuttall, 101.
39. Nuttall, 101.
40. Nuttall noted that the settlement was begun by a Colonel Mooney. This is probably Daniel Mooney who had settled between the St. Francis River and Mississippi River about 1797 in present-day Phillips County, Arkansas. He served as sheriff and rose in the ranks of the militia. See Clifft, "Phillips County"; Shinn, *Pioneers and Makers of Arkansas*.
41. Nuttall, *Travels into the Arkansas Territory*, 101–2.
42. Nuttall, 102.
43. Nuttall, 102–3.
44. Nuttall, 104.
45. Nuttall, 105.
46. Nuttall, 106.
47. Nuttall, 107.
48. Nuttall, 109.
49. Nuttall, 108.
50. Nuttall, 110. The surnames of the farm owners mentioned by Nuttall in the area are Morrison, Dardenne, Mason, Vaugin, and Embree. Other than Lewismore Vaugine, it is unclear from Nuttall's journal whether or not he met any of these men or their families. Métis are people of mixed Indian and European ancestry.
51. Nuttall, *Travels into the Arkansas Territory*, 111.
52. Nuttall, 111.
53. Nuttall, 110.
54. Nuttall, 112.
55. Nuttall, 111.
56. Nuttall, 112.
57. Nuttall, 111–12.
58. Nuttall, 112.
59. Nuttall, 113.
60. Nuttall, 113.
61. Nuttall, 113.
62. Nuttall, 113.
63. Nuttall's Monsieur "LaFeve" might have been Pierre LeFevre, with

whom Dunbar and Hunter traveled and who died in Little Rock in 1820. According to Josiah Shinn, Wright Daniels was "one of the oldest settlers of Pulaski, a most industrious man, the owner of a grist mill, and the father of beautiful daughters." Edmund Hogan (ca. 1780–1828) was a representative to the Territorial General Assembly of Missouri in 1816 and 1818 and served as the first justice of the peace for Pulaski County. Hogan also operated a ferry across the Arkansas River at Little Rock. See Gieringer, "Edmund Hogan (1780–1828)"; Shinn, *Pioneers and Makers of Arkansas.*

64. Nuttall, *Travels into the Arkansas Territory*, 114.
65. Nuttall, 114.
66. Nuttall, 114.
67. Nuttall, 114.
68. Nuttall, 115.
69. Nuttall, 116.
70. Nuttall, 115.
71. According to Josiah Shinn, Lemuel R. Curran was sheriff of Pulaski County from 1818 to 1821 and was "one of the leading spirits of Cadron and died there on March 8, 1821." See Shinn, *Pioneers and Makers of Arkansas.*
72. Nuttall, *Travels into the Arkansas Territory*, 117.
73. Mr. Blair might have been W. P. L. Blair, the clerk of Clark County at the time of Nuttall's visit. It is also possible that "Blair" was David or Jonathan Pharr who had settled in the area near Crystal Hill. James, Jacob, and John Pyeatt settled upstream from Crystal Hill. James operated a ferry across the Arkansas River and Jacob founded a settlement at Cadron in 1815. See Shinn, *Pioneers and Makers of Arkansas*; Allison, "Crystal Hill (Pulaski County)."
74. Nuttall, *Travels into the Arkansas Territory*, 118.
75. Nuttall, 119.
76. Nuttall, 119.
77. Nuttall, 119, 121.
78. Nuttall, 122.
79. Nuttall, 122.
80. Nuttall, 124.
81. Nuttall, 125.
82. Nuttall, 125.
83. Nuttall, 127.
84. Nuttall, 127.
85. Nuttall, 128.
86. Nuttall, 128.
87. Mr. Petis was probably a private deputy surveyor under contract with William Rector, the U.S. surveyor general for the Missouri District until 1824. The township and range survey of public lands in Arkansas began with the establishment of the Fifth Principal Meridian in eastern Arkansas in 1815. According to David Smith, "Much of the early survey work of Arkansas lands performed by the contracted deputies was of poor quality . . . either due to carelessness, faulty equipment, incompetence, or malfeasance, and a substantial amount of the initial effort was either rejected by the office of the surveyor general serving Arkansas or by the GLO in Washington DC. 'Resurveys' of prior work were often necessary." See Smith, "Public Land Surveys."

88. Nuttall, *Travels into the Arkansas Territory*, 129.
89. Nuttall, 128–29.
90. Nuttall, 129.
91. Nuttall, 130.
92. Nuttall, 130.
93. Nuttall, 131.
94. Nuttall, 132.
95. Nuttall, 132.
96. Nuttall, 133.
97. Nuttall, 133.
98. Nuttall, 133.
99. Nuttall, 134.
100. Nuttall, 134.
101. Nuttall, 136.
102. Nuttall, 135.
103. Nuttall, 136–37.
104. Nuttall, 138.
105. Nuttall, 139.
106. Nuttall, 136. It is unclear why Drope decided not to continue to Fort Smith. The rising river's strong current could have made him decide to turn back. It is also possible that he had run out of supplies to trade and decided to return downstream.
107. Nuttall, *Travels into the Arkansas Territory*, 143.
108. Nuttall, 142.
109. Nuttall, 145.
110. Nuttall, 145.
111. Nuttall, 146.
112. Nuttall, 149–50.
113. Nuttall, 147.
114. Nuttall, 147.
115. Nuttall, 145. The only Cherokee that Nuttall mentions by name is John Rogers, the nephew of John Jolly and Tahlonteeskee. Nuttall described Rogers as a "very respectable and civilized Cherokee."
116. Nuttall, *Travels into the Arkansas Territory*, 141.
117. Nuttall, 140. One of the ridges that Nuttall climbed was probably present-day Sunrise Point.
118. Nuttall, *Travels into the Arkansas Territory*, 141.
119. Nuttall, 142.
120. Nuttall, 143.
121. Nuttall does not indicate with whom he stayed or where he ate during his two weeks in Dardanelle. His reference to Walter Webber on April 9 and again on April 20 suggests that he may have taken accommodations in his house.
122. Nuttall, *Travels into the Arkansas Territory*, 152. According to Samuel Dorris Dickinson, Charbonniere Creek may be present-day Cane Creek. He noted that "since charbonniere in French is a woman who burns or sells charcoal or who heaves coal, Nuttall probably got the gender wrong and should have spelled the name charbonnier." Dickinson, "Colonial Arkansas Place Names," 158.
123. Nuttall, *Travels into the Arkansas Territory*, 152.
124. Nuttall, 153.
125. Nuttall, 153.
126. Nuttall, 153. Nuttall referred to Short Mountain as the Cassetete or Tomahawk mountain after the names used by French hunters.
127. Nuttall, *Travels into the Arkansas Territory*, 154.
128. Nuttall, 154.
129. Nuttall, 154.
130. Nuttall, 154.

131. Nuttall, 155.
132. Nuttall, 159. Fort Smith was named for General Thomas Smith, the Commander of U.S. Army Rifle Regiment. Bradford and his men were charged with maintaining peace between the Osages and Cherokees.
133. Nuttall, *Travels into the Arkansas Territory*, 159.
134. Nuttall, 155–56.
135. Nuttall, 157–58.
136. Nuttall, 161.
137. Nuttall, 162.
138. The Kiamichi River flows into the Red River south of present-day Fort Towson, Oklahoma. This is approximately fifty miles from the convergence of the present state lines of Arkansas, Texas, and Oklahoma. One of the riflemen on the expedition was Peter Caulder, a free black man who had enlisted in the U.S. Army and served under Major Bradford. See Higgins, *Stranger and a Sojourner.*
139. Nuttall, *Travels into the Arkansas Territory*, 166.
140. Nuttall, 166.
141. Nuttall, 170.
142. Nuttall, 172.
143. Nuttall, 170–71.
144. Nuttall, 174.
145. Nuttall, 176.
146. Nuttall, 170.
147. Nuttall, 179.
148. Nuttall, 180.
149. Nuttall, 180.
150. Fort Gibson, Oklahoma, was established here five years after Nuttall's visit.
151. Nuttall, *Travels into the Arkansas Territory*, 192.
152. Nuttall, 191.
153. This may have been Tom Slover, who was in the area of the Three Forks by this time. See Baird, "Westward Expansion, 1803–1861."
154. Nuttall, *Travels into the Arkansas Territory*, 202.
155. Nuttall, 204–5.
156. Nuttall, 212.
157. Nuttall, 226.
158. Nuttall, 226.
159. Nuttall, 227.
160. Nuttall, 228.
161. Nuttall, 228.
162. Nuttall, 228.
163. Nuttall, 228.
164. Nuttall, 232.
165. Nuttall, 232.
166. Nuttall, 233.
167. Nuttall, 233.
168. Nuttall, 237.
169. Graustein, *Thomas Nuttall.*
170. Nuttall, *Travels into the Arkansas Territory*, 238.
171. Nuttall, 238.
172. Nuttall, 239.
173. Nuttall, 243.
174. James Miller was a native of New Hampshire who had served as a general in the War of 1812. Although appointed Governor of Arkansas Territory in March 1819, Miller did not arrive in the territory until December of that year. See Clements, "James Miller (1776–1851)."
175. Nuttall, *Travels into the Arkansas Territory*, 248–49.
176. Nuttall, 247.
177. Frederick Notrebe (1780–1849) came to the United States—probably New Orleans—from France in about 1810

and became connected with other traders and merchants in the Lower Mississippi River Valley. He amassed wealth in Arkansas Post and eventually owned more than five thousand acres of land and more than one hundred slaves. See Cande, "Frederick Notrebe (1780–1849)."

178. Nuttall, *Travels into the Arkansas Territory*, 247–49; Graustein, *Thomas Nuttall*, 150–51. Nuttall arrived in New Orleans approximately one month after departing Arkansas Post. He spent four or five days in Natchez, Mississippi, where he visited with Samuel Postlethwaite, the son-in-law of William Dunbar, and learned about Mississippi agriculture, horticulture, and ethnology. On his way to New Orleans, Nuttall commented on the misguided Indian removal policies, the ugliness and injustice of the slavery, and the lack of education and culture in New Orleans. He was back in Philadelphia by the end of April 1820.

5. A Savage Sort of Country

1. Featherstonhaugh, *Excursion through the Slave States*, 63.
2. Featherstonhaugh, 63.
3. Featherstonhaugh, 64; emphasis in original.
4. Featherstonhaugh, 69.
5. George Featherstonhaugh Jr. was born in October 1814, so he was near his twentieth birthday when he and his father made their tour of Arkansas. George Jr. lived until at least 1900, when he was enumerated on the U.S. federal census as a resident of Lake County, Illinois.
6. Featherstonhaugh, *Excursion through the Slave States*, 72.
7. Featherstonhaugh, 73.
8. Featherstonhaugh, 73.
9. Featherstonhaugh, 77.
10. Featherstonhaugh, 75.
11. Featherstonhaugh, 75.
12. Featherstonhaugh, 76.
13. Featherstonhaugh, 78.
14. Featherstonhaugh, 74.
15. Featherstonhaugh, 78.
16. Featherstonhaugh, 81.
17. Featherstonhaugh, 81.
18. Featherstonhaugh, 82.
19. Featherstonhaugh, 83.
20. Featherstonhaugh, 85.
21. Featherstonhaugh, 85.
22. Featherstonhaugh, 85.
23. Featherstonhaugh, 86.
24. Featherstonhaugh, 86.
25. Featherstonhaugh, 86.
26. This was probably the household of James Russell and Parthena Bridges Russell who were married in Randolph County in 1832. The 1840 U.S. federal census enumerated a household of nine, including five children under ten and a woman over sixty.
27. Featherstonhaugh, *Excursion through the Slave States*, 86. Fenston noted that Mr. Russell had moved his family to Arkansas twenty-four years earlier.
28. Featherstonhaugh, 86.
29. Featherstonhaugh, 86.

30. Featherstonhaugh, 86.
31. Featherstonhaugh, 86. Mrs. Newland was probably the widow of William Newland, who died around the time of Fenston's tour. The Newlands were taxed in Strawberry Township of Lawrence County, which would place them along Fenston's route.
32. Featherstonhaugh, 86.
33. Featherstonhaugh, 86.
34. Featherstonhaugh, 87.
35. The Meriwethers were probably John Martin Meriwether (1787–1844) and Martha "Patsy" Duncan Meriwether (1799–1863). They were residents of Black River Township, Independence County, in 1835 and are buried in Pleasant Hill Cemetery, Sulphur Rock, Arkansas.
36. Featherstonhaugh, *Excursion through the Slave States*, 87.
37. Featherstonhaugh, 87.
38. Featherstonhaugh, 87.
39. Featherstonhaugh, 87.
40. Featherstonhaugh, 87.
41. Featherstonhaugh, 87.
42. Featherstonhaugh, 88.
43. Featherstonhaugh, 89.
44. Featherstonhaugh, 89.
45. Featherstonhaugh, 89.
46. Featherstonhaugh, 89. This man may have been Payton Tucker, who served as postmaster in 1832 and 1833 in White Run Township, Independence County.
47. Featherstonhaugh, 91.
48. Joseph and Obadiah Hernby lived in Lawrence County, Arkansas, in 1831. No other records could be found to verify the identity of the "Hornby" that Featherstonhaugh described.
49. Featherstonhaugh, *Excursion through the Slave States*, 92.
50. Featherstonhaugh, 92–93.
51. Featherstonhaugh, 94.
52. Featherstonhaugh, 93.
53. Featherstonhaugh, 94.
54. Featherstonhaugh, 94.
55. Featherstonhaugh, 94.
56. Featherstonhaugh, 96.
57. Featherstonhaugh, 95.
58. Featherstonhaugh, 95; emphasis in original.
59. Featherstonhaugh, 95.
60. Featherstonhaugh, 95.
61. Featherstonhaugh, 95.
62. Featherstonhaugh, 95.
63. William Stevenson (1768–1857) was one of the first Methodist circuit-riding preachers in Arkansas. He moved to Louisiana in 1826, but the description of the Rev. Stevenson in Little Rock that Featherstonhaugh gives fits William Stevenson. According to his autobiography, Stevenson damaged one of his eyes around age eighteen when a horse he was riding got away from him and he gouged his eye on the branch of a tree. See Stevenson, *Autobiography*; Johnson, "William Stevenson (1768–1857)."
64. Featherstonhaugh, *Excursion through the Slave States*, 95.
65. Featherstonhaugh, 95.
66. Featherstonhaugh, 96.
67. Featherstonhaugh, 97.
68. John Pope (1770–1845) served Kentucky as U.S. senator from 1807 to 1813 and was appointed territorial governor of Arkansas in 1829 after the election of President Andrew

Jackson. Frances Watkins Walton Pope (ca. 1772–1843) was John Pope's third wife following the deaths of his first two wives and was the Mrs. Pope that Featherstonhaugh would have met. Pope's tenure as territorial governor ended in 1835, shortly after Featherstonhaugh's visit, and he returned to Kentucky. The Pope's are buried at Cemetery Hill Cemetery, Springfield, Washington County, Kentucky. See Bender, "John Pope (1770–1845)."

69. Featherstonhaugh, *Excursion through the Slave States*, 97.
70. Featherstonhaugh, 97.
71. William E. Woodruff (1795–1885) was a native of New York who worked for newspapers in Kentucky and Tennessee before coming to Arkansas in 1819 to seek opportunities in the newly-formed territory. Thomas Nuttall passed through Arkansas Post about three months after Woodruff's arrival in the new territorial capital. When Featherstonhaugh met Woodruff fifteen years later, Woodruff had established the very successful Arkansas Gazette newspaper. See Kwas, "William Edward Woodruff (1795–1885)."
72. Featherstonhaugh, *Excursion through the Slave States*, 97.
73. Featherstonhaugh, 96; emphasis in original. Regarding newspapers in Arkansas, Featherstonhaugh included a footnote that "the *National Intelligencer* of the City of Washington well deserves the high character it has everywhere acquired."
74. Featherstonhaugh, *Excursion through the Slave States*, 97.
75. Featherstonhaugh, 97.
76. Featherstonhaugh, 99–100.
77. Featherstonhaugh, 97.
78. Featherstonhaugh, 97.
79. Featherstonhaugh, 98.
80. Featherstonhaugh, 98–99.
81. Featherstonhaugh, 100; emphasis in original.
82. Featherstonhaugh, 100.
83. Featherstonhaugh, 100.
84. Featherstonhaugh, 100; emphasis in original.
85. Featherstonhaugh, 100.
86. Featherstonhaugh, 101.
87. Featherstonhaugh, 101.
88. Featherstonhaugh, 101.
89. Featherstonhaugh, 102.
90. Featherstonhaugh, 102.
91. Featherstonhaugh, 102.
92. Featherstonhaugh, 102.
93. Featherstonhaugh, 102.
94. Featherstonhaugh, 102.
95. Featherstonhaugh, 102.
96. Alexander Starbuck (ca. 1787–1839) was a native of Massachusetts and arrived in Pulaski County, Arkansas, by 1830. His wife, Olive Elliott Starbuck (ca. 1790–1843), was the daughter of Benjamin Elliott (ca. 1762–1848) and Frances Pankey Elliott (ca. 1762–1854). The Elliotts were also residents of Pulaski County by 1830.
97. Featherstonhaugh, *Excursion through the Slave States*, 103.
98. Featherstonhaugh, 103.
99. Featherstonhaugh, 104.
100. Featherstonhaugh, 104.
101. Featherstonhaugh, 104; emphasis in original.

102. Featherstonhaugh, 104.
103. Featherstonhaugh, 105.
104. Featherstonhaugh, 104.
105. Featherstonhaugh, 105; emphasis in original.
106. Featherstonhaugh, 105.
107. Featherstonhaugh, 106.
108. Featherstonhaugh, 106.
109. James S. Conway (1796–1855) was a native of Tennessee and nephew of surveyor general William Rector. In 1826 he married Mary Jane "Polly" Bradley (1809–78), the niece of Captain Hugh Bradley. The Bradleys were among the early settlers on Long Prairie near the Red River. At the time of Featherstonhaugh's visit, the Conways were building a summer cottage at Magnet Cove to complement their two-thousand-acre plantation with eighty slaves in Lafayette County. Conway would be elected the first governor of the new state of Arkansas in 1836. See Williams, "James Sevier Conway (1796–1855)."
110. Featherstonhaugh, *Excursion through the Slave States*, 107.
111. Featherstonhaugh, 107.
112. Featherstonhaugh, 107. Helen Pennington writes that "until recently, the available data indicated that there were more distinct minerals found in the five-square-mile radius of the cove than were found anywhere else on the planet; a small location in Russia is now believed to be comparable to Magnet Cove's mineral deposits, many of which are microscopic." She also notes that "the current general consensus of opinion is that [Magnet Cove] was formed of intrusive (below the ground) igneous rock. Minerals formed in thin veins as a result of the passage of vapors and fluids released by the cooling magma penetrating outward." Pennington, "Magnet Cove."
113. Featherstonhaugh, *Excursion through the Slave States*, 108.
114. Featherstonhaugh, 108.
115. Featherstonhaugh, 108–9. Mr. Percival may have been John H. Percivall (1754–1835), a native of Cheshire, England, who had moved to Arkansas by 1820. He lived in Hot Springs by 1828 and died there in the summer of 1835, about six months after Featherstonhaugh stayed with him.
116. Featherstonhaugh, *Excursion through the Slave States*, 109.
117. Featherstonhaugh, 109.
118. Featherstonhaugh, 109.
119. Featherstonhaugh, 110.
120. Featherstonhaugh, 110.
121. Featherstonhaugh, 109.
122. Featherstonhaugh, 109.
123. Featherstonhaugh, 111; emphasis in original.
124. Featherstonhaugh, 113.
125. Featherstonhaugh, 111. If Featherstonhaugh had gone to Fort Towson, he would have observed the territory that Thomas Nuttall visited in 1819 on the excursion to remove white settlers from the area.
126. Featherstonhaugh, *Excursion through the Slave States*, 111.
127. Mr. Mitchell is probably Moses H. Mitchell, who was enumerated on the 1830 U.S. federal census in Fenter Township, Hot Springs County, as the head of a household that included

two slaves, three young children, three men in their twenties, and two women in their twenties. Moses Mitchell appears on county tax rolls throughout the 1830s.

128. Featherstonhaugh, *Excursion through the Slave States*, 114.
129. Featherstonhaugh, 114.
130. Featherstonhaugh, 114.
131. Featherstonhaugh, 114.
132. Featherstonhaugh, 114.
133. Jacob Barkman married Rebecca Davis in his native Kentucky and moved to Louisiana and then Arkansas around 1811. By 1815, he started constructing his two-story brick house that served as the first courthouse and first post office of Clark County. Before Featherstonhaugh's arrival, the house had become a stagecoach stop. The house was destroyed after Barkman's death in 1852. Rebecca Davis Barkman died about three years after Featherstonhaugh's visit. See Sesser, "Jacob Barkman (1784–1852)."
134. Featherstonhaugh, *Excursion through the Slave States*, 114.
135. Featherstonhaugh, 115.
136. Featherstonhaugh, 115.
137. Featherstonhaugh, 115.
138. Featherstonhaugh spelled Terre Noire Creek as "Tournoise Creek" and Hignight's name as "Hignite." According to his headstone along Arkansas State Highway 26 near Terre Noire Creek, Abner Hignight (ca. 1790–1857) came to Arkansas in 1810, brought the first seed corn to Clark County, and was "a farmer, road overseer, deputy sheriff, and noted bear and buffalo hunter." For the names of pioneer citizens, including Abner Hignight, see Pinkston, "Greenville (Clark County)."
139. Featherstonhaugh, *Excursion through the Slave States*, 115. Fenston made note of what he called "this bandying about of court-houses" and explained that this was due to the "state of the settlements in this new country" where "the counties are ten times as large as they are eventually destined to be, and everything is a matter of expediency until population fills up the space a little." Thus, the cabin of a settler was used as a temporary courthouse and the location was changed occasionally to serve settlers in various sections of the county.
140. Featherstonhaugh, *Excursion through the Slave States*, 115.
141. Featherstonhaugh, 115. Mr. Tunstall was most likely Thomas Todd Tunstall (ca. 1787–1862) who was the Captain of the Waverly, the first steamboat on the upper White River, and the owner of a large farm on Dota Creek in Independence County where he bred and raced horses. See Rorie, "Dota (Independence County)."
142. Featherstonhaugh, *Excursion through the Slave States*, 115.
143. Featherstonhaugh, 115.
144. Featherstonhaugh, 115.
145. Featherstonhaugh, 115; emphasis in original.
146. Featherstonhaugh, 116.
147. Featherstonhaugh, 116.
148. Featherstonhaugh, 116.
149. Featherstonhaugh, 116.
150. Featherstonhaugh, 117.
151. Featherstonhaugh, 117.

152. Featherstonhaugh, 117.
153. Featherstonhaugh, 117.
154. Featherstonhaugh, 117.
155. Featherstonhaugh, 117.
156. Edward Cross (1798–1887) was a native of Tennessee who moved to Arkansas in 1826 after earning a law degree. He was appointed U.S. judge for Arkansas in 1830 and was serving in this capacity when Featherstonhaugh visited him in 1834. Cross later served as U.S. surveyor general for Arkansas (1836–1838), U.S. congressman (1839–1845), Arkansas Supreme Court judge (1845–1855), president of the Cairo and Fulton Railway (1855–1862), and attorney general of Arkansas. He is buried in Marlbrook Cemetery in Blevins, Arkansas. See "Cross, Edward," Biographical Dictionary of the United States Congress.
157. The "Double-Cabin" style of the Cross home that Featherstonhaugh described was probably a "Double Pen" house. For more on regional architectural styles, see Nostrand, *Making of America's Culture Regions.*
158. Featherstonhaugh, *Excursion through the Slave States*, 117.
159. Featherstonhaugh, 118.
160. Featherstonhaugh, 118.
161. Featherstonhaugh, 118.
162. Featherstonhaugh, 118.
163. Featherstonhaugh, 118.
164. Featherstonhaugh, 118.
165. Featherstonhaugh, 118.
166. Featherstonhaugh, 119.
167. Featherstonhaugh, 119.
168. Featherstonhaugh, 119.
169. Featherstonhaugh, 120; emphasis in original.
170. Featherstonhaugh, 121. Featherstonhaugh spelled the name "Prior." Richard Pryor was likely the "Mr. Prior" with whom Fenston journeyed from Washington to his cabin since he fits the description of the wealthy Virginian and the Spring Hill township residents. The 1840 U.S. federal census indicated that Pryor owned nineteen slaves. According to the 1850 U.S. federal census, Richard Pryor was born in Virginia in 1798, lived in the Spring Hill township with his wife, Virginia, and owned $6,000 in real estate. The 1850 census also lists an Edward L. Pryor living in Washington, Hempstead County, who was born in Virginia in 1805.
171. Featherstonhaugh, *Excursion through the Slave States*, 121; emphasis in original.
172. Featherstonhaugh, 121.
173. Featherstonhaugh, 121.
174. Featherstonhaugh, 121.
175. Featherstonhaugh, 122.
176. Featherstonhaugh, 122.
177. Featherstonhaugh, 122.
178. Featherstonhaugh, 122.
179. Featherstonhaugh, 122.
180. Featherstonhaugh, 122–23.
181. Featherstonhaugh, 123.
182. Featherstonhaugh, 123.
183. Featherstonhaugh, 123.
184. Featherstonhaugh, 123.
185. Featherstonhaugh, 123. Fenston's comments can be placed within the context of his frustrations over the boundary dispute between the United States and Canada in Maine and New Brunswick. He understood American expansionism firsthand. His writing

appears prophetic regarding Mexico's loss of Texas, but since the book was not published until after Texas achieved independence he may have been applying the benefit of hindsight here.

186. See Christ, "Dooley's Ferry Fortifications Historic District."
187. Featherstonhaugh, *Excursion through the Slave States*, 124.
188. Featherstonhaugh, 124; emphasis in original.
189. Dr. Jones is most likely Isaac Newton Jones (1797–1858), a native of North Carolina and a physician in Washington, Arkansas. He was serving as postmaster of Lost Prairie at the time of Featherstonhaugh's visit.
190. Featherstonhaugh, *Excursion through the Slave States*, 124.
191. Featherstonhaugh, 124. For more on cotton in Texas, see Torget, *Seeds of Empire*.
192. Featherstonhaugh, *Excursion through the Slave States*, 124.
193. Featherstonhaugh, 125; emphasis in original.
194. Featherstonhaugh, 124–25. For more on slavery in Texas, see Campbell, *Empire for Slavery*.
195. Featherstonhaugh, *Excursion through the Slave States*, 125.
196. Featherstonhaugh, 125.
197. Featherstonhaugh, 125. Featherstonhaugh probably did not venture far enough west to have been in present-day Texas. He does not give a detailed itinerary or set of locations, but he crossed the Red River east of Texarkana and probably spent most of this portion of the journey in what is present-day Miller County, Arkansas, about ten to fifteen miles from the current state line.
198. Featherstonhaugh, *Excursion through the Slave States*, 127.
199. Featherstonhaugh, 128.
200. Featherstonhaugh, 128–29.
201. Featherstonhaugh, 129.
202. Featherstonhaugh, 129.
203. Featherstonhaugh, 129.
204. Featherstonhaugh, 129.
205. Featherstonhaugh, 129.
206. Featherstonhaugh, 129.
207. Featherstonhaugh, 130.
208. Featherstonhaugh, 130.
209. Featherstonhaugh, 130.
210. Featherstonhaugh, 133. Featherstonhaugh probably meant to spell the word "stercoraceous," which Merriam-Webster defines as "relating to, being, or containing feces."
211. Featherstonhaugh, 133.
212. Featherstonhaugh, 134.
213. Featherstonhaugh, 134.
214. Featherstonhaugh, 134.
215. Featherstonhaugh, 135.
216. Featherstonhaugh, 135.
217. Featherstonhaugh, 136.
218. Featherstonhaugh, 137.
219. Featherstonhaugh, 136; Cochran, "'Low, Degrading Scoundrels.'" It is important to recognize that the men Fenston was labeling as low, degraded scoundrels were not residents of Arkansas but rootless outlaws.
220. Featherstonhaugh, *Excursion through the Slave States*, 133.
221. Featherstonhaugh, 133.
222. Antoine Barraque (1773–1858) established the settlement of New Gascony and served as agent to the Quapaw. He arrived in Arkansas in about 1816 and developed partnerships with

other French businessmen in the area such as Frederick Notrebe. His wife, Maria Therese Dardenne, was the daughter of his friend Joseph Dardenne and a Quapaw woman. At the time of Fenston's visit, Barraque had begun focusing his efforts on cotton. See Teske, "Antoine Barraque (1773–1858)."

223. Featherstonhaugh, *Excursion through the Slave States*, 133; emphasis in original.
224. Featherstonhaugh, 134.
225. Featherstonhaugh, 134.
226. Featherstonhaugh, 134.
227. Featherstonhaugh, 134–35.
228. Featherstonhaugh, 135.
229. Featherstonhaugh, 135.
230. Featherstonhaugh, 137. This cutoff is the same path that Thomas Nuttall followed when he entered Arkansas.
231. Featherstonhaugh, 137.
232. Featherstonhaugh, 137.
233. Featherstonhaugh, 137.

6. Deep Mapping Travelers' Perceptions of the Arkansas Past

1. Peters and Woolley, "Presidential Debate in East Lansing, Michigan."
2. The method for creating perception maps for this chapter is similar to the one I used in my article "Mapping Travelers' Cultural and Environmental Perceptions." The maps for this chapter built upon this experience, but I used different data gathering and mapping techniques. First, the journals were read again and mapped using GoogleEarth. For each traveler observation, a GoogleEarth placemark was added. The features of the placemark were changed to white for descriptive observation, red for negative perceptions, and green for positive perceptions. Descriptive observations were those in which a traveler described environmental or cultural features without offering his judgment or opinion about those features. Positive perceptions were those in which a traveler described an environmental or cultural feature and then offered a judgment or adjective that indicated that he approved of or took pleasure in this feature. Negative perceptions were those in which a traveler described an environmental or cultural feature and then offered a judgment or adjective that indicated that he disapproved of or was disgusted by this feature. Separate folders were created in GoogleEarth to group the descriptive observations, cultural perceptions, and environmental perceptions of each traveler. Next, the GoogleEarth maps were saved as kmz files and delivered to Erin Greb Cartography. The locations and attributes of each kmz file were used to create the illustrations that appear in chapter six of this book. Hollow squares were chosen to symbolize descriptive observations, plus signs to symbolize positive perceptions, and negative signs to symbolize negative perceptions. When observations and perceptions closely overlapped in space and could not be symbolized effectively at a statewide

scale, they were organized in rows to capture the frequency of the observation and perceptions at the expense of precise locations. While some locations were easy to determine, others required estimation rooted in the distance, direction, and likely travel paths of a traveler.

3. Figures 6.7 and 6.8 include symbols depicting Schoolcraft's descriptions and perceptions during the very beginning of his journey. The symbols around and west of Potosi, Missouri, illustrate statements from the beginning of Schoolcraft's journal. These statements are consistent with those described when referring to figures 6.5 and 6.6, so there is no further discussion of them in the paragraphs about figures 6.7 and 6.8.

Bibliography

Allen, John L. "Thomas Jefferson and the Mountain of Salt: Presidential Image of Louisiana Territory." *Historical Geography* 31 (2003): 9–22.

Allison, Julanne S. "Crystal Hill (Pulaski County)." Encyclopedia of Arkansas History and Culture, February 22, 2018. http://www.encyclopediaof arkansas.net/encyclopedia/entry-detail .aspx?search=1&entryID=2706.

Arnold, Morris S. *Colonial Arkansas, 1686–1804: A Social and Cultural History*. Fayetteville: University of Arkansas Press, 1991.

———. "Indians and Immigrants in the Arkansas Colonial Era." In *Arkansas: A Narrative History*, 46–74. Fayetteville: University of Arkansas Press, 2002.

———. *The Rumble of a Distant Drum: The Quapaws and Old World Newcomers, 1673–1804*. Fayetteville: University of Arkansas Press, 2000.

Baird, W. David. "Westward Expansion, 1803–1861." The Encyclopedia of Oklahoma History and Culture. Accessed July 28, 2018. http://www .okhistory.org/publications/enc/entry .php?entry=WE021.

Bender, Robert Patrick. "John Pope (1770–1845)." Encyclopedia of Arkansas History and Culture, September 2, 2014. http://www.encyclopediaof arkansas.net/encyclopedia/entry -detail.aspx?search=1&entryID=318.

Berkeley, Edmund, and Dorothy Smith Berkeley. *George William Featherstonhaugh: The First U.S. Government Geologist*. Tuscaloosa: University of Alabama Press, 1988.

Bigelow, Jacob. "Review of Thomas Nuttall's *A Journal of Travels into the Arkansa Territory during the Year 1819*, with Occasional Observations on the Manners of the Aborigines. Illustrated with a Map and Other Engravings." *North American Review* 16, no. 38 (January 1823): 59–76.

Blevins, Brooks. *Arkansas/Arkansaw: How Bear Hunters, Hillbillies, and Good Ol' Boys Defined a State*. Fayetteville: University of Arkansas Press, 2009.

Bodenhamer, David J., John Corrigan, and Trevor M. Harris, eds. *The Spatial Humanities: GIS and the Future of Humanities Scholarship*. Bloomington: Indiana University Press, 2010.

Bodenhamer, David J., Trevor M. Harris, and John Corrigan. "Deep Mapping and the Spatial Humanities." *International Journal of Humanities and Arts Computing* 7, no. 1–2 (2013): 170–75.

Bolton, S. Charles. *Arkansas, 1800–1860:*

Remote and Restless. Fayetteville: University of Arkansas Press, 1998.

Bremer, Richard G. *Indian Agent and Wilderness Scholar: The Life of Henry Rowe Schoolcraft*. Mount Pleasant: Clarke Historical Library, Central Michigan University, 1987.

Burns, Louis F. *A History of the Osage People*. New ed. Tuscaloosa: University of Alabama Press, 2004.

Campbell, Randolph B. *An Empire for Slavery: The Peculiar Institution in Texas, 1821–1865*. Baton Rouge: Louisiana State University Press, 1989.

Cande, Kathleen H. "Frederick Notrebe (1780–1849)." Encyclopedia of Arkansas, August 11, 2011. http://www.encyclopediaofarkansas.net/encyclopedia/entry-detail.aspx?entryID=4126.

Christ, Mark K. "Dooley's Ferry Fortifications Historic District." Encyclopedia of Arkansas, June 11, 2015. http://www.encyclopediaofarkansas.net/encyclopedia/entry-detail.aspx?entryID=7499.

Clark, Daniel. Daniel Clark Jr. to Thomas Jefferson, February 12, 1799. https://www.loc.gov/resource/mtj1.021_0881_0884/.

Clements, Derek Allen. "James Miller (1776–1851)." Encyclopedia of Arkansas History and Culture, May 9, 2007. http://www.encyclopediaofarkansas.net/encyclopedia/entry-detail.aspx?search=1&entryID=2872.

Clifft, Billy Steven. "Phillips County." Encyclopedia of Arkansas History and Culture, December 29, 2017. http://www.encyclopediaofarkansas.net/encyclopedia/entry-detail.aspx?search=1&entryID=797.

Clouston-Becker, Audrey Lee. *The Lives and Legends of the Ozark Yoakums: Westward Migration from Pennsylvania to the Ozarks and beyond*. Edited by Marilyn Jean Jackson-Pfitzner. Conway: Arkansas Research, 2008.

Cochran, Robert B. "'Low, Degrading Scoundrels': George W. Featherstonhaugh's Contribution to the Bad Name of Arkansas." *Arkansas Historical Quarterly* 48 (1989): 3–16.

Cosgrove, Denis E. *Geography and Vision: Seeing, Imagining and Representing the World*. New York: I.B. Tauris, 2008.

Cresswell, Tim. *Place: A Short Introduction*. Malden, Mass.: Blackwell, 2004.

"Cross, Edward." Biographical Dictionary of the United States Congress. Accessed April 27, 2017. http://bioguide.congress.gov/scripts/biodisplay.pl?index=C000930.

DeRosier, Arthur H., Jr. *William Dunbar: Scientific Pioneer of the Old Southwest*. Lexington: University Press of Kentucky, 2007.

Dickinson, Samuel Dorris. "Colonial Arkansas Place Names." *Arkansas Historical Quarterly* 48, no. 2 (1989): 137–68.

Dunbar, William. William Dunbar to Thomas Jefferson, August 18, 1804. https://www.loc.gov/item/mtjbibo13735/.

———. William Dunbar to Thomas Jefferson, February 2, 1805. https://www.loc.gov/resource/mtj1.032_0438_0441/?sp=1.

———. William Dunbar to Thomas Jefferson, June 1, 1804. https://www.loc.gov/item/mtjbib013476/.

———. William Dunbar to Thomas Jefferson, May 13, 1804. https://www.loc.gov/item/mtjbib013428/.

———. William Dunbar to Thomas Jefferson, November 9, 1804. Manuscript/mixed material. https://www.loc.gov/resource/mtj1.031_0648_0651/?sp=4.

Dunbar, William, and George Hunter. *The Forgotten Expedition, 1804–1805: The Louisiana Purchase Journals of Dunbar and Hunter.* Edited by Trey Berry, Pam Beasley, and Jeanne Clements. Baton Rouge, LA: Louisiana State University Press, 2006.

Dunbar, William, and Eron Rowland. *Life, Letters, and Papers of William Dunbar: Of Elgin, Morayshire, Scotland, and Natchez, Mississippi: Pioneer Scientist of the Southern United States.* Jackson: Press of the Mississippi Historical Society, 1930.

Dunn, Stuart, Lesley Kadish, and Michael Pasquier. "A Religious Centre with a Civic Circumference: Towards the Concept of a Deep Map of American Religion." *International Journal of Humanities and Arts Computing* 7, nos. 1–2 (2013): 190–200. https://doi.org/10.3366/ijhac.2013.0089.

DuVal, Kathleen. "'A Good Relationship, & Commerce': The Native Political Economy of the Arkansas River Valley." *Early American Studies: An Interdisciplinary Journal* 1, no. 1 (2003): 61–89.

———. "Debating Identity, Sovereignty, and Civilization: The Arkansas Valley after the Louisiana Purchase." *Journal of the Early Republic* 26, no. 1 (2006): 25–58.

Featherstonhaugh, George. *Excursion through the Slave States: From Washington on the Potomac, to the Frontier of Mexico; with Sketches of Popular Manners and Geological Notices.* New York: Harper, 1844.

———. *Geological Report of an Examination Made in 1834, of the Elevated Country between the Missouri and Red Rivers.* Washington, D.C.: United States Congress, 1835.

———. George W. Featherstonhaugh to John Murray, February 3, 1844. National Library of Scotland, John Murray Archive.

Fishkin, Shelley Fisher. "'Deep Maps': A Brief for Digital Palimpsest Mapping Projects (DPMPs, or 'Deep Maps')." *Journal of Transnational American Studies* 3, no. 2 (2011): 1–31.

Freeman, Thomas, and Peter Custis. *Southern Counterpart to Lewis and Clark: The Freeman and Custis Expedition of 1806.* Edited by Dan L. Flores. Norman: University of Oklahoma Press, 1985.

Gieringer, Dana. "Edmund Hogan (1780–1828)." Encyclopedia of Arkansas History and Culture, August 15, 2016. http://www.encyclopediaofarkansas.net/encyclopedia/entry-detail.aspx?search=1&entryID=4265.

Goodspeed. *Biographical and Historical Memoirs of Northeast Arkansas: A Condensed History of the State, a Number of Biographies of Distinguished Citizens of the Same, a Brief Descriptive*

History of Each of the Counties Named Herein, and Numerous Biographical Sketches of Prominent Citizens of Such Counties. Chicago: Goodspeed Publishing, 1889.

Graustein, Jeannette. *Thomas Nuttall: Naturalist, Explorations in America, 1808–1841*. Cambridge: Harvard University Press, 1967.

Harris, Matthew L., and Jay H. Buckley, eds. *Zebulon Pike, Thomas Jefferson, and the Opening of the American West*. Norman: University of Oklahoma Press, 2012.

Heat Moon, William Least. *PrairyErth: (A Deep Map)*. Boston: Houghton Mifflin, 1991.

Higgins, Billy D. *A Stranger and a Sojourner: Peter Caulder, Free Black Frontiersman in Antebellum Arkansas*. Fayetteville: University of Arkansas Press, 2005.

Holmes, Jack D. L. "Casa Calvo, Marques de," June 12, 2010. https://www.tshaonline.org/handbook/online/articles/fca80.

Jackson, Donald. *Thomas Jefferson and the Rocky Mountains: Exploring the West from Monticello*. Norman: University of Oklahoma Press, 1993.

Jefferson, Thomas. Thomas Jefferson to William Dunbar, June 24, 1799. Founder's Online Archive. http://founders.archives.gov/documents/Jefferson/01–31–02–0120.

———. Thomas Jefferson to William Dunbar, January 12, 1801. https://www.loc.gov/item/mtjbib009582/.

———. Thomas Jefferson to William Dunbar, July 17, 1804. Library of Congress. https://www.loc.gov/item/mtjbib013639/.

———. Thomas Jefferson to William Dunbar, March 14, 1805. https://www.loc.gov/resource/mtj1.032_0815_0815/.

Johnson, Michael. "William Stevenson (1768–1857)." Encyclopedia of Arkansas History and Culture, April 23, 2014. http://www.encyclopediaofarkansas.net/encyclopedia/entry-detail.aspx?entryID=3537.

Keighren, Innes M., Charles W. J. Withers, and Bill Bell. *Travels into Print: Exploration, Writing, and Publishing with John Murray, 1773–1859*. Chicago: University of Chicago Press, 2015.

Kilpatrick, Dr. "Historical and Statistical Collections of Louisiana." *DeBow's Southern and Western Review*, 1852.

Koelsch, William A. "Thomas Jefferson, American Geographers, and the Uses of Geography." *Geographical Review* 98, no. 2 (2008): 260–279.

Kuhlman, Betty L. "Bogy, Joseph (ca. 1749–?)." The Encyclopedia of Oklahoma History and Culture. Accessed July 28, 2018. http://www.okhistory.org/publications/enc/entry.php?entry=BO003.

Kwas, Mary L. "William Edward Woodruff (1795–1885)." Encyclopedia of Arkansas History and Culture, June 8, 2016. http://www.encyclopediaofarkansas.net/encyclopedia/entry-detail.aspx?search=1&entryID=2533.

Maher, Susan Naramore. *Deep Map Country: Literary Cartography of the Great Plains*. Lincoln: University of Nebraska Press, 2014.

Masterson, James R. *Arkansas Folklore: The Arkansas Traveler, Davey Crockett, and Other Legends*. Little Rock: Rose, 1974.

McWhiney, Grady. *Cracker Culture: Celtic Ways in the Old South*. Tuscaloosa: University of Alabama Press, 1988.

Meinig, D. W. *Continental America*. Vol. 2. The Shaping of America: A Geographical Perspective on 500 Years of History. New Haven: Yale University Press, 1986.

Mercer, Henry Chapman. "On the Track of 'The Arkansas Traveler.'" *The Century* 51 (1896): 707–12.

Miller, Mary Cooper, and Denny Elrod. "John Lafferty (1759–1816)." Encyclopedia of Arkansas History and Culture, April 26, 2018. http://www.encyclopediaofarkansas.net/encyclopedia/entry-detail.aspx?entryID=2582.

Milson, Andrew. "Mapping Travelers' Cultural and Environmental Perceptions: Thomas Nuttall and Henry Rowe Schoolcraft in Arkansas, 1818–1819." *Historical Geography* 45 (2017): 172–87.

Mumford, Jeremy. "Mixed-Race Identity in a Nineteenth-Century Family: The Schoolcraft's of Sault Ste. Marie, 1824–27." *Michigan Historical Review* 25, no. 1 (Spring 1999): 1–23.

Nostrand, Richard L. *The Making of America's Culture Regions*. Lanham: Rowman & Littlefield, 2018.

Nuttall, Thomas. *A Journal of Travels into the Arkansas Territory during the Year 1819*. Edited by Savoie Lottinville. Norman: University of Oklahoma Press, 2012.

Owsley, Frank Lawrence. *Plain Folk of the Old South*. Baton Rouge: Louisiana State University Press, 1949.

Oxx, Katie, Allan Brimicombe, and Johnathan Rush. "Envisioning Deep Maps: Exploring the Spatial Navigation Metaphor in Deep Mapping." *International Journal of Humanities and Arts Computing* 7, no. 1–2 (2013): 201–27. https://doi.org/10.3366/ijhac.2013.0090.

Pennington, Helen. "Magnet Cove." Encyclopedia of Arkansas, September 17, 2014. http://www.encyclopediaofarkansas.net/encyclopedia/entry-detail.aspx?search=1&entryID=4129.

Peters, Gerhard, and John T. Woolley. "Presidential Debate in East Lansing, Michigan." The American Presidency Project, October 19, 1992. http://www.presidency.ucsb.edu/ws/?pid=21625.

Pinkston, Lori. "Greenville (Clark County)." Encyclopedia of Arkansas, March 24, 2014. http://www.encyclopediaofarkansas.net/encyclopedia/entry-detail.aspx?search=1&entryID=1201.

Pope, William F., and Dunbar H. Pope. *Early Days in Arkansas: Being for the Most Part the Personal Recollections of an Old Settler*. Little Rock: F. W. Allsopp, 1895.

Pratt, Mary Louise. *Imperial Eyes: Travel Writing and Transculturation*. New York: Routledge, 1992.

Ridge, Mia, Don Lafreniere, and Scott Nesbit. "Creating Deep Maps and Spatial Narratives through Design." *International Journal of Humanities and Arts Computing* 7, no. 1–2 (2013): 176–89.

Rollings, Willard H. *The Osage: An Ethnohistorical Study of Hegemony on the Prairie-Plains*. Columbia: University of Missouri Press, 1995.

Ronda, James P. "Exploring the West in the Age of Jefferson." In *North American Exploration: A Continent Comprehended*, 3:9–74. Lincoln: University of Nebraska Press, 1997.

Rorie, Kenneth. "Dota (Independence County)." Encyclopedia of Arkansas, December 22, 2016. http://www.encyclopediaofarkansas.net/encyclopedia/entry-detail.aspx?entryID=9184.

Schoolcraft, Henry R. *A View of the Lead Mines of Missouri; Including Some Observations on the Mineralogy, Geology, Geography, Antiquities, Soil, Climate, Population, and Productions of Missouri and Arkansaw, and Other Sections of the Western Country*. New York: Charles Wiley, 1819.

———. *Narrative Journal of Travels through the Northwestern Regions of the United States Extending from Detroit through the Great Chain of American Lakes to the Sources of the Mississippi River, Performed as a Member of the Expedition under Governor Cass in the Year 1820*. Albany: E & E Hosford, 1821.

———. *Personal Memoirs of a Residence of Thirty Years with the Indian Tribes of the American Frontiers: With Brief Notices of Passing Events, Facts, and Opinions, A.D. 1812 to A.D. 1842*. Philadelphia: Lippincott, Grambo and Co., 1851.

———. *Rude Pursuits and Rugged Peaks: Schoolcraft's Ozark Journal, 1818–1819*. Edited by Milton D. Rafferty. Fayetteville: University of Arkansas Press, 1996.

———. *Scenes and Adventures in the Semi-Alpine Region of the Ozark Mountains of Missouri and Arkansas*. Philadelphia: Lippincott, Grambo and Co., 1853.

Sesser, David. "Jacob Barkman (1784–1852)." Encyclopedia of Arkansas History and Culture, April 7, 2016. http://www.encyclopediaofarkansas.net/encyclopedia/entry-detail.aspx?entryID=9197.

Shinn, Josiah Hazen. *Pioneers and Makers of Arkansas*. Little Rock: Democrat Printing and Lithographing, 1908.

Smith, David A. "Public Land Surveys." Encyclopedia of Arkansas History and Culture, January 13, 2017. http://www.encyclopediaofarkansas.net/encyclopedia/entry-detail.aspx?search=1&entryID=7829.

Stevenson, William. *The Autobiography of the Rev. William Stevenson*. Edited by Ted A. Campbell. Dallas: Tuckapaw Media, 2012. http://www.smu.edu/~/media/Site/Perkins/PDF/PublicProgs/LaySchool/ Autobiography%20of%20William%20Stevenson.ashx.

Sturges, Mark. "A Deep Map of the South: Natural History, Cultural History, and William Bartram's Travels." *South Atlantic Review* 79, nos. 1–2 (2015): 43–67.

Teske, Steven. "Antoine Barraque (1773–1858)." Encyclopedia of Arkansas, June 21, 2010. http://www.encyclopediaofarkansas.net/encyclopedia/entry-detail.aspx?search=1&entryID=2962.

Thompson, Carl. *Travel Writing*. New York: Routledge, 2011.

Torget, Andrew J. *Seeds of Empire: Cotton, Slavery, and the Transformation of the Texas Borderlands, 1800–1850*. Chapel Hill: University of North Carolina Press, 2015.

Townsend, John Kirk. *Narrative of a Journey across the Rocky Mountains, to the Columbia River, and a Visit to the Sandwich Islands, Chili, &c. with a Scientific Appendix*. Philadelphia: Henry Perkins, 1839.

Turnbo, S. C. *The White River Chronicles of S.C. Turnbo: Man and Wildlife on the Ozarks Frontier*. Edited by James F. Keefe and Lynn Morrow. Fayetteville: University of Arkansas Press, 1994.

Valenčius, Conevery Bolton. *The Lost History of the New Madrid Earthquakes*. Chicago: University of Chicago Press, 2013.

Weaver, H. Dwight. *Missouri Caves in History and Legend*. Columbia: University of Missouri Press, 2008.

Whayne, Jeannie M. "The Turbulent Path to Statehood: Arkansas Territory, 1803–1836." In *Arkansas: A Narrative History*, edited by Jeannie M. Whayne, Thomas A. Deblack, George Sabo III, and Morris S. Arnold, 75–108. Fayetteville: University of Arkansas Press, 2002.

Whayne, Jeannie M., and Willard B. Gatewood, eds. *The Arkansas Delta: Land of Paradox*. Fayetteville: University of Arkansas Press, 1993.

Williams, C. Fred. "James Sevier Conway (1796–1855)." Encyclopedia of Arkansas History and Culture, February 16, 2018. http://www.encyclopediaofarkansas.net/encyclopedia/entry-detail.aspx?search=1&entryID=97.

———. "The Bear State Image: Arkansas in the Nineteenth Century." *Arkansas Historical Quarterly* 34 (1980): 99–111.

Winders, Jamie. "Imperfectly Imperial: Northern Travel Writers in the Postbellum US South, 1865–1880." *Annals of the Association of American Geographers* 95, no. 2 (2005): 391–410.

Wylie, John. *Landscape*. New York: Routledge, 2007.

Index

C

D

E

F

O

P

Q

R

S

T

Y